# EXPLORING EAST END WATERS

A Natural History and Paddling Guide

## Also by Mike Bottini
## Trail Guide to the South Fork

## Help keep this book up-to-date!

The author welcomes comments regarding your experience with this guide and how you feel it could be improved and kept up-to-date. Please e-mail your comments and suggestions to **mike@peconic.org** or mail them to:
Mike Bottini, 34 Chapel Lane, East Hampton NY 11937.

Thanks for your input and enjoy paddling the East End's waters!

**Visit Mike on the web at www.MikeBottini.com**

# EXPLORING EAST END WATERS

## A Natural History and Paddling Guide

## Mike Bottini

New York | Sag Harbor
Harbor Electronic Publishing

**HEP**

www.HEPDigital.com
2005

Printed in the United States of America.
First printing: June 2005

This print version of the book does not include an index. Readers who need an index are directed to the eBook version, which is fully word-searchable.

**Credits**
Edited by Charles Monaco
Cover design by Joseph Dunn
Maps hand-drawn by Mike Bottini, edited by Joseph Dunn
Cover photograph by John Todaro (view more at *www.johntodaro.com*)
Photographs by Mike Bottini

**A Note on the Type**
This book is set in Adobe Garamond. Based on the design of sixteenth-century typesetter Claude Garamond, the many Garamond faces have proved among the most durable and popular typefaces of the last 400 years. Adobe designer Robert Slimbach went to the Plantin–Moretus museum in Antwerp, Belgium, to study the original Garamond typefaces. These served as the basis for the design of the Adobe Garamond romans; the italics are based on types by Robert Granjon, a contemporary of Garamond's. This elegant, versatile design, especially suited to both screen and print, was the first Adobe Originals typeface, released in 1989.

For my parents:

Dolores Bottini, who insisted I write home during my traveling years,
and
Gerard Bottini, who taught me that anything is possible.

# CONTENTS

**Photographs:**

## Spotlight Topics

# Main Key

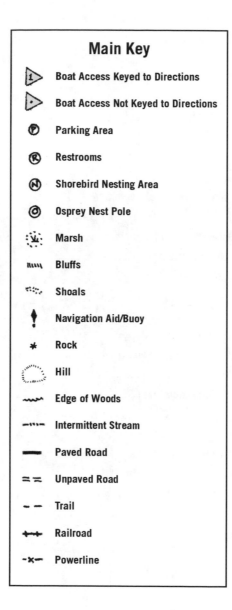

- ▷1  Boat Access Keyed to Directions
- ▷  Boat Access Not Keyed to Directions
- Ⓟ  Parking Area
- Ⓡ  Restrooms
- Ⓝ  Shorebird Nesting Area
- Ⓞ  Osprey Nest Pole
- Marsh
- Bluffs
- Shoals
- Navigation Aid/Buoy
- Rock
- Hill
- Edge of Woods
- Intermittent Stream
- Paved Road
- Unpaved Road
- Trail
- Railroad
- Powerline

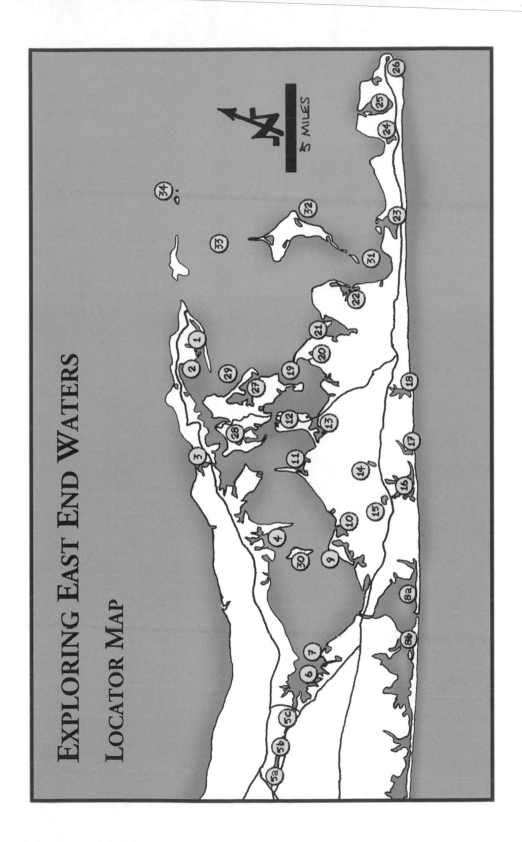

# ACKNOWLEDGMENTS

Jack Pigott, my college roommate at St. Lawrence University, first introduced me to canoeing and the unique camaraderie that develops on paddling trips. John Kulish showed me the advantages of exploring nature and viewing wildlife by paddle craft.

Rob Battenfeld, Kurt Billing, Judy Cooper, Richard G. Hendrickson, Deb Reed, Rick Salter, Russ Tillman, John Todaro, and George Velmachos kept me company on many East End paddling adventures, some of which found their way into this book. Their companionship is something I will always cherish.

Over the past 17 years, I have been fortunate to have worked with many knowledgeable naturalists, scientists, historians, land managers, and environmental advocates, most of whom have contributed in some way to this book. Special thanks to the following: NYSDEC staff Byron Young, Chart Guthrie, Michelle Gibbons, Brian Swift, and Bill Fonda, who provided information on fisheries, Mute Swans, and bird nesting areas; Bob Conkling, who shared his knowledge of the Alewife and the Peconic River fish ladder; Richard G. Hendrickson, Rick Whalen, John Strong, Marlene Haresign, and Peter Corwith, who contributed valuable local knowledge and historical information; The Nature Conservancy's Mike Scheibel, one of the most knowledgeable people on the East End when it comes to Ospreys; Bill Sickles and Nick Gibbons of Suffolk County Parks; Jim Ash, Pete Weis, and Eric Salzman of the South Fork Natural History Society; the extremely patient and helpful marine biologist Howard Reisman of Southampton College and his colleagues at CRESLI Sam Sadove, Paul Forestell, and Artie Kopelman; American Littoral Society naturalists Steve Finn, Don Reipe, Mickey Cohen, and Rob Villani, who taught me many things on their Montauk Natural History Weekends; Southampton Town environmentalist Marty Shea; East Hampton Town Natural Resource Director Larry Penny; Denise Markut of the Peconic Land Trust, Jim McMahon of Southold Town, and Doug Murphy of Eagle's Neck Paddling Company, who helped me learn about the North Fork's beautiful paddling areas; Jay Damuck of Shelter Island Kayak; and Jim Dreeben of Peconic Paddler in Riverhead. A special thanks to Rob Battenfeld who, in his professional capacity as a research librarian, helped me navigate through online databases. Writer and friend Greg Donaldson's advice and comments were helpful, as always.

This book is based on stories I've written for the South Fork Outdoors column in the *Southampton Press*. Thanks to publisher Joe Louchheim and editor Joe Shaw for giving me the opportunity to do a weekly column, and for their encouragement over the years.

Last but far from least, many thanks to the environmental advocacy organization Group for the South Fork. Among their many activities on the East End, the Group has a long history of supporting efforts to educate and involve paddlers in environmental initiatives. The roots of this book can be traced back to the years I spent working for them as an Environmental Planner. Special thanks to staff members Steve Biasetti and Bob DeLuca, who have been extremely helpful and always available to share their expertise.

# FOREWORD: THE PECONIC BAYKEEPER

*by Kevin McAllister*

Linking the North and South Forks of eastern Long Island, the Peconic Bay Estuary System is a vast resource of beauty and bounty for Long Island communities. The Peconic Estuary encompasses hundreds of miles of shoreline, vast marshlands, and numerous inlets, harbors, and tidal creeks. The estuary contains the highest concentration of rare and endangered species in the entire State of New York. In recognition of its ecological value, in 1992 the Peconic Estuary was included in the National Estuary Program, whose mission is to promote wise management of estuaries threatened by pollution and development.

Paddling has opened to us the bay's treasures and has allowed us to interact and explore nature quietly, under the power of our own stroke. Whether you choose to navigate the ghost forest at Hubbard Creek and alight on a sandy beach for a picnic lunch, trace the surprising stony beaches and cliffs along Jessup Neck, or tackle the sometimes turbid Orient Bay to behold some of the most pristine beaches on the island, you are privy to natural serenity and beauty that might otherwise be missed.

Paddling is the best way to experience the diverse wildlife and breathtaking scenery of the Peconic Estuary. Hunting Ospreys and diving terns and Plovers are often seen flying overhead. Egrets and Great Blue Herons stand motionless along the shorelines while Cormorants and a variety of ducks float nearby. Diamondback Terrapins break the water's surface and, in the right season on a moonlit night, phosphorescent jellyfish glow and swirl with a paddle stroke. By canoe, kayak, or other vessel, paddling offers a unique opportunity for people of any age to participate in the natural world around us and experience first-hand the splendor the Peconic Bay offers.

One paddle I enjoy is through Bullhead Bay and Sebonac Creek where one can see the flourishing Eelgrass beds which suggest that the embayment experiences good water quality and is not suffering from excessive nitrogen loading. Nevertheless, this trip always reminds me of how vulnerable the bay is to encroachment and contamination. It is increasingly vital that we—who spend time outdoors, value the spectacular waterscapes that the East End offers, and understand the significance of a sustainable estuarine system—enjoy and preserve these invaluable resources in a responsible way.

Fostering public awareness of and stewardship for the Peconic and South Shore bays is my full-time job at Peconic Baykeeper®, a non-profit education and advocacy organization charged with protecting these precious biomes. Like a "cop on the beat," we respond to citizen concerns about events or actions that threaten the integrity of the estuarine ecosystem. We work with government and civic officials to develop progressive conservation and management policies, and, of significant importance, ensure that laws protecting water quality and habitats are enforced. For more information about the Peconic Baykeeper program, call 631-727-7346 or visit us online at *www.peconicbaykeeper.org*.

I urge you to explore, learn more, and do what you can to help protect this resource. Avoiding bird-nesting areas (particularly in the spring and early summer) and leaving surrounding marshes untouched are integral to sustaining the diverse wildlife of the system. Equally important is the need to return from your journey with everything, leaving no waste behind and—in this sense of common responsibility—picking up litter negligently left behind by others. With continually increasing development threats to our bays, there is a growing need for citizen activism. Showing support through attendance and speaking out at government meetings, writing letters to the editors of local newspapers, and supporting environmental advocacy groups helps to make citizen activism powerful and our elected officials accountable.

Your guide in exploring the Peconic Bay and its environs, Mike Bottini, will help you chart your course for secluded inlets, dramatic bluffs, and pristine, untouched beaches. His encyclopedic knowledge of estuarine flora and fauna will help you understand the nuances and subtleties inherent in an ecosystem that is as sensitive and complex as it is resilient and forgiving. Enjoy it and protect it.

**Visit the Peconic Baykeeper at *www.PeconicBaykeeper.org*.**

# Introduction

*About the East End*

The East End of Long Island is split into two long peninsulas called the North and South Forks. Nestled between them is a large estuary encompassing hundreds of distinct but interconnected bays, coves, and tidal creeks that comprise what is called the Peconic Estuary. This waterway, which extends east beyond the Peconic Bays to include Gardiners Bay and a portion of Block Island Sound, has over 1,000 miles of shoreline for sea kayakers and canoeists of all abilities and interests to explore, and a wealth of historical, scenic, and ecological assets, including:

- Native American archeological sites
- the earliest English settlements in New York State
- a long and varied maritime history including whaling (Sag Harbor) and oystering (Greenport)
- a vibrant commercial fishery
- over 30 state-designated "Significant Coastal Fish and Wildlife Habitats"
- eight National Audubon Society "Important Bird Areas"
- two of Long Island's eight National Wildlife Refuges
- over 6,000 acres of State parkland, 8,000 acres of County parkland, and several thousand acres of parkland and preserves owned by the five East End towns bordering the estuary (these figures only include parks with waterfront on the estuary)
- numerous waterfront preserves owned by The Nature Conservancy (including the 2,100-acre Mashomack Preserve on Shelter Island with over 10 miles of coastline), Peconic Land Trust, and various homeowner associations
- Gardiners Island, a 3,000-acre island that has been in the same family ownership since the 1600s; although there is no public access to the island, most of it has been protected through a 20-year conservation easement.

The waterway's many attributes enabled it to receive federal recognition as part of the National Estuary System. It also has its own Baykeeper and is one of the Nature Conservancy's designated "Last Great Places." Jimmy Buffett claims that the best way to view this particular Last Great Place is from the air by small plane. While I have enjoyed that spectacular vantage point, I disagree. The absolute best way to view and experience the East End waterways is by canoe or kayak.

Paddling through a quiet backwater of the estuary is a great way to observe wildlife and view the East End's magnificent scenery. Our moderate climate enables paddlers to enjoy a very long paddling season throughout the spring, summer, and fall months, generally early May into November. It is not unusual to have a warm spell during the winter and, with the proper equipment and safety precautions, a paddle can be very enjoyable even then.

Many of the small tidal creeks and harbors are well protected and suitable for novice paddlers. For the more experienced and adventurous, a circumnavigation of one of the estuary's islands (Robins, Shelter, or Gardiners) provides a rewarding and challenging day trip. For those interested in an overnight outing, there are many motels and B&Bs, and two Suffolk County Park campgrounds, accessible by boat.

Feeling adventurous but don't have the time to spend a whole day on the water? After work, pack a dinner and paddle to one of many secluded, sandy beaches for a picnic. The evening light lasts until at least 8 P.M. between late April and the end of August, and a sunset viewed while paddling quietly along a waterway can be an unforgettable experience. Pick an evening several days before, or during, a full moon and return from your picnic spot by moonlight... a magical trip!


*About Safety*

I would be remiss not to mention a few words about safety. Respect the sea. It is a beautiful but temperamental environment that can change dramatically in a short time. Be aware of water temperatures; they often hover in the 50s (°F) in spring and fall when mild air temperatures can lull you into a false sense of security. Check the weather forecast before setting out, and remember that our summer southwesterly sea breeze can freshen into a formidable wind by early afternoon. That local phenomenon might not be in the regional forecast.

An accidental capsize can happen to anyone in any sea condition. Consider the scenario of reaching behind your seat for a water bottle or windbreaker: it gets hung up momentarily; you tug on it and it suddenly comes free, throwing you off balance to one side; you overreact and capsize on the opposite side. Practice getting back into your boat *before* this happens to you (or a paddling buddy). You may learn that your boat is missing some key pieces of safety equipment.


*About This Book*

The chapters in this book are arranged around 34 specific paddling areas I have explored, some dozens of times and others just once. The bulk of each chapter describes one trip journal of that particular area, with details on the flora and fauna sighted, weather and currents encountered, and some historical notes I found interesting. I have listed the month of the trip so that the reader can better relate to the wildlife sightings and changes in shoreside vegetation noted. All of these appeared at some time in my South Fork Outdoors column published by the *Southampton Press.*

Also included in each chapter are access information, directions, and paddling distance, as well as a detailed map of the waterway. A stand-alone box containing detailed natural history information on a specific "spotlight topic" is found in each chapter, although the theme of each is applicable to many other East End waterways. My use of capital letters for the common names of species warrants explanation: to distinguish descriptive adjectives from proper names I have chosen to capitalize the proper names of species (e.g. Great Black-backed Gull).

The Appendix contains useful information for planning a trip, including how to obtain access and parking permits. These are necessary during the ever-lengthening "summer season" when local towns and villages beef up their parking ordinance enforcers. Take note of parking regulations; even the most remote access points are regularly patrolled during the summer months.

This is not a comprehensive guide. There are many ponds, creeks, and stretches of coastline—perhaps your favorite waterway—not included here. Their exclusion is a matter of limitations imposed on the size of this book, and should not be taken as an indication that they are not worth paddling.

Finally, a few words as to why I wrote this book. When I first arrived on the East End to work at the Group for the South Fork I was surprised to learn that there were very few paddlers in this area, and no paddling outfitters east of Riverhead. The skeptical reaction of my some of my colleagues to my suggestion that we offer canoe outings in addition to our nature walks was also a surprise. That was 1988.

Since then, the number of paddlers in general, and kayakers in particular, on the East End has mushroomed. As a user group, there is no question we are impacting the waterways we paddle. This can be a negative impact, as seen all too often when paddlers come too close to nesting Ospreys or land near a nesting colony of terns and waterbirds. On the other hand, we can have a positive impact on our waterways by supporting and getting involved in protection efforts, educating ourselves about good stewardship practices, and putting those practices to use.

It is my hope that this book will be a useful, informative and educational resource for the growing number of recreational canoeists and kayakers paddling on the East End, and will instill in this important user group a sense of stewardship towards the estuary and its surrounding watershed.

*Mike Bottini*
*Springs*
*May 2005*

# I | NORTH FORK

# 1 | HALLOCK BAY

*Orient, Town of Southold*

DISTANCE:  The bay, including its many tidal creeks, smaller embayments, and dredged channels, has over 10 miles of shoreline to explore by canoe or kayak.

ACCESS:  1) Orient Beach State Park: No permit needed (pay State parking fee at park entrance). From Greenport, drive 7.6 miles east on Rte. 25 to the well-marked entrance of Orient Beach State Park and follow the park causeway to where it ends at a circle. Look for a sign marking the boat drop-off halfway around the circle. Park in the nearby lot and carry over the gravel road to the put-in (30 yards to Hallock Bay and 50 yards to Gardiners Bay).

2) Narrow River Road: Town of Southold parking permit is required. Eastbound on Rte. 25, travel 5.6 miles from the intersection of Rte. 25 and Rte. 48 north of Greenport and turn right onto Narrow River Road. The access is just past the Narrow River Marina.

3) Orient Harbor: No permit needed for the NYSDEC-owned portion. Follow Narrow River Road (see directions above) to its southwestern end on Orient Harbor. Parking on the road requires a Southold Town permit. The NYSDEC parking area is on the east side of the road. NOTE: This puts you in a fairly exposed part of Orient Harbor, with a 0.75-mile-long paddle to the entrance of Hallock Bay.

NOTES:  Orient Beach State Park naturalist Mary Laura Lamont hosts excellent natural history programs at this outstanding park. Call the park (631-323-2440) for information and schedule.

*December*

The sun is as high as it gets in late December when Rob Battenfeld and I park at Potato Beach on the west side of Narrow River. On the one hand, the sun has done its work, warming the frosty morning air to a delightful 50°F. On the other, considering December's short days, we are getting a very late start for a paddle around Hallock Bay.

Hallock Bay is named for George W. Hallock, the Thomas Edison of agriculture. In 1870, Hallock took over a run-down farm bordering Orchard Street and the west side of Narrow River. In those days farming practices often depleted the soil of minerals and nutrients and, according to a publication of the Oysterponds Historical Society entitled *Historic Orient Village* (1976), the Orient farms of the 18th and early 19th centuries never produced much above subsistence level. Hallock, through careful management of the soil, increased crop yields tenfold and completely revolutionized farming.

Some maps and charts label this stretch of water Long Beach Bay, referring to the four-mile-long sliver of barrier beach that comprises Orient Beach State Park. Long Beach forms the bay's eastern and southern border, separating and protecting it from Gardiners Bay. Gardiners Bay, having a long fetch to the east here, can be a rough stretch of water. It is constantly rearranging the barrier beach's shoreline and wreaking havoc on the paved causeway that provides access to Orient Beach State Park.

Part of Hallock's very successful operation included his own steamship to ship produce to New England markets. Potato Beach was close to, if not the actual site of, Hallock's wharf. While Rob and I begin unloading boats and gear, we strike up a conversation with a gentleman packing up after a successful morning of clamming. Hallock Bay is well known among baymen for its shellfishing, and at one time it was one of the most productive scallop areas on the East End. "Any Bay Scallops show up in your clam rake?" I inquire. "Naw, just a few bugs," a reference to small, one-year-old scallops.

A long discourse ensues on the various theories attributed to the mysterious decline of scallops. When we are ready to go, we wave to the clammer watching us from his truck and set out across the mouth of Narrow River. We are planning to do a clockwise paddle around Hallock Bay, and hope to have enough time to explore some of its tidal creeks, man-made lagoons and ditches, and a long, narrow appendage of Hallock Bay called Little Bay.

We are headed for a point of land labeled Barnfield Point on some maps, Eagle Point on others. This area has a long history of use by a Native American group called the Corchaugs and English settlers, the latter dating back to 1661. As a result, many of its prominent geographical features have a number of different names. For example, the whole area east of the Rte. 25 causeway and Dam Pond was once known by its Indian name, Poquatuck. The early English settlers called it Oysterponds. In 1836 its name was changed to Orient.

At Barnfield Point we pass by one of over a dozen Osprey nest poles found in the Hallock Bay area. Ospreys are still rebounding from a population decline related to the spraying of DDT (an insecticide used to kill mosquitoes) on these marshes between 1940 and 1970. If you are paddling during their nesting season, please keep your distance to avoid flushing incubating adults off their nests.

By December the Ospreys are all far to the south, some as far as Brazil. But another magnificent piscivore, the Great Blue Heron, stalks for prey in our waterways all winter long. On our approach, one takes flight with a loud "Arawnk!" and disappears around the bend.

A large channel cuts into the salt marsh east of Barnfield Point, and we turn in to

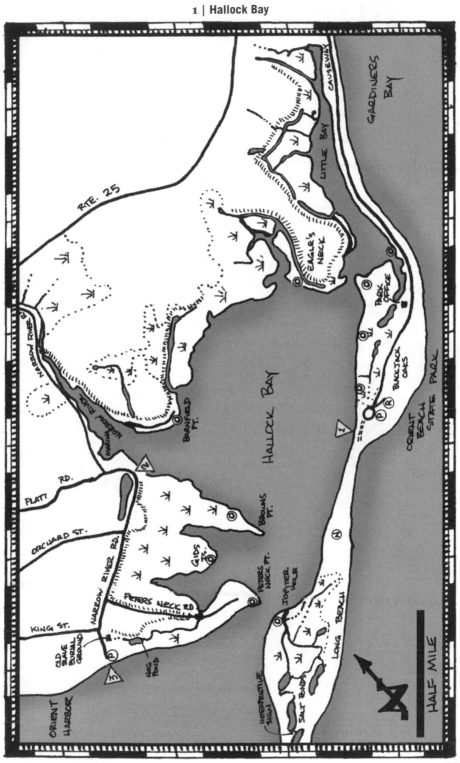

explore. My USGS topographic map shows approximately 10 of these curious channels along the north and west sides of the bay. Most parallel the bay's shoreline and are located on the landward side of the salt marsh, adjacent to farmland. They are clearly man-made features, but much wider than the ubiquitous, grid-like mosquito control ditches.

We follow the channel for a third of a mile, where it dead-ends. It reminds me of the lagoons adjacent to Moriches Bay that were created for raising ducks, but I am not aware of any reference to duck farms in Orient. Along its entire length, on our left, is a tall, steep-sided earthen berm, most likely the spoils from the dredged channel. Examining my map more carefully,

Bug Light at the southwest end of Long Beach.

I notice the symbol for levee where the berm is located, and a series of these disconnected levees extending along most of the bay's northern shoreline.

A post-paddle call to local historian Elinor Williams solved this mystery. Storm surges periodically inundated low-lying portions of farmland bordering the bay. The salt water not only damaged crops but ruined the soil for the next growing season. The Hurricane of 1938 did extensive damage. It took years before rainfall flushed the salt out of the soil and crops could be grown again. Sometime in the 1940s, to prevent this from happening again, the berms were built. Instead of using valuable topsoil to construct them, farmers dug into what they considered at the time to be worthless salt marsh, creating lagoons in the process.

Continuing east along the edge of the marsh, we pass a large area of Cordgrass (*Spartina alterniflora*) that has been heavily grazed, probably by geese. A large waterway on the west side of Eagle's Neck leads into another dredged channel bordered by a steep-sided berm. Both Eagle's Neck and Barnfield Point, as well as the west side of Narrow River, are depicted on an Oysterponds Historical Society map as sites of Poquatuck Indian camps. Roy Latham, in addition to being a great naturalist, was an amateur archeologist. Some of the Poquatuck artifacts he uncovered in this area can be viewed at the Southold Indian Museum.

Despite the names of the neck and point, there are no records of eagles nesting in this area, at least as far back as the late 1800s. However, some readers might be surprised to learn that Latham reported a pair of bald eagles nesting on Gardiners Island up until the 1930s. Wouldn't it be something to see them return to nest some day!

Turning in my kayak to look for the source of an odd, soft grunting sound drifting across the bay, I could barely make out the dark blotch on the water that marked a large raft of Long-tailed Ducks. Formerly known by the politically incorrect name Oldsquaw, these striking sea ducks are making quite a racket.

Paddling through the narrows off Eagle's Neck and entering Little Bay, we head for its far end. There, alongside a rubble-strewn levee, both of us make an awkward exit to stretch cramped legs and have a bite to eat. Following one of many deer paths through Groundselbush that marks the upper edge of the salt marsh, we make our way to the causeway where there is a great view over Gardiners Bay. From north to south, Orient Point, Plum Island, the Ruins at Gardiners Point, Gardiners Island, Springs, and the sandy bluffs of Hedges Banks in East Hampton Town are visible on the horizon.

Long Beach, or what is now Orient Beach State Park, has never been privately owned. Since the area was settled by the English in the 1600s until 1929 when it was deeded over to New York State for a public park, Long Beach was held and managed as common lands belonging to all the male inhabitants of the Orient area. Leases were drawn up for uses such as pasturing, beach rights and, from 1865 to 1895, a fish factory that processed Menhaden into oil and fertilizer.

In addition to outstanding views over the surrounding bays, the park boasts a number of rare and unusual plants and is designated a National Natural Landmark. This is the only place on the East End that I have seen the Blackjack Oak (*Quercus marilandica*). I was surprised to learn from the Suffolk County Soils Map that most of the park's upland area, including the nature trail through the Blackjack Oak forest, is classified as fill.

Back in Hallock Bay we hug the park's shoreline, enjoying the late afternoon sunlight that illuminates the golden-browns of the marsh grasses and greens of the Eastern Red Cedars. Waterfront signage here reflects a tug-of-war between boaters coming ashore to picnic and park managers trying to avoid disturbance to rare plants and nesting birds. Until 2004, canoes and kayaks were actually prohibited from the park.

Fortunately, this policy has been changed. With that change comes the responsibility to practice good stewardship that all paddlers should heed. Steer clear of nesting birds, avoid trampling sensitive beach and dune vegetation, and leave nothing behind but your wake.

At Jupiter Hole we follow the incoming tide into a small creek, bearing right at the first fork on the narrow waterway. Soon the creek opens up into a small salt

The East End's only native cactus, the Prickly Pear, in bloom.

### Prickly Pear Cactus (*Opuntia humifusa*)

This is our only native cactus. As with other members of this group of desert specialists, the Prickly Pear has a large water storage capacity and a very low surface area-to-volume ratio to reduce water loss. The large, chlorophyll-filled pads where photosynthesis occurs are actually not leaves but modified stems and branches. The leaf structure has evolved into thin spines, which grow from small, wart-like nodes scattered over the pads.

Just above the spines are very fine and tiny barbed spines that are unique to the *Opuntia* genus. These are more difficult to see, and much more difficult to remove once lodged in the skin. Its flower is anything but tiny. The two-to-three-inch-wide yellow flowers bloom in early June, and mature to form a red—and tasty—fruit.

The pads tend to orient their flat surfaces to the east or west, avoiding the more intense southern exposure, and it grows low to the ground, a strategy that serves it well on our windy shores. These special adaptations come at a cost: Prickly Pear grows very slowly.

There are large numbers of this plant at Sammy's Beach (Goose Creek), Orient Beach State Park (Hallock Bay), and Indian Island County Park near Riverhead.

pond that appears to be a dead end. I became familiar with this area last winter while on the Orient Christmas Bird Count, and knew that a short navigable section of mosquito ditch linked this with another, larger salt pond approximately a half-mile in from the bay.

Soon Rob and I are standing next to an interpretive sign on an old roadway, enjoying some of the most beautiful scenery on Long Island. At our feet are hundreds of specimens of Long Island's only native cactus, the Prickly Pear Cactus (*Opuntia humifusa*), and in the woods nearby are remnants of the fish factory that operated and housed a small village of workers in the 1800s. The Park Superintendent has some great photos of the fish factories, an interesting era of East End history. I would love to see these ruins made more accessible and interpreted some day.

Paddling back to the bay, I try to photograph the oddly-shaped, multi-stemmed Eastern Red Cedars that border the marsh and salt ponds here. The low, late afternoon sunlight seems to illuminate my subject perfectly, but it just doesn't look quite the same in my viewfinder.

Back in the bay, we cross over to Peters Neck Point to explore the small embayment formed by it and Brown's Point. It is now getting late, and we are pushing our luck with getting back to the cars before dark, but neither one of us has been in this section of the bay before. It turns out to be well worth the time and effort. An island of oaks called Gid's Island divides the embayment in two, with the southern arm leading to a small but navigable tidal creek that passes under Peters Neck Road. A beautiful stretch of water, this creek hugs the back edge of the bay dune and winds its way westward to Hog Pond, not far from the site of the Old Slave Burial Ground on Narrow River Road.

The historic burial ground has an informative monument and is worth visiting. Unfortunately, the well-protected creek does not appear to be navigable all the way to Hog Pond; my guess is it's two-tenths of a mile short of Narrow River Road.

The sun has now set but there is plenty of twilight to navigate by. Noticing a series of ditches running along the landward side of Gid's Island and Brown's Point, Rob and I hope our good luck will hold as we try to cut across the marshland and avoid the longer paddle around the island and point.

The channel separating Gid's Island is wide and a nice passage; the contorted route across Brown's Point is another story that ends with an awkward carry and wet feet. But we have managed to explore quite a few of the nooks and crannies in Hallock Bay, one of the East End's outstanding waterways, and it has been an exceptional day on the water. ✕

# 2 | ORIENT HARBOR

DISTANCE:   3 mile loop.

ACCESS:   1) Rte. 25 causeway: No permit needed. Located 3.1 miles east of Rte. 48 and Rte. 25 intersection (Greenport). Park on the causeway's wide shoulder at its far eastern end. Most of the causeway's seaward edge is armored with rock, but the eastern end has a sandy beach suitable for launching a canoe or kayak.

2) Trumans Beach/NYSDEC access: No permit needed. From intersection of Rte. 48 and Rte. 25 (Greenport) drive 3.4 miles east to access on the north side of Rte. 25.

3) Harbor River Road: Southold Town permit needed. Facing water, launch from cobble beach on right.

*November*

Our delightful Indian summer weather held through early November, and all sorts of people were out on the water. Kayakers and sailors in boats, scallopers in chest waders hunched over their homemade underwater viewfinders, and rod and reelers trying their luck from shore. There were even a few scuba divers taking advantage of the excellent visibility found in the bay at this time of year.

I was picking up a friend at the Orient ferry, and lashed a canoe to the truck in hopes of doing a short paddle in that area before the sun set. Orient refers to the area of the North Fork east of Dam Pond, a pretty mosaic of farmland, woods, marshes, beaches, tidal creeks, and bays that totals 3,000 acres. It was once home to the Poquatuck Indians. The first permanent English settlers moved in around 1661 and named the area Oysterponds. It was changed to Orient in 1836.

We park and launch from the NYSDEC access on the north side of Rte. 25, shoving off into Long Island Sound and heading west along Truman Beach. Surfcasters nod a quiet hello as we pass them to port. Off to starboard the water-filled horizon extends eight miles to the low coastal hills of Connecticut.

Truman Beach's cobbles are piled too high to see over from the canoe's low vantage point, but it is fairly obvious when we are abreast of Dam Pond. Our plan is to portage across the narrow beach and into Dam Pond, a picture-perfect stretch of water whose outlet flows into Orient Harbor. Be aware that most of the narrow, steep cobble beach separating the Sound from the pond is privately owned, and

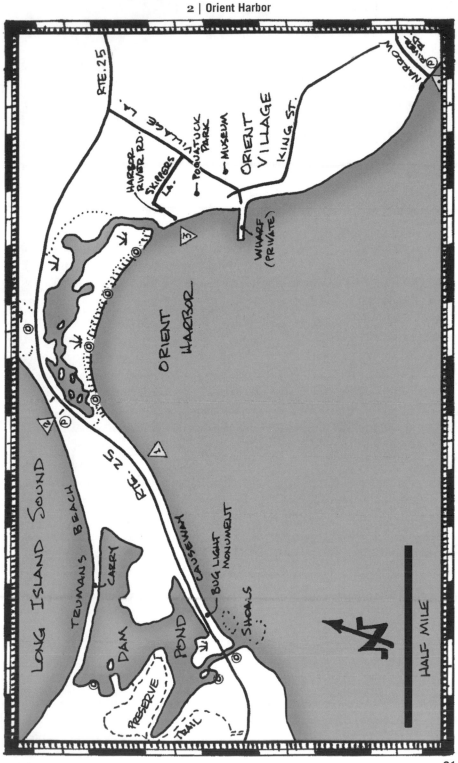

please respect that fact. Look for signs marking a 150-foot-wide section of Town-owned beach, and portage there (see map).

The recent acquisition by Southold Town of this half-acre lot was funded through the town's Real Estate Transfer Tax. Southold Town residents and public officials have a strong commitment to preserving open space, including the remainder of the cobble beach here should the owners be willing to sell at some time in the future.

The beach here, quite unlike anything on the South Fork, is entirely composed of smooth, rounded, egg-sized rocks, mostly quartz. I find the lack of sand material here interesting, and can only surmise that it is somehow related to the process of glaciation. The south side of both the Ronkonkoma and Harbor Hills terminal moraines were the recipients of large amounts of fine sediments, including sand, that were carried southward from the glacier's leading edge by glacial meltwater. These deposits created the outwash plains that extended far beyond the southern limit of the glacial ice mass. South of the Ronkonkoma moraine, this outwash plain now extends well out to sea and provides the raw material for our world-class, perfectly textured ocean beaches.

The outwash plain associated with the Harbor Hills moraine extends south into what is now the Peconic Bay–Gardiners Bay estuary, and provides the raw material for the bayside beaches on the North Fork. It may also be the raw material for the bayside beaches on the South Fork, having moved into position through the action of tidal and wind driven currents over the 10,000 years since the glaciers melted.

Perhaps the beaches on the North Fork's Sound side, as in the case of Truman Beach, are short on sand material because they are not located on or near an outwash plain. In any event, Truman Beach has a few other characteristics worth noting. During Colonial times it was called Hard Beach. Despite that name, eight storms over the last 300 years have punched through the beach and isolated Orient from the rest of the North Fork.

In his book *Eastern Long Island Geology With Field Trips* geologist Les Sirkin makes specific reference to some of the unique geological features of the Truman Beach–Dam Pond area. The low-lying sliver of land that includes Dam Pond and the unnamed tidal marsh to the east is a cut in the Harbor Hill moraine carved out by glacial meltwater. The meltwater channel crossed what is now Gardiners Bay as a tributary of the main channel that cut through the Ronkonkoma moraine in the vicinity of Napeague.

Truman Beach to the north and the unnamed beach bordering Orient Harbor to the south form a double tombolo connecting, only recently in geologic time, Orient with the rest of the North Fork.

After making the easy, short portage, we resume paddling in the quiet waters of Dam Pond. Most of the pond's west shoreline has been preserved through joint County and Town acquisitions. Again, revenue from the Town's Real Estate Transfer

## Community Preservation Fund (a.k.a. Real Estate Transfer Tax)

In 1984, several East End environmental groups and public officials lobbied New York State government to allow the Town of East Hampton to establish a real estate transfer tax to be used to fund open space acquisitions. This important environmental initiative, modeled after the successful Nantucket transfer tax, was killed by the powerful New York State Realtors Association and Builders Association lobby groups.

In 1998, with development clearly threatening many of the qualities that its residents cherish, a broad coalition of the East End's environmental, political and business leaders, including many local realtors, descended on Albany and prevailed in getting the enabling legislation for the transfer tax passed. This time, all five East End towns surrounding the Peconic Estuary were included.

While the success of this initiative was due to its widespread community support, several people who played a major role in the effort are worth noting. They are Kevin McDonald of the Group for the South Fork, NYS Assemblyman Fred Thiele, Stuart Lowrie of The Nature Conservancy, and Edwin "Buzz" Schwenk. Buzz initially represented the Long Island Builders Institute; when they refused to support the initiative, he resigned and continued to work with the coalition on his own.

Called the Community Preservation Fund (CPF), the program generates land acquisition funds via a 2% real estate transfer tax on land and home sales. The tax is based on the purchase price less a fixed exemption that is designed to avoid impacting low income purchasers. For example, on the purchase of a $475,000 house in Southampton, $250,000 is deducted before calculating the transfer tax, which amounts to $4,500.

Since its inception in April of 1999, the Community Preservation Fund has generated $237 million (through 12/04) and has protected 5,000 acres of land throughout the East End. It has become one of our most popular environmental initiatives. The original CPF had a sunset date for December 2010, but residents overwhelmingly passed a recent proposal to extend the CPF another 10 years.

This important program is helping to ensure that our East End waterways remain a beautiful place to paddle for future generations.

Tax enabled the preservation of this and many other significant open spaces in the area since the tax's inception in 1998.

The preserve is a beautiful mix of salt marsh, glacial erratics, forest, and shrubs. In 2003, the Town and County began removing some of the shrubs and restoring the grassland plant community. The only drawback to paddling here is the fairly constant sound of automobiles carried by the prevailing southwesterly wind across the otherwise tranquil waters.

According to *Historic Orient Village*, a publication by the Oysterponds Historical Society, at one time a tide mill with a huge water wheel was located at the pond's outlet. There appears to be plenty of water for paddling the pond and negotiating the outlet at all tidal stages. Once clear of the bridge and into the bay, however, the pond's channel splinters into a network of narrow, shallow chutes bisecting a series of even shallower shoals that are high and dry at low tide.

Passing the causeway access point, we paddle parallel to a narrow, low ridge of upland adorned with four Osprey poles. Many of these nesting platforms, as well as quite a few others in the Orient area, were erected by local naturalists and interested volunteers. I've heard that Bob Gloria is responsible for organizing much of this work. The sites were well chosen, as they've usually been occupied and produced young.

The USGS topographic map for this area marks this low ridge with the map symbol for levee. From the canoe it appears to be a low dune vegetated with typical bayside shrubs and grasses. But upon closer inspection, pieces of concrete and asphalt are found in the mix. Back in the office, I check the Soil Conservation Service maps and find that the low ridge is labeled as "fill." The rationale for the levee and the date it was built are unknown to me, as is the name of the salt pond behind it.

A small rock jetty marks the entrance to the salt pond at the levee's east end. It's best to time a paddle into the pond with the end of the flood tide, as the current moves fast out of the narrow outlet, and the pond itself is quite shallow. The pond and adjacent salt marsh are owned by the Orient–East Marion Park District. Although the pond's upper end comes quite close to Rte. 25 across from the starting point, the marsh separating the two is posted with "no trespassing" signs. To complete the circuit, take out at the east end of the causeway (access point #1 on the map), and walk the two-tenths of a mile back to the start.

At some point you might consider going ashore and stretching your legs with a walk around Orient Village, a very attractive and historic area well worth a visit. Given its location on Orient Harbor, this is not as simple as it sounds. The Village's entire waterfront is privately-owned with the exception of an awkward public access where Harbor River Road ends on the water (access #3 on the map). The road end and northwest side are bulkheaded and armored with concrete and rock. Facing the road from the water, take out at the cobble beach to your left. But stay as close as possible to the road (within its 50-foot-wide right-of-way) to avoid trespassing on the adjacent residential property's beach.

It's a short (two-tenths of a mile) enjoyable walk to the Orient Country Store for a coffee and bite to eat. Also consider visiting the Oysterponds Historical Society complex a few blocks further south on Village Lane. ✕

# 3 | HASHAMOMUCK POND

*Town of Southold*

DISTANCE: 4 miles R/T between its headwaters at the western end of Long Creek and its outlet on Southold Bay.

ACCESS: 1) Bayview Avenue: Southold Town permit required. Traveling east on Rte. 48, continue 0.7 miles past Hashamomuck Beach (on Long Island Sound) and turn right onto Albertson Lane. Make the next right onto Colony Road and turn left onto Bayview Avenue. Continue to end and look for the launch site on the right. (NOTE: Launch sites at the north end of Southold Bay can also be used to access the pond.)

*September*

Nautical charts and USGS topographical maps label the largest of the North Fork's fresh and tidal ponds as Hashamomuck Pond. It also goes by the name Arshamomaque Pond, another tongue-twister of Native American derivation. The pond occupies a relic meltwater channel carved through a portion of the Harbor Hill Moraine (called the Roanoke Point Recessional Moraine between Smithtown and East Marion) during the last glacial era thousands of years ago. According to geologist Les Sirkin, this particular channel swung eastward at Shelter Island Sound to flow along the north side of Jennings Point and the dramatic kame known as Shelter Island Heights.

The main pond, combined with a narrow western arm called Long Creek and its outlet to Shelter Island Sound known as Mill Creek, is two miles in length. Its northwestern end is separated from Long Island Sound by a tombolo a mere 200 yards wide. Unfortunately, private property and privately owned roads prevent public access to Hashamomuck Town Beach and the possibility of a portage from Pond to Sound, or vice versa.

This portage route was part of an historic event. On May 23, 1777 thirteen whaleboats carrying 170 men of the Continental Army crossed the Sound from Guilford, Connecticut, dragged the boats across the low sand spit into Hashamomuck Pond, and continued on to surprise the British at Sag Harbor. There they took 90 prisoners before returning to Guilford. The entire journey, known as Meig's Raid in honor of the Lt. Col. who led the troops, took 25 hours.

While replicating Meig's Raid is not possible today, there are a variety of public access points which can be used to explore this beautiful and historic waterway. On a summer-like September day, I am joining friends Greg Donaldson and John Todaro for a paddle to Hashamomuck by way of Shelter Island. We launch from

**35**

Crescent Beach near the Pridwin Inn, approximately one and a half miles from the entrance to Mill Creek.

The narrow section of water separating Shelter Island from Conkling Point on the North Fork is surprisingly deep, with several 90-foot marks recorded on the chart. Tidal currents can be strong, and as they flow over the uneven bottom here they create unusual boils on the surface. A foul tide in the narrows is easily avoided by paddling close to shore (watch for rocks) and crossing to the North Fork west of Camp Quinipet's gazebo at Jennings Point. There, the waterway widens significantly and the tidal current is less noticeable.

This Osprey has constructed a nest atop an abandoned chimney on Mill Creek.

We regroup near the dilapidated brick chimney that has been converted into a nest by Ospreys. The chimney may be a remnant of one of the brickyards that operated here until 1939. Large areas of Canadice Silt Loam, a soil type high in fine clay, are found nearby. This natural resource, along with abundant fisheries, excellent agricultural soils, freshwater, and a large stand of White Pines attracted settlers to the area, both Native Americans (the Corchaug) and later, the English. The English harvested the White Pines for lumber and used its resinous sap to make turpentine. An historic marker on the east side of the Rte. 25 bridge over Mill Creek reads:

Hashamomack

or

Arshamomaque

1636–37

Hashamomack was the first place of English Occupation in Southold Town, oldest Town founded by English speaking people in New York State. By letters patent from the Earl of Sterling, seekers of Sperrits Resin (turpentine) came to dwell on ye Necke called Hashamomack.

I should mention that there's been a long-standing debate between Southold and Southampton about the "oldest town founded by English speaking people in New York State" claim.

The entrance to Mill Creek is marked by two navigational buoys. Once inside we turn right and pass through a narrows, hugging the creek's west shore to avoid a large area of shoals and the brunt of an ebb current. Both the Rte. 25 and LIRR bridges have plenty of clearance, but be careful of the swifts under the railroad

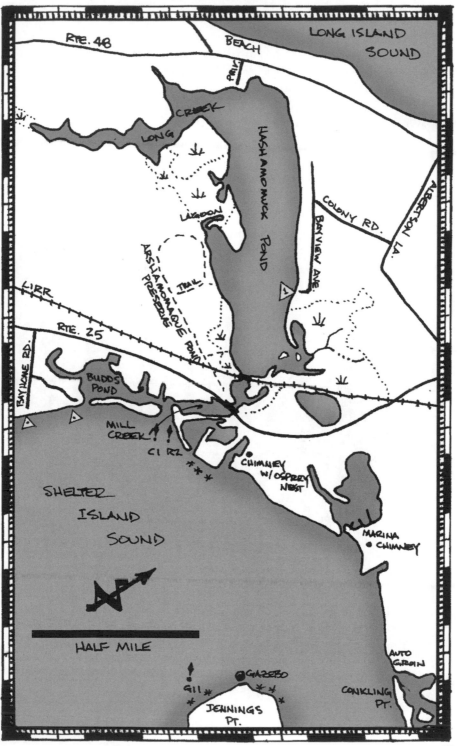

bridge. They flow at an angle to the bridge such that they could pin your boat to one of the pilings and cause a dangerous capsize.

Soon after the first English settlers arrived, a mill was constructed here to harness the strong tidal current. An earlier name for this waterway was Tom's Creek, in reference to the first miller, Thomas Benedict. Water-powered mills turned grindstones to make flour from grain, saws to make lumber from logs, and paddles to make fabric from wool and flax. One operated here until the 1870s.

Once under the trestle and in the pond, we follow the undeveloped west shoreline along the Town's Arshamomaque Pond Preserve, created in 2000. An acquisition in 2004 doubled the size of the preserve to nearly 50 acres. The preserve's entrance and start of its mile-long nature trail are located on the north side of Rte. 25 just west of the bridge. For paddlers wishing to stretch their legs, the trail can be accessed from the water at the two points on the map where it swings close to the pond.

En route to the pond's west end, I make a short diversion to explore a shallow cove. There, an obviously man-made lagoon leads around the back side of a pretty oak hummock but does not reconnect back to the pond. Barely visible through the

## Native Americans

In the 1600s, when the first European settlers arrived on the East End of Long Island, the area was inhabited by four groups of Native Americans. The Corchaugs occupied the North Fork, the Manhasetts resided on Shelter Island, and the Shinnecocks and Montauketts claimed western and eastern portions, respectively, of the South Fork. All four groups were closely-related and not considered separate tribes. In fact, in the mid-1600s, the Sachems, or leaders, of all four groups were brothers.

The routes described in this book were once traveled by Native Americans, and several pass close by known village sites, burial grounds and encampments. Theirs were dugout canoes, essentially hollowed-out trees, the largest of which were made from the Tulip and Sycamore, and were capable of carrying 10 to 30 men. Both of these tree species were part of a forest community that no longer exists on the East End today, having been cleared long ago for farming.

Many of the placenames in use on Long Island today were adopted by the first English and Dutch settlers from their Native American neighbors three and a half centuries ago. Some, like Mashashimuet in Sag Harbor and Hashamomuck in Southold, are tongue twisters that take some time to learn. But all, such as Sebonac, Cutchogue, Mashomack, Napeague, are beautiful sounding words whose literal translation often aptly describes this lovely and interesting landscape. I have tried to include information about the origin and meaning of these placenames, as well as those of English origin, in this book.

Phragmites is the reason for the lagoon: a source of fill to construct a simple road over the tidal marsh to the wooded hummock.

Turning into Long Creek, I am surprised to see both sides of this waterway developed with homes. Fortunately, most of the current homeowners have kept the natural shoreline vegetation intact, including some large oaks, American Beeches, Red Maples, and Tupelos. A Great Blue Heron, Little Green Heron, Belted Kingfisher, and several Ospreys—all piscivores—are perched on branches overhanging the creek.

The reason for the collection of fish-eaters soon becomes apparent. In the shallows near the far end of Long Creek, the placid water periodically erupts with silvery fish flying through the air in every direction. Hundreds of two-to-three-inch-long fish travel in tight formations beneath our kayaks, obviously being pursued by larger, and hungry, fish. One of the eruptions results in a half-dozen fish being stranded atop a mat of floating Sea Lettuce (*Ulva lactuca*). Curious as to the identity of the abundant silvery prey, I paddle over and scoop one up. It is a member of the Herring family, of which there are 10 species found in this area. The young are difficult to identify by species, but this one is strongly compressed, deep body with a brassy tint and dark spot on its sides is most likely that of an Atlantic Menhaden (*Brevoortia tyrannus*), also known as Bunker.

Making our way back out into Shelter Island Sound, we follow the west shore of Conkling Point, passing a bizarre collection of rusted automobile chassis exposed by the falling tide. They are being used as a groin to shore up the beach from the scouring action of tidal currents. Just east of the auto graveyard we turn into a pretty stretch of salt pond behind the point, and spend some time exploring its quiet waters until a combination of grumbling stomachs, fading light, and thirsty mouths call for turning back to Crescent Beach and leaving the exploration of Pipes Cove for another day. ✕

# 4 | CUTCHOGUE HARBOR

*Cutchogue, Town of Southold*

DISTANCE: The harbor, along with several tidal creeks and coves that feed into it, has at least 10 miles of shoreline to explore. The circumnavigation of Little Hog Neck is 6 miles. The crossing from the South Fork (North Sea Road) to Nassau Point on Little Hog Neck is 2 miles (one way).

ACCESS: 1) Nassau Point Beach: Town of Southold permit needed for road end access; Cutchogue–New Suffolk Park District permit needed for bathing beach parking lot. From Rte. 25 in Cutchogue turn south on Skunk Lane (13.9 miles east of Rte. 105). Travel 1.8 miles from Rte. 25 to road end access or 1.9 miles to parking lot on left.

2) Pequash Avenue Beach (a.k.a. Fleet's Neck Beach): Park District permit needed for park; Town of Southold permit needed for road end access. From Rte. 25 in Cutchogue turn south on Pequash Avenue (10.7 miles east of Rte. 105). Go to end (1.1 mile from Rte. 25). Road end access is straight ahead; park is on the right.

3) New Suffolk Beach: Southold Town permit required. From Rte. 25 in Cutchogue turn south on New Suffolk Road (10.3 miles east of Rte. 105). Travel 1.6 miles from Rte. 25, turn left onto Jackson St. and continue to end. Park is on the right.

4) North Sea Road: No permit needed. From Rte. 27 near Southampton Village turn north onto North Sea Road and follow it for 4.2 miles (avoid the right turn onto Noyac Road) to a dead end on the bay.

NOTES: Cutchogue Harbor is located in the northwest corner of Little Peconic Bay and framed by Little Hog Neck on the east, Fleets Neck on the north, and New Suffolk (once called Robins Island Neck) on the west. The source of the harbor's name, as well as that of the surrounding land and nearby hamlet, is "Corchaug," the name of the group of Native Americans residing on the North Fork in the 1600s when the first European settlers arrived. Corchaug means "principal place of refuge" and refers to the stockaded fort that the Corchaugs built on the west shore of Downs Creek, one mile west of the harbor.

There are five well-protected coves and creeks adjacent to the harbor that are worth exploring: Wickham Creek, East Creek, Mud Creek, and Wunneweta Pond on the west side of Little Hog Neck, and the Haywater Cove and Broadwater Cove waterway. My favorites were Wickham and Mud Creeks and Wunneweta Pond. I also enjoyed the six-mile circumnavigation of Little Hog Neck.

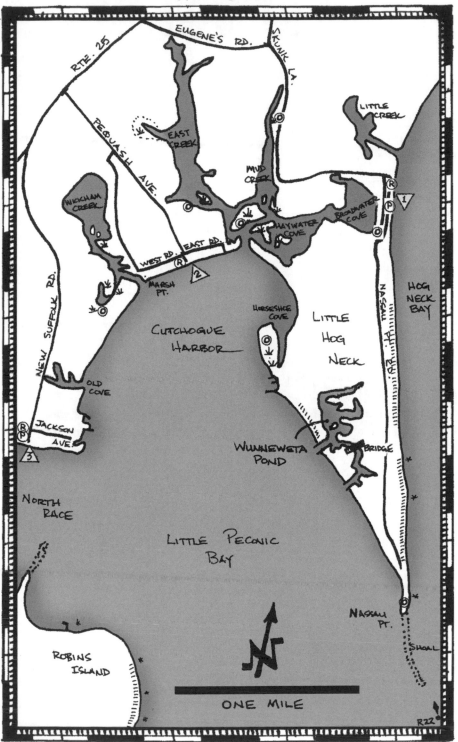

CUTCHOGUE HARBOR

LITTLE PECONIC BAY

ONE MILE

*July*

Standing on the beach where North Sea Road meets Little Peconic Bay, the forecasted 25-knot southwesterly wind is not readily apparent. There, in the lee of Cow Neck, the bay appears quite calm. Nassau Point, my landfall on the North Fork, is clearly visible two miles away. I am getting a late start but still have plenty of daylight to make the crossing and locate some friends barbecuing on the northwest corner of Little Hog Neck.

Despite what I see before me, the weather forecast had called for a rough crossing, so I prepare for one. My spray skirt in place, I tether the chart case to the deck, stow my camera in a waterproof container, and lash that to the kayak as well. Since I am paddling alone, I tuck my paddle float securely under some decklines in the event of a capsize. And, of course, I am wearing my lifejacket. I check everything (or so I think) once more and, satisfied, shove off.

I am making good time and within 10 minutes the South Fork falls a half-mile astern. Now I am beginning to feel that 25-knot wind, and the waves it is generating. The incoming tide, working against the wind, is making the seas particularly steep and choppy. As the kayak is tossed around I brace my knees against the underside of the deck for more stability. This is my first rough water paddle of the year, and it takes me awhile to relax and enjoy the exhilarating conditions.

Another half-mile out and wind and waves increase even more. Now, with the kayak wanting to turn up into the wind, I am struggling to keep on course. This is a common problem where wind and waves are on the beam (perpendicular to the direction of travel) or are quartering aft (about 45° off the stern). My boat has a rudder for such situations, but when I attempt to engage it I realize I haven't removed the bungee cord that keeps it from flopping around atop my car. I am able to compensate for this by doing some sweep strokes, but it is tiring work.

Fortunately, an incoming tide seems to be compensating for the effect of the wind, and I manage to keep on a fairly straight line for Nassau Point. Passing navigational aid R22, I turn east and, with wind and waves dead astern, paddle and surf toward the shoals. In their lee I find some shelter from the seas and can sort out my rudder. Ahead I can see waves breaking over the barely submerged sandy spit. I am hoping that I can catch a wave and ride over the shallows.

I do. Although the east side of the shoal offers no protection from the wind, the water there is flat. I land on an exposed section of the shoal to take a photo, sort out my rudder, and stretch my stiff back and tight hamstrings. Then I slide my boat over the sand and prepare to get back into the stormy bay.

Wading far enough from shore to avoid breaking waves, I wiggle into the cockpit and paddle another 20 feet to deeper water. That is the easy part. Now I have to secure the spray skirt to the rim of the cockpit before the wind pushes me back into the breaking waves and onto the shoal. On the third try, after having to pick up my paddle twice to gain more sea room, all is secured, my rudder is engaged, and I am underway.

Not for long. Applying pressure on the rudder pedal to turn north, the starboard cable snaps. Back to shore for repairs and another wet launch. But it is worth the effort. With the rudder in place I can paddle more efficiently and soon cruise by the shorebird nesting area and occupied Osprey platform at Nassau Point. Just beyond some steep bluffs I turn into a small inlet and leave the stormy sea and noisy wind behind.

According to my chart, this unnamed tidal creek runs under a road and joins Wunneweta Pond. I am hoping that the creek is navigable, and that I can float through the bridge or culvert underneath the road. Luck is with me on both counts. The winding waterway is a delightful paddle, and the salt pond is full of waterbirds: Great and Snowy Egrets, Canada Geese, Common Terns, and Great Black-backed and Herring Gulls. Like myself, they are probably here seeking refuge from the stormy bay.

Back out into the bay via Wunneweta Pond inlet, it is a short paddle down the beach to a bonfire, dry clothes, food, and friends. I have packed a light and planned to return to the South Fork later in the night. Paddling at night, under the right conditions, is a wonderful experience. But the wind never lets up, so I stay over and plan to paddle back the next morning.

Morning finds the wind still blowing hard out of the west-southwest. I pull out my well-tattered xerox of the topographical map for this area, and study it. There are three tidal creeks nearby, all flowing into Cutchogue Harbor. Although the map depicts quite a few roads in the area, most likely an indication of fairly dense development, there are enough blank spaces on the map to pique my interest. Since I have never paddled this area before and am not in a rush, I decide to explore the creeks before continuing clockwise around Little Hog Neck and re-crossing the bay.

In a finger of salt marsh owned by the Nature Conservancy near Horseshoe Cove, I watch a pair of our smallest and most common falcons. Hovering in place just 10 feet above the marsh grasses, the Kestrels periodically dart down at suitable prey, possibly grasshoppers and other large insects in this case. The preserve is also home to a pair of Ospreys. An adult, perched on a tall stake not far from the nest pole, picks at some type of flatfish it has pinned in its right foot, while a fledgling, nearly as large as the adult, cries pitifully from the edge of the stick nest. Despite the racket it is making, the adult seems unperturbed.

Wickham Creek is the westernmost of the harbor's tidal creeks that I want to explore, and I head there next, hugging Fleet Neck to get some protection from the wind. The west side of its entrance is marked by a pretty sandy beach at the foot of a small, sparsely vegetated hill. According to the County soil map, the hill is not a natural feature but a man-made one resulting from deposition of fill, probably sand dredged up from the creek's entrance many years ago.

Although not posted and a tempting spot to land and go ashore, the beach and hill may be privately-owned. Much of the west side of the creek is owned by the Wickham family, whose ancestors were among the first English speaking settlers to begin farming on the North Fork several hundred years ago. A significant portion of their farm and adjacent wetlands has been preserved through a PDR, or Purchase of Development Rights, program. Hopefully the scenic hill is also part of the preserved area.

Just inside the creek are a small marina on the right (east) and a large expanse of salt marsh on the left. The latter, quite a pretty stretch of landscape, wraps around behind the man-made hill and is bisected by a narrow, but navigable, tributary of the main creek. My map indicates that the narrow creek eventually opens up into a small salt pond, and the side trip looks appealing.

A short way in I realize that the Ospreys occupying the nest on the edge of the pond are not happy with my approach, and I turn back. It is late July and many of this year's hatchlings have already left their nests. But the unusually cold spring could have delayed some nesting.

Near the northern end of the main creek, a young family is busy clamming. Most of the shoreline has a narrow band of wetland grasses and shrubs that effectively screens the farm fields a stone's throw away. Aside from the small marina and a handful of houses, the creek's shoreline is quite undeveloped and makes for a very scenic paddle.

Back in the harbor, I make a note that Marsh Point is situated on the bold shoreline of Fleet Neck and it is unlikely that it ever supported a marsh. Later, back at home with soil and topographical maps, I would surmise that the creek's inlet may have been further west, with the salt pond and narrow tributary having been the original creek bed before the area was dredged. If so, Marsh Point once extended as much as a quarter-mile further to the southwest as a low-lying spit of sand and marsh.

Passing the protected bathing beach, playground, and rest rooms that mark the Town Park on Fleets Neck, I turn north and ride an incoming tide through an inlet which quickly branches in three different directions. I choose the westernmost arm of water which leads into East Creek.

A very short Osprey platform on a marshy island at the confluence of the three waterways has an active nest. In contrast to Wickham Creek, most of East Creek's shoreline is lined with homes. Two other Osprey nesting platforms are unoccupied. The nicest stretch of the creek is at the far northern end. There I startle a large Snapping Turtle that surfaces next to my kayak, and paddle under the watchful eyes of a Great Egret perched in a creekside tree.

## Hog Neck

The derivation of placenames is something that has always intrigued me. I noticed that Hog Neck is a name found in several places on the East End, including Little Hog Neck and Great Hog Neck on the North Fork, and North Haven (once known as Hog Neck) on the South Fork. They all share a common feature: all are points of land that nearly form an island.

In *Changes in the Land: Indians, Colonists, and the Ecology of New England*, author William Cronon points out that hogs had several characteristics that set them apart from most other livestock brought over by the early settlers. Most importantly, they could hold their own against predators, including the wolves and bears that populated Long Island into the 1700s. And they could eat almost anything.

Hogs had one serious drawback. They could do major damage to cultivated crops, and needed to be isolated from those areas. The solution used by early settlers was simple. Hogs were let loose on necks or peninsulas that required a minimum of fencing where it connected to the mainland. Hog ears were notched to distinguish ownership, and they were left alone until fall when a portion of the fattened adults were harvested and the young of the year were marked. And so, the names of these necks reflected their use as areas to raise hogs.

En route to Mud Creek, I manage to safely negotiate through a flock of 10 Mute Swans. In some waterways, boaters have made a habit of feeding them, changing their behavior from that of an aggressive but wary animal to that of an aggressive, in-your-face creature which is not happy if you have nothing to offer. From the low sitting position of most kayaks, this can result in a very uncomfortable eyeball-to-eyeball confrontation.

Much of Mud Creek's eastern side is relatively undeveloped and quite scenic. The northern third of the creek is very narrow, coursing through a pretty salt marsh owned by the Nature Conservancy. An Osprey nesting structure there is occupied and the nesting pair have successfully fledged one young. One of the adults is perched on another platformless pole, busily tearing chunks of flesh off of a nice-sized fish in its talons.

From Mud Creek I paddle up into Broadwater Cove. Except for a narrow belt of sand at Little Hog Neck's northeast corner, the cove separates the neck from the mainland of the North Fork. Littoral (shoreline) currents carrying sand northward from the neck's eroding bluffs facing Hog Neck Bay create a tombolo over which I have to make a short portage.

Just north of an unoccupied Osprey pole is a sandy beach suitable for landing and carrying over to Nassau Point Beach, a pretty Town bathing beach on Hog Neck Bay. It is possible that, many years ago, easterly storms periodically cut through the tombolo and made a temporary waterway linking Hog Neck Bay and Broadwater Cove. Sometime prior to the 1970s, fill was brought in to shore up the tombolo and better protect it, and Nassau Point Road, from storm damage.

Except for narrowly missing a large rock whose barnacle-covered top was barely out of sight, the paddle south along Little Hog Neck's east shore is uneventful. The towering bluffs completely shield me from the west winds. Residential development spans the length of the steep shoreline, in places rising 70 feet above the bay, and much of the shoreline here is bulkheaded.

The steep bluffs here are what's left of kames, or conical hills, formed by the retreating glacier. Little Hog Neck was part of a recessional moraine deposit that included Robins Island to the west and Great Hog Neck, Shelter Island, Gardiners Island, and Corn Neck (Block Island) to the east.

The west wind greets me again at Nassau Point. Hugging the east edge of the shoals I am afforded some protection from the waves. Standing nearby on the gravel spit, beaks into the wind, are two odd-looking birds that I am surprised to see in late July. The male of this species has a spectacularly long tail that is hard to confuse with anything else bobbing around on the bay, marking them Long-tailed Ducks. According to John Bull's *Birds of New York*, large numbers of these birds are found on the East End bays in winter, but they are very uncommon between April and October. These two are either injured or young birds that are not yet mature enough to breed.

Continuing on, I run the length of the Nassau Point shoal and soon lose its protection from the bay's steep waves. A direct line to my car at North Sea Road puts me on a heading that is almost straight into the wind and waves, so I fall off a bit to port and make for the tall, sandy bluff that marks Homes' Hill. This distinctive landmark stands just west of the entrance to North Sea Harbor. Once there, I am again shielded from the wind and waves and turn west, following the shoreline a short distance to my takeout. With lunch at Cromer's Market in Noyac on my mind, I quickly pack up, take a swim, and get on the road. ✕

# 5 | PECONIC RIVER

*Towns of Riverhead, Brookhaven, and Southampton*

DISTANCE:  10 miles from the Connecticut Avenue access to Flanders Bay.

ACCESS:  1) Connecticut Ave.: No permit needed. From LIE exit 71 (0.0 mile) turn left and pass under the LIE, over the Peconic River, and turn left onto River Road (0.3 mile). Pass the Peconic River Herb Farm (0.6 mile) and turn left onto Connecticut Avenue (unmarked; 2.0 miles). The parking area/launch site is well-marked on the left (2.3 miles).

2) Mill Road (NOTE: some maps label this South River Road): NYS-DEC Permit needed. From L.I. Expressway exit 71, turn left onto Rte. 24/Edwards Ave., pass under the LIE, and take the first left onto Mill Road. Travel 0.6 mile on Mill Road to the access on the right marked by the sign: NYSDEC Upper Peconic River Access.

3) Edwards Avenue: No permit needed. Located 0.2 mile north of LIE exit 71. Park on paved shoulder on west side of Edwards Ave. NOTE: There is no public access to the river on the east side of the road.

4) South River Road: From LIE exit 71 (0.0 mile), turn right onto Rte. 24 (heading towards Riverhead), make the first left onto South River Road (unmarked; 0.2 mile) and look for the access on the left marked by the sign "Forge Pond NYSDEC Access" (0.7 mile).

5) West Main Street: No Permit needed. Located 0.3 mile east of Forge Road and 2.1 miles west of Center Drive. This newly refurbished and hideous-looking access, a joint design venture between County Parks and the NYSDOT, is hard to miss.

6) Mill Road: No Permit needed (NOTE: There is no street sign marking this as Mill Road). It is located off West Main Street near the Snowflake Ice Cream Shop, 1.1 miles east of Forge Road and 1.0 mile west of Center Drive. Park in the NYSDEC lot.

7) Rte. 24–Peconic Avenue. The eastern terminus of the freshwater portion of the Peconic River is not very canoe or kayak friendly. The best place to exit or launch is at the earthen dam at river right. Curbing and a lack of a shoulder to park on along Rte. 24 makes loading and unloading boats here impractical. Park in the big municipal lot on the northeast side of the river, and carry across Peconic Ave. Be careful: this will be the most dangerous part of your trip down the river.

NOTES:  From its headwaters in a Red Maple swamp just west of the William Floyd Parkway, the Peconic River meanders eastward for 15 miles before reaching sea level, a drop of 60 feet in elevation or 1 foot per 0.25 mile. This is a statistic that would turn away paddlers looking for whitewater thrills, but the river has much to offer to those interested in local history or ecology, and those looking to get outdoors for a relaxing paddle through a beautiful area.

Including a tidal section spanning 3 miles, the Peconic River has a total length of 19 miles, making it the longest river on Long Island. However, with the exception of a short section in Manorville, little more than half of that distance, the 10-mile section downstream from Connecticut Avenue out into Flanders Bay, is navigable by canoe or kayak.

The river is largely groundwater fed; surface water runoff adds little to its volume. This characteristic has important ecological ramifications. Being groundwater fed, it can be contaminated indirectly by discharging pollutants into groundwater flowing towards the river, necessitating wide buffer areas for long-term protection of its water quality.

This latter point was driven home when it was discovered that the river's water, in addition to its acidic, iron-laden, nutrient-poor qualities which reflect its groundwater origin, had picked up some new characteristics as it traveled through the Brookhaven National Lab facility: the radioisotopes tritium and strontium-90. As of 2005, cleanup efforts were still underway in sections of the river three miles upstream of the Connecticut Avenue launch site.

Being largely groundwater fed also means that it is not subject to the tremendous seasonal fluctuations in height and volume that can be found on many rivers up north. Even so, some sections are quite shallow and a drop of a few inches in water level can mean the difference between floating and grounding. I recommend doing the river in the spring and fall when water levels are generally highest. These are also times when you are likely to have the river to yourself.

With the exception of the Edwards Avenue bridge, where fast water makes travelling upstream difficult and private property on its entire east (downstream) side makes portaging impossible, the entire route below Connecticut Avenue can be paddled in both directions. This makes the logistics of planning a trip much simpler, particularly for those travelling solo, as a variety of loops are possible.

A three-mile loop is feasible from any of the three access points (1, 2, 3) in the upper section (Connecticut Avenue–Edwards Avenue). Any of the access points below Edwards Avenue can be used to paddle loops measuring up to nine miles in length.

Don't overlook the possibility of a late day paddle after work. Being on the river for the sunset, paddling through the evening twilight, and then by the light of the moon, even if not full, can be a magical experience.

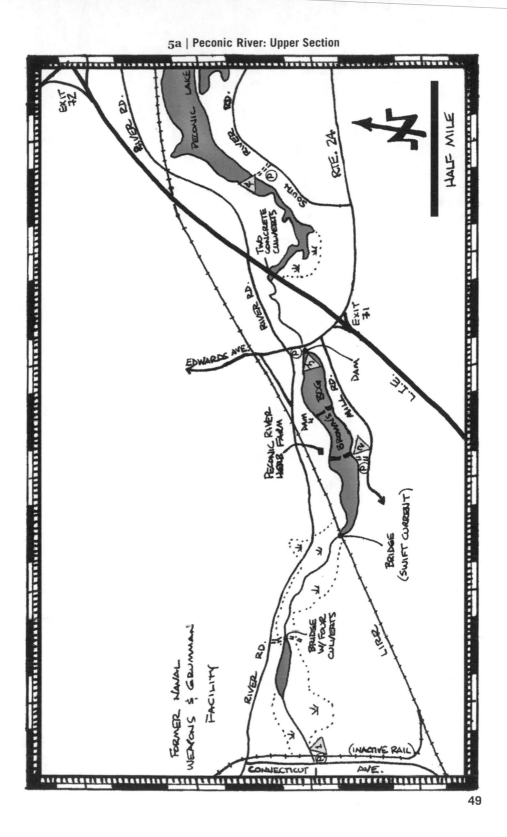

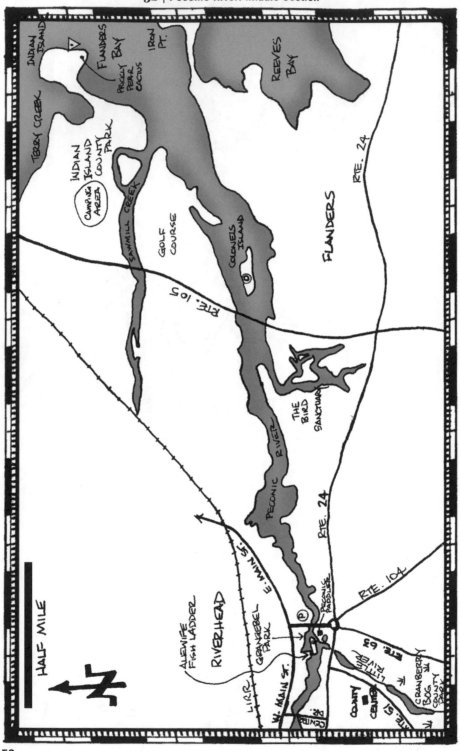

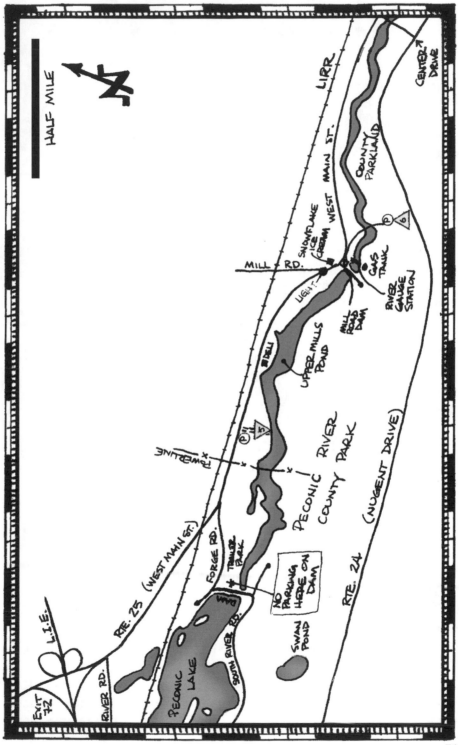

*Upper Section: Connecticut Avenue to Edwards Avenue (1.5 miles–one way)*
*October*

Autumn is a great month for paddling along our local waterways and enjoying our brilliant fall foliage, which peaks slightly ahead of our upland forests. Among our many canoeable waterways, the upper section of the Peconic River rates high for its outstanding scenery and fall colors, and September and October are perfect months to paddle it.

The launch area on the east side of Connecticut Avenue is well-marked. Walk over the train tracks (an abandoned rail line connecting the LIRR–Riverhead line with the old Grumman facility at Calverton to the north) and follow the gravel path to a wooden launch ramp. If you're lucky, the nearby Peconic River Sportsmen Club won't be having target practice, enabling you to enjoy the waterway's tranquility in addition to its scenery.

The river here is quite narrow and winds through a thick forest of Red Maples whose branches reach completely across the waterway in many places. Novice canoeists will find this first section, with its tight turns, a challenge. Don't get too distracted with the maneuvering, as there are many interesting plants to note here. Not far from the put-in, on both sides of the river, are two Willows that tower above the Red Maples, and a bit further along on the right is a large and unusually contorted Red Maple.

The shoreline is thickly vegetated with typical wetland shrubs: Speckled Alder, Sweet Pepperbush, Arrowwood, Highbush Blueberry, Swamp Honeysuckle, Fetterbush, Meadowsweet, Buttonbush, and Sweet Gale, to name but a few. Each has started to turn its own distinctive color, and what might have appeared to be a uniform wall of green shrubs a month ago is now a mass of easily distinguishable, individual species.

Adding to the riot of leaf colors are the bright red berries of the Swamp Rose and Winterberry Holly, the latter being a deciduous relative of the American Holly. Speaking of berries and foliage colors, you will hopefully recognize the pale berries and scarlet-to-purple leaves of Poison Ivy, very common and quite robust in growth along this stretch of river. If you can't pick it out, try to avoid reaching for nearby branches to straighten out your errant craft; contact with any part of this plant could leave you with the telltale rash and blisters.

The river gradually opens up with the overhanging Red Maples retreating further back from the river's edge, and a wider band of wetland shrubs developing along the immediate shoreline. Here, a few Tupelos are visible with their sharply angular branches largely barren against the sky. This early leaf-turner, putting on a spectacular display of deep reds and scarlets, has already peaked and dropped most of its leaves.

Approximately one half-mile from the start is a bridge formed by four steel culverts, all of which are usually passable. If in doubt, try to discern which of the four the main current seems to be headed through; that will likely be the best route. Overhead is an old abandoned dirt road that, to the left, connects with River Road and provides another access point to the river for fishermen. Beyond the culverts, the river continues to meander through a mix of wetland types: marshes, shrub swamps, and forested swampland. All are excellent wildlife habitats and beautiful landscapes.

Further along on the left are the remnants of an old dock and a dilapidated wooden shack. Between the two is a grassy clearing where you can easily get ashore. Another quarter-mile beyond the shack is the LIRR bridge (one mile from the start), carrying trains to and from the North Fork along the Riverhead–Greenport line. Again, the water under the bridge is easily navigable. At this point the river widens a bit more and cuts through a wetland dominated by emergent plants such as Smartweeds (*Polygonum* spp.) and Swamp Loosestrife (also known as Water Willow) which provide some interesting colors and textures of their own. Off to the sides of the main channel, you may notice faint paths through the thick aquatic vegetation. These are turtle trails. The most common turtle in this area is the Painted Turtle, but biologists have documented a total of six species in the river.

Just ahead is a long earthen dam, one of eight crossing the river and one of three between here and Edwards Avenue. This first dam has a narrow sluiceway that is passable in a canoe. The three dams on this section of the river were constructed as part of a commercial cranberry operation. They were necessary in order to regulate water levels at various times of the year to promote the growth and harvest of cranberries. The cranberry operations started here in 1870, and at least one along the river continued as late as 1974.

The shoreline here, on the right side, changes dramatically with steep, wooded slopes rising sharply to over 50 feet in elevation, then more gradually to over 100 feet above the river. At this point the river has run into the northern slopes of the Ronkonkoma moraine. You may notice a trail leading up the slope from the dam; this is another access point that is reached from Mill Road.

Off on the left side of the river is the Peconic River Herb Farm, a picturesque facility well worth a visit. Leaving the main channel, work your way over towards the far shore and find a good place to land. The river here is covered with Duckweed, a tiny floating plant that completely covers the surface of the river, making it look as if it has been painted green. More troublesome is the thick submergent vegetation, identified by Paul Stoutenburgh as Fanwort, that makes paddling awkward.

After touring the herb farm and perhaps purchasing some plants to return home with, continue downstream to the second earthen dam where a historic signpost

The upper Peconic River has some outstanding scenery.

marks this as part of the Browns Bog cranberry farm and includes a brief description of its operation.

At this point, those making a loop might want to start heading back. Although the return trip is upstream, the current is negligible with two minor exceptions where the river narrows to flow under a bridge or through the culverts; even there, the short swifts are easily negotiated and you will find the paddle back upstream as enjoyable as your earlier downriver run.

Should you want to continue down the river, be aware that although the sluiceway through this dam is often not navigable, the portage is a simple slide over the concrete spillway. Just ahead is Edwards Avenue and the third dam with a longer, but extremely canoeist-friendly, portage.

*Middle Section: Edwards Avenue to Forge Road (2 miles—one way)*
*May*
Seeing an appealing stretch of backwater to explore, I lay my paddle across the cockpit of the kayak, pull out my map, and begin jotting down some notes. Moments later, the sound of rapidly approaching, rushing water causes me to look up, more with curiosity more than alarm. There are no rapids and very little current, with the exception of several very brief sections immediately downstream of dams and spillways, to negotiate on the Peconic River. Yet the source of the noise is potentially as dangerous and less predictable than a challenging section of white water: a Mute Swan!

Quickly stowing the map and pen, I keep a close eye on the approaching swan as I back-paddle in retreat. Knowing its eight-foot wingspan includes a knobby bone which packs quite a wallop, one that broke the arm of a biologist who was addling its eggs, I maintain a good distance between us. We proceed downstream in this strange fashion, facing each other in silence except for the sound of our propulsion through the water, for a quarter mile. Satisfied, the swan finally abandons pursuit and lets me enjoy the riverside scenery.

It is a perfect evening for a paddle. The air is warm, the breeze light, and the clear sky holds the possibility of a spectacular sunset. It is too early in the season for bothersome insects, and at this time of the year I am assured of having plenty of water to negotiate the river's shallower sections without grounding. To top it off, with the exception of a few fisherman, I have the river to myself.

I had launched on the west (upstream) side of Edwards Avenue just below a dam where the NYSDEC provides public access to the river. Not long ago, this access point was in dispute, but fortunately it has been resolved. An erosion problem and tricky put-in have also been corrected, and today the portage is much improved.

Between Edwards Avenue and the Long Island Expressway underpass, the river is a narrow, twisting labyrinth through a forest of Willow and Red Maples. Early in the paddling season, before maintenance crews have been out, branches, fallen trees, and logs may test your maneuvering skills. At several points, the river forks and offers a choice of routes, none an obvious main channel. At these forks, compare the amount of current flowing into each, and choose the route with the most current.

Either of the two concrete culverts under the Long Island Expressway is passable. The tunnels are quite long and some might find the length and low clearance disconcerting and a bit claustrophobic. Kayakers will have difficulty using their paddles because of the tunnel's narrow width. Try propelling your boat by pushing against the roof with your hands. It is a shame that the construction of these culverts did not incorporate a more canoe and kayak-friendly design.

Once clear of the LIE tunnel, the river opens up and is bordered by a beautiful mix of low wetland shrubs and aquatic plants. If not for the constant roar of the LIE, one could imagine being in a remote wilderness setting. The somewhat shrubby plant that forms dense thickets here is Water Willow. On the river's south side, this interesting plant community is quite extensive and intersected by navigable backwaters. A quick side trip into it is well worth the time and effort; I am rewarded with sightings of muskrat and painted turtles, the latter seen soaking up the day's last rays of sunlight.

Most of the southern shoreline (river right) is New York State parkland, and includes a State access point (#4). Beyond the access the river gradually widens into an area called Peconic Lake that extends east to a dam at Forge Road. I usually paddle the lake's more wild-looking south side. Look for a series of uprooted Red Maples that form an unusual riverside facade of exposed roots. These trees were toppled by strong northerly winds blowing uninterrupted across the wide lake, the result being a shoreline that appears to have been neatly peeled back.

Across the lake a railway briefly hugs the shore. At one time ice was hauled out of the river here and stored in a three-story ice house before shipment to New York City by train. Not far ahead is the dam at Forge Road. For those continuing downstream, the take-out and portage is river left.

*Lower Section: Forge Road to Peconic Avenue (2.5 miles—one way)*
*June*

Forge Road is named for the large iron forge built nearby in the late 1700s. The raw iron came from the river and adjacent swamp and bog soils—thin deposits called bog iron that precipitated out of groundwater as they entered the wetland systems. Much of the iron was made into anchors and ballast for ships. As far as I know, nothing remains of the old forge itself.

For approximately 100 yards below the spillway, the river's current is quite swift before abruptly resuming its more characteristic sluggish pace. As a general rule, fast-flowing water is able to carry more suspended sediments than water moving at a slower speed. Where there is a dramatic change in current speed from fast to slow, as there is here, the river will drop much of its suspended sediments. The result is the formation of a series of sand bars which are difficult to cross even in a shallow-draft canoe or kayak. To avoid running aground, keep in mind another general rule of river dynamics: where there is a bend in the river, the current flows quickest along the outside of the bend. Although a course paddled along the inside of the bend is the shortest distance, this is where the shallows and sand bars will be most developed.

As the river widens and slows, I come upon an interesting scene. By land, sea, and air, a multi-faceted assault on the river's fish resources is underway. Along the river's edge, a Great Blue Heron silently stalks the shallows. A Double-crested Cormorant plies the deeper waters mid-stream. The aerial assault is led by a Common Tern, noisily flying less than 20 feet above the river's surface, and an Osprey, circling quietly much higher in the sky.

All four piscivores are hunting for fish, yet each has evolved a unique hunting technique that focuses its efforts on a slightly different part of the river, and perhaps different sizes of target species. These factors, when combined, comprise an important part of each species' niche and enable them to coexist without direct competition for the Peconic River's diverse fisheries resources.

Rounding out the assault team is a representative from *Homo sapiens*, casting about from an aluminum boat in hopeful pursuit of one of the river's larger-sized fish. Not far downstream a Muskrat swims by, its widening V-shaped wake pointing to a head barely visible above the water's surface. This aquatic mammal is too slow to chase down any of the river's finfish, but it periodically supplements its largely vegetarian diet to dine on freshwater mussels, making it an omnivore.

The current now is negligible, and I am paddling through a section of the river whose name, Upper Mills Pond, reflects just that: a mill pond. Nearly all of the river's southern shoreline along this stretch is protected from development; along the north side the reverse is true. In the 1980s, a moratorium on riverside development was put in place while a future land use and management plan was worked out. Most of the river corridor was designated "scenic" or "recreational" under the New York State Wild, Scenic, and Recreational Rivers Act, and both the County and State committed funding for open space acquisitions. Since 1998, Riverhead and Southampton Towns have had Real Estate Transfer Tax monies to add to the open space acquisition pot, expediting several purchases.

Today, the river's land use map reveals large swaths of publicly-owned open space in the river corridor. Still, there is some concern over the potential impacts of redevelopment along the northern shoreline just west of downtown Riverhead, an area of mostly commercial properties sandwiched between the river and Rte. 25. One exception on the north shore is a small, unmarked parcel of County parkland wedged between a residential trailer park and a long stretch of commercial property. This is an okay spot to pull up for a stop; a dock for launching was constructed there in 2005.

The preserved southern shoreline is more interesting to paddle along. From a point just east of the overhead powerlines, nearly all the way to Mill Road, there are many barely submerged pilings on the south side of the river. Beware. If struck, these unseen obstacles can cause a capsize as you over-react to the sudden pitch of the boat. These pilings may possibly be remnants of the original Atlantic White Cedar forest that grew in the wet soils along the river corridor before the Mill Road dam was constructed.

There are several other potential stops worth noting along the way to Mill Road. There is an accessible, isolated, cleared area where the powerlines cross the south side of the river. A deli and an ice cream parlor are on the north. The latter is on West Main Street, a short walk up from the NYSDEC parking lot and fishing access on Mill Road and, according to a colleague, has excellent ice cream.

At the Mill Road dam are two culverts through which the overflow enters. They are pitched at an angle, and one has enough headroom to slide through. In a plastic canoe, this was fun, but the combination of fast water, boat, and protruding paddles in a confined tube is a recipe for all sorts of bizarre disasters. As of spring 2005, one culvert had been replaced and work was ongoing on the site. On my last outing, I felt uncomfortable taking my kayak through and decided to make the short portage (river left) as most people do.

This aluminum fish ladder at the Grangebel Park dam will eventually be replaced with a permanent, concrete step pool system.

As I mentioned, most of the river's southern shoreline has been preserved through public open space acquisitions by the County and State. To give you an idea how extensive these holdings are, paddlers with some time to spare can hike through County parkland from Mill Road south to the summit of Bald Hill and the Pau-manok Path, approximately three miles away as the crow flies.

Mill Road, not surprisingly, was the site of a water-powered woolen mill in operation around 1900. There was also a small water-powered plant for generating electricity. Within 200 feet of Mill Road is another dam built to monitor the river's flow. Although barely a two-foot drop, the water is quite shallow on the downstream side where it runs over a concrete apron. This combination is awkward to run as your boat will briefly bridge between the top of the dam and the apron, creating an unstable situation that can cause a capsize and possibly some damage to your boat. The portage is on the south side (river right) and does not require carrying the boat. Simply climb out onto the concrete edge of the gauge station, slide the boat over the dam, and climb back in.

From here it is a mile paddle to the Center Drive bridge just north of the County center complex, and another half-mile to Grangebel Park and the take-out where the Little River meets the Peconic in downtown Riverhead. Grangebel Park, now owned and managed by the Town of Riverhead, has an interesting series of waterworks, paths, and gardens carved out of what was once a swamp. Created by Timothy Griffing in the late 1800s, the park is named for his three daughters: Grace, Angeline, and Mabel.

A fish ladder was recently installed at the dam there to allow Alewives (a type of herring) to reach their historic spawning areas in the freshwater reaches of the river. The ladder is a portable device that is removed after the main run is over, sometime in late May. According to NYSDEC biologist Mark Lowery, this interesting project is being monitored by Riverhead High School students and DEC fisheries staff.

For those ending their trip here, work your way over to the take-out on the far right, near the intersection of Rte. 24 and the traffic circle.

For those wishing to continue east and venture out into Peconic Bay, the dam in Grangebel Park can be portaged but the next bridge just downstream (Peconic Avenue) doesn't have enough clearance for boats at most tide levels. Jim Dreeben welcomes paddlers to portage through his property (Peconic Paddler, river right) to Peconic Avenue, and continue across the road to the put-in on the south side of the river. It is a challenge to cross busy Peconic Avenue under normal circumstances; be careful with your canoe or kayak in tow. A mile downstream, just before the next bridge (Rte. 105), is a tributary that leads into a pretty wildlife sanctuary which is definitely worth exploring. ✕

## Dams and Fish Ladders

In much of the Alewife's range, dams (and in some cases road culverts) have blocked access to freshwater spawning areas. The Peconic River has over 300 acres of suitable spawning and nursery habitat that have been blocked by a series of dams since colonial times. Until recently, Alewives have had to make do with an acre of spawning habitat found below the Grangebel Park dam in Riverhead.

That changed in the spring of 1995 when a group of volunteers led by Bob Conklin began netting Alewives and lifting them over the Grangebel Park dam. In March 2000, working with the U.S. Fish and Wildlife Service, Cornell Cooperative Extension, and the NYSDEC, Conklin installed a temporary aluminum fish ladder there. This box-like device is fabricated with baffles every 16 inches to create turbulence that allows fish to swim up the inclined device against the current.

The ladder was installed at one end of the dam and watched carefully. Alewives could be seen congregating nearby, but none entered the ladder. A decision was made to move the ladder to the opposite end of the dam, and it was an instant success. Alewives were observed swimming up while it was being put in place! Later that spring, one and a half miles above the dam, several thousand Alewives were captured on film successfully overcoming the next obstacle: a two-foot-tall concrete spillway below the Upper Mills dam. This was all the evidence some needed to deem the project a success. To others, notably NYSDEC fisheries biologist Chart Guthrie, the goal was not just to move fish upstream but to have them spawn. Success would be measured by the presence of juvenile Alewives later in the summer.

Unfortunately, subsequent surveys in the Peconic River upstream from the ladder have not revealed any juveniles. However, adults that made their way over the dam on the Little River (a tributary of the Peconic that leads to Swezey Pond), Cranberry Bog County Park, and Wildwood Lake (someone may have netted and lifted them over) successfully spawned. In the fall of 2004, a large school of juveniles was observed passing over the Little River dam on their way to the sea.

The absence of juvenile Alewives in the Peconic River above the fish ladder remains a mystery. Despite that, in August of 2004 the USFWS announced a proposal and funding to install additional fish ladders in the area: one at the dam on the Little River, another at the Mill Road dam, and a permanent, concrete "step pool" system at the south dam in Grangebel Park. USFWS biologist Tom Halavik also reported that the concrete sill at the USGS Gauge Station below Mill Road will be notched to ensure that Alewives make it over that obstacle even when water levels are low. These projects are currently being reviewed by local agencies, and will hopefully be implemented soon.

NOTE: An excellent video covering the ecology of the Alewife and the installation of the Peconic River fish ladder is available at the Riverhead Public library.

# II | SOUTHAMPTON TOWN

# 6 | SMITHERS PRESERVE

*Flanders, Town of Southampton*

DISTANCE: From the access at Birch Creek, a R/T paddle to the south end of Goose Creek is 3.5 miles, to the south end of Mill Creek is 3 miles, and to the entrance to Hubbard Creek is 5.5 miles. Birch Creek has 1.5 miles of shoreline to explore.

ACCESS: 1) Birch Creek Road: No permit needed. From Sunrise Highway (Rtc. 27) take Exit 65 North onto Rte. 24, traveling 3.4 miles to an unpaved and unmarked road on the right (first right after Spinney Road just beyond a sharp curve). Follow this for 0.4 miles to an excellent launch site on Birch Creek.

*August*

A cool, moist wind blows from the east as I ferry my kayak, paddle, lunch, and assorted notes and maps down to the creek's edge. Fog is enveloping the North Fork, giving Flanders and Peconic Bays a far greater sense of size than in actuality. Launching from the remote and scenic north end of Birch Creek Road, I decide to first explore the protected waters of this creek before venturing out onto the choppy bay. Turning south, Birch Creek quickly narrows to a width of 30 to 50 feet. A thin band of salt marsh separates it from a classic pine barrens forest to the east, while its western shoreline hugs a substantial expanse of marshland, as much as 200 yards in width, before subtle gradient changes enable Eastern Red Cedar and Post Oak, among other forest edge species, to thrive.

Not far down the narrows, I begin herding a family of Mute Swans. The largest of the threesome, an adult male, or cob, takes up the rear, placing himself between my boat and the young of the year, or cygnet, while the female leads them away. The cygnet is already quite large, nearly the size of its mother, but its plumage is still the telltale gray of an immature. Fortunately, the adults are wary of my approach but do not appear aggressive and keep moving ahead. This same scenario earlier in the summer might have evoked quite a different response and I may have found myself back paddling furiously at this point, barred from this end of the creek by an ornery, more territorial cob.

Nearing a sharp bend in the creek, I come upon a series of metal posts in the water, possibly used to secure a duck blind during the autumn waterfowl hunting season. Nearby is a "posted" sign, identifying the area as a "Licensed Shooting Preserve" owned by R. Brinkley Smithers of Mill Neck, NY. While this area is still used for hunting, it was acquired from the Smithers family in 1996 by Suffolk County, and is now open to all County residents for hiking, birding and paddling in addition to hunting.

Following the family of swans to a point not far from Rte. 24, the creek splits into a series of narrow and shallow slots that wind through the marsh grasses. Into one of these, too narrow and shallow for my boat to proceed at this tide, the swans disappear from sight. Off to the south is a grove of typical swamp trees: Red Maple and Tupelo. The presence of both signifies an area where the soil is saturated with freshwater. Not far away, just on the other side of Rte. 24, an impoundment of Birch Creek created Birch Pond, a beautiful, long, linear waterbody visible from the road. The headwater of Birch Creek is another two-tenths of a mile south of Birch Pond: a tiny natural pond visible from the Paumanok Path called Owl Pond.

Heading back toward the Birch Creek inlet and Flanders Bay, I pass close by a sandy spit that hooks into the creek from its east side and gives me good protection from the easterly wind and building seas. An assortment of birds hunkered down in the lee of this peninsula—Double-crested Cormorants, Common Terns, Herring and Black-back Gulls, a Snowy Egret, and several Willets—eye me warily as I paddle by, but most are reluctant to take flight. The exceptions are the Willets, who scold noisily as they take flight, displaying their striking white patterns on the topsides of their wings.

At the northernmost point of the spit, I turn the kayak into the wind and waves, wondering if I shouldn't pull out the spray skirt tucked behind my seat. I have one of those nylon skirts which is very effective at collecting every little drop of water that falls on it into a growing pool located directly over my lap. Within minutes, the pool begins to seep through the fabric and soon a steady drip develops, soaking my pants and eventually reforming into another pool on my seat.

I leave the skirt tucked away and continue on around the small westernmost headland that separates Birch Creek from Mill Creek. Here the sandy shore gives way to a stretch of peat sparsely vegetated with severely stunted Cordgrass (*Spartina alterniflora*). The presence of such a thick mass of peat indicates that this was once an ideal location for the growth of marsh grasses, and such ideal locations are only found where there is excellent protection from wave action. Another possibility is that most of the peat formed when this area was a freshwater bog. Either way, this area must have changed significantly over time, since neither salt marsh nor bog vegetation could survive in the current exposed location.

Clearing the headland, I turn into a small protected embayment to get a close look at an Osprey nest. The mosquito ditch leading further into the upper marsh and a small tide pool would provide a better view of the nest and might be navigable at a higher tide, but not now. Having done a census of Osprey platforms earlier in the summer, I know that this one produced young. I can see an Osprey perched on the edge of the nest platform, but I can't say for certain that this individual

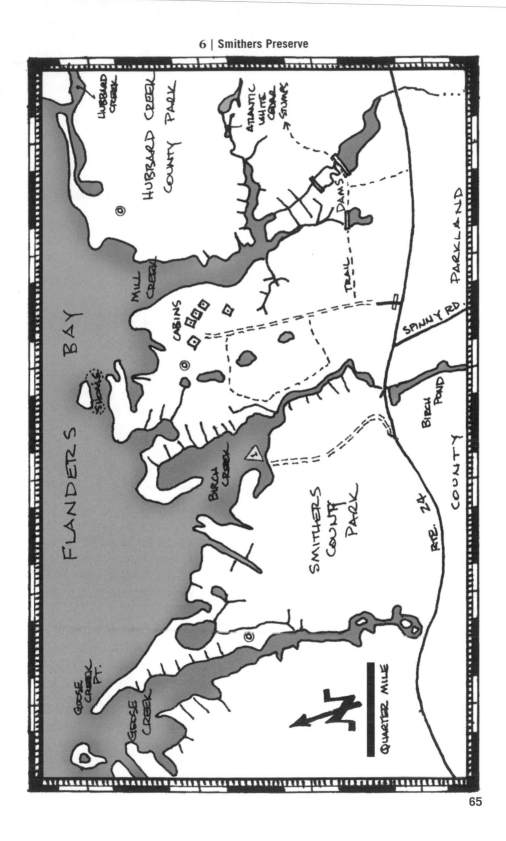

nested there. It is well past the nesting season and this may be a migrating bird resting on its way south to the Caribbean or South America.

Back on the bay, I continue east, barely sliding over the shoals between a small island and the entrance to Mill Creek. Turning right to enter the creek, I pass a large house and a cluster of cottages. The buildings were lodgings for members of the Flanders Club, a group of waterfowl and upland game hunters. I am not sure of the exact connection between this group and the Smithers family but I believe the club members leased the property from the Smithers for many years until their lease expired and the County took ownership. Another successful Osprey nest is off to the left, located along the dirt road that leads past the Black Duck Lodge in the adjacent Hubbard Creek County Park.

The County currently houses seasonal staff here, including biologists employed by the conservation organization Ducks Unlimited. These biologists have been involved in salt marsh restoration projects, and some of their work—the construction of earthen and plywood dams—can be seen on the ditches leading from the west side of Mill Creek. There has been some discussion about the possibility of utilizing the cottages as overnight accommodations for hikers (they are one mile from the Paumanok Path) and sea kayakers (as part of the East End Water Trail). This would make an excellent place from which day trippers could explore the Peconic–Flanders Bays area west of Robins Island. Other paddlers could make the more than 20-mile passage from here to Cedar Point County Park, where there are camping facilities, in a long day.

Soon after leaving the cottages astern, Mill Creek divides into four smaller channels. The westernmost channel doesn't go very far before petering out at the edge of the oak forest, but the other three can be traveled for quite some distance. On another trip I had paddled down the main channel that leads to two dammed ponds (worth carrying over to explore) and eventually connects, by intermittent streambed, to Sears Pond. This time I wanted to explore the other two significant tributaries.

There are four earthen impoundments on Mill Creek that I know of; at least one was used to power a saw mill between 1800 and 1850. Others may have been built during the past century to enhance waterfowl habitat during its heyday as a private hunting estate. Heading south toward the western impoundment, I come across what appears to be old foot bridge footings and, partially sunken in the creek mud, the single log which must have spanned the creek. Soon after this point the creek bed is exposed and I proceed on foot, luckily over firm, wet sand. At one point the creek seems to dead-end at an impenetrable wall of Phragmites but, hearing running water, I cross a small boggy area to a tiny trickle of water that I follow through the thick Phragmites to the steel culvert protruding from the side of an earthen dam. Clambering up the impoundment, I am rewarded with a view over a beautiful pond dotted with snags at its far end.

Back in my boat, I paddle east past the deceptively narrow main channel and pole my way up the eastern tributary as far as I can. Exiting the kayak, I find a small grouping of tree stumps exposed in the creek bed, their fluted connections between roots and trunks indicative of the now rare Atlantic White Cedar. If so, this location was once well above the influence of tides and seawater and is more evidence of sea level rise over the period of time since these trees were alive.

With dusk approaching, I begin the return paddle, realizing I will have to leave exploring Goose Creek, on the far western boundary of the Smithers Preserve, for another day. ✕

## Salt Marsh Zones

You don't have to be a botanist to be able to pick out the distinct plant communities, or zones, found in the salt marsh. Plant zones are created by changes in the physical and biological environment that favor one or more species over others. In salt marshes, zones are created by changes in the frequency and degree of exposure to salt water. The latter is related to elevation above mean sea level and often very subtle, difficult to discern changes in the topography of the marsh surface.

Tides fluctuate twice daily here, with two high and two low tides over a 24 hour, 50 minute period. In addition, tidal range fluctuates over the course of approximately two-week cycles, with a large tidal range (a very high and very low tide) associated with a new moon or full moon (called a "spring tide"), and a smaller tidal range on the quarter moons (a "neap tide").

Following a straight line, or transect, from the upland edge of the forest to the water, the forest edge zone is usually made up of trees that have some degree of tolerance for salt-laden air, such as Post Oak (*Quercus stellata*) and Eastern Red Cedar. The trees mark an elevation above mean sea level that is just out of reach of most storm tides.

The next zone, also above the highest spring tides but periodically flooded by storms, is characterized by two very similar-looking woody shrubs: Marsh Elder (*Iva frutescens*) and Groundsel-bush (*Baccharis halimifolia*). They are easily distinguished by taking a close look at the arrangement of their leaves or buds along a twig. Marsh Elder's leaves are paired; those on Groundsel-bush are offset, or alternate. Of the two, Marsh Elder is often found growing lower down the topographic gradient toward the intertidal zone. Both can be found growing far out into the salt marsh alongside mosquito control ditches. A close look at this situation reveals that they have colonized the small berm created by ditch spoils.

Seaward of the shrubs is the actual salt marsh where grasses dominate. A careful look at the grasses, even from a distance, reveals patterns of height, texture and color. For those naturalists who would like to learn to distinguish the various marsh grasses from one another, late summer and fall, when flowers or seeds are evident, is a good time to visit.

The salt marsh has two basic zones, and both are represented by *Spartina* species. A word of caution here: the terminology for these zones, as well as the common names of the plants, are interchangeable and confusing among the popular reference books on this topic.

The upper marsh, dominated by two grasses and a rush, is flooded every two weeks by the spring tides. This is the classic salt meadow in which one of the main grasses, Salt Hay (*Spartina patens*), forms matted, cowlick patterns. Its seeds are arranged in a row along one side of the stem like the teeth on a comb, and its thin, wiry leaves are rolled inward lengthwise, so that if you were to slice it across its width, it would appear U-shaped in cross-section.

The other grass here is Spike Grass (*Distichlis spicata*). It has short, flat, pointed leaves and yellowish flowers that are easily picked out from a distance. The third common plant here is Black Grass (*Juncus gerardi*). It is actually a rush, and is easy to pick out from its very dark flowers and seeds which are visible most of the year at the top of its stem.

Forming the lowest salt marsh zone—which is flooded twice daily by even the lowest (neap) high tide—is Cordgrass (*Spartina alterniflora*). This wide-bladed grass is the pioneer plant of the salt marsh, colonizing new shoals or overwash fans. It often forms a fringe around the upper marsh and lines the edges of mosquito ditches.

Look for the salt marsh's two keystone species in the Cordgrass zone: the Ribbed Mussel and the Fiddler Crab. Keep in mind that in the upper part of its zone, Cordgrass is often very stunted, attaining a height of several inches and easily overlooked.

Growing on the mussel's shell, at the lowest edge of the Cordgrass zone, is an interesting marine alga called Rockweed (*Fucus* spp.). Its leaves are tipped with air bladders that float them up toward the sunlight as the tide rises. The lower limit of Cordgrass is marked by the tidal elevation that allows seedlings enough air exposure to develop.

# 7 | HUBBARD CREEK

*Flanders, Town of Southampton*

DISTANCE: 1.5 miles R/T from the Upper Red Creek Road access to Flanders Bay. There are several additional miles of waterway to explore in Hubbard Creek.

ACCESS: 1) Upper Red Creek Road: No permit needed. From Sunrise Highway, take exit 65 North and follow Rte. 24 to a right turn onto Red Creek Road (2.0 miles). Where Hubbard Creek flows under the road (2.4 miles) access is possible but awkward. Watch out for Poison Ivy and Catbrier. Continue on Red Creek Road and take the left fork onto Upper Red Creek Road (2.6 miles), looking for a derelict cinder block garage and metal gate on the left at 2.9 miles. Park on the shoulder. Carry 200 feet down the path behind the metal gate and launch on the edge of the marsh.

*July*

Having launched where Hubbard Creek flows under Red Creek Road, I find myself pushing my kayak along this very shallow and narrow section of the tidal creek by using my paddle like a pole. The paddle, seven and a half feet in length, is a bit longer than the creek is wide at this point. Other than having to carry my boat through Poison Ivy to reach the creek, I am not sorry I chose to launch at this awkward spot.

The shoreline vegetation is interesting and, although this is clearly within the influence of bay tides, freshwater plants dominate. Jewelweed, Narrow-leaved Cattail, a variety of ferns, sedges, and rushes—in addition to an overhanging canopy of Red Maples and Tupelos—surround me. Within a quarter-mile, this changes. The forest recedes from overhead, the creek widens and deepens, and the diversity of the shoreside flora decreases dramatically, reflecting the influence and associated stresses of a more saline environment.

Near the indiscernible boundary marking where the freshwater wetland ends and the salt marsh begins, I stop to examine a series of narrow posts spanning the creek—perhaps at one time a rustic boardwalk providing access to the eastern marshes for duck hunters staying at the Black Duck Lodge, a half-mile to the west by trail.

The lodge and surrounding woods and marshes were owned and visited by a number of famous and wealthy families over the last two centuries. In the early 1800s, when the area was owned by the Astor family, much of the forest was cut and sold as cordwood. The lodge was built in the late 1800s by the Hubbard family, owners of the marshes, fields and second growth forest surrounding the creek between 1815 and 1937 and for whom the park is now named. In 1937, E.F. Hutton purchased the property as a private hunting preserve, for which it was used until 1974 when the County acquired it. Today, Hubbard Creek County Park remains an important deer and waterfowl hunting area but is now open to the public for such purposes. In addition, it provides a greenbelt trail linkage for the Paumanok Path and excellent wildlife viewing and nature study opportunities for park visitors.

As I push off from the nearest pole and picked up my paddle again, a White-tailed Deer emerges from the wall of Groundsel and Marsh Elder shrubs rimming the marsh and begins feeding. Thinking it would easily spook if I move, I freeze and let the kayak drift slowly along. It, in turn, catches my scent and also freezes. As the light wind pushes me within 30 feet of where it stood, I am treated to a close look at its gleaming reddish summer coat (a striking contrast to the lush green of the surrounding vegetation) and deep dark eyes. At this time of year, males should be showing at least a small stub of velvet-covered antler growth, so this particular animal must be a female. Several minutes pass and, sensing no danger, the deer resumes feeding and I paddle on.

The creek continues to widen and an Osprey pole comes into view on the right. One of three such structures bordering Hubbard Creek, I had helped erect this one with Group for the South Fork staff and volunteers in 1989 but it had never been occupied. The others, taller and located closer to the bay, have attracted nesting pairs in most years.

Another 150 yards further the creek widens dramatically, losing all semblance of being a creek, and the wind freshens. Working my way along the western shoreline, I pick my way between two small islands and around a marshy point where the creek becomes a labyrinth of twisting channels, tributaries, shoals, and islands. Many of these can be navigated by canoe or kayak, but a sharp eye is needed on a low tide.

The exposed marsh banks are riddled with Fiddler Crab holes and, just below the Cordgrass stems, dotted with barnacle-encrusted Ribbed Mussel shells. There are a number of small tributaries leading off through the upper marsh grasses, and in some cases to an upper marsh salt pond. These are best explored on an incoming, near high, tide. The longest of these tributaries winds through the eastern reach of the Hubbard Creek marsh.

Given the tide and time of day, I opt to explore the channel which parallels the outer barrier beach on the west side of the creek's inlet. Several Snowy Egrets and a Great Blue Heron are wading in the shallows, stopping frequently to peer into the water in search of a fish meal. Upon reaching the small pond at this tributary's headwaters, an Osprey flushes off the nearby nest with a half-eaten fish in its talons. It flies into the wind and circles around to land on a snag at the edge of a hummock of woods on Flanders Bay. Later, as I am portaging over the narrow barrier beach and into the bay, the fish hawk takes flight again, returning to the nest. A light rain

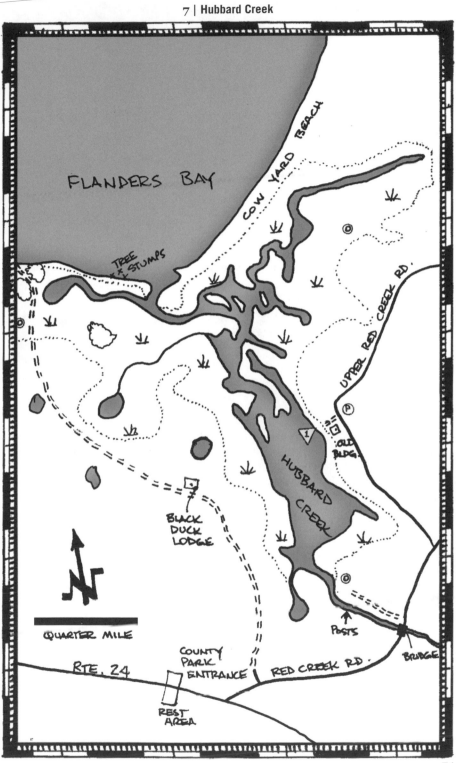

has begun to fall, and in the gray light I can't determine whether it is a fledgling or adult, even with binoculars.

Paddling back towards the inlet, I pass close by a section of bay bottom dotted with tree stumps, now exposed by the outgoing tide. According to a County brochure that refers to this as a "ghost forest," these are remnants of an Atlantic White Cedar grove, considered a freshwater wetland plant community. Obviously, the location of this grove in the intertidal zone is a clue that conditions here were much different many years ago when the cedars were alive. Mean sea level was lower and the bay beach and salt marsh were located further out in what is now the bay's sublittoral zone.

Even over the short term, from year to year and seasonally, visitors to this dynamic boundary between land and sea will note dramatic changes. The location of the inlet and shoals, establishment of *Spartina* grasses on formerly bare mud flats, storm over-wash blanketing the marsh with a layer of sand which is colonized by beachgrass, all these and more are part of the ever-changing nature of the barrier beach–inlet–salt marsh ecosystem: a fascinating place to visit and observe coastal processes at work. ⅄

## Ribbed Mussel (*Modiolus demissus*)

This ubiquitous, keystone species of the salt marsh is easily overlooked, but once you carefully peer among the Cordgrass stems at the water's edge you are likely to be astounded by the number of mussel shells protruding from marsh peat.

Related to the smoother-surfaced Blue Mussel served in restaurants, the Ribbed Mussel, as the name suggests, is covered with raised ridges running the length of its shell. Some claim it is edible, but I'll stick with *M. edulis* for personal consumption. Both have thin but tough byssal threads that anchor them in place: on rocks, pilings and other hard surfaces in the case of the Blue Mussel, the roots of Cordgrass for Ribbed Mussels. These anchor lines can be cast off if the mussel needs to reposition itself. By using its foot and newly attached threads, in a process that sounds much like kedging a boat off a shoal, it can very slowly move a short distance to a new location.

Ribbed Mussels are filter feeders, and are only active when covered by the tide. Because their feeding time is restricted, they have evolved to siphon water in at the relatively fast rate of one gallon per hour. The seawater is filtered through mucous-coated gills to remove potential food (gills are also used in respiration), and this material is passed onto the palps where the finer, digestible material is separated out and sent to the mouth. The large, coarse material left is excreted. Called pseudofeces, this material is rich in plant nutrients and is taken up by the Cordgrass roots to which the mussel is anchored. This ecological relationship is an example of mutualism, where both species benefit: the Ribbed Mussel gets an anchor point and the Cordgrass gets nutrients.

# 8 | SHINNECOCK BAY

*Southampton Village and Hampton Bays, Town of Southampton*

*The following is a description of two paddling trips on different sections of the bay, one at its eastern end and the other in the vicinity of the Ponquogue Bridge.*

DISTANCE: From Taylor Creek at its eastern end, to Penniman Creek on the west, the bay extends 10 miles and has over 50 miles of shoreline to explore by canoe and kayak.

ACCESS:  *Eastern Shinnecock:*

You can reach the following access points from Montauk Hwy. (Rte. 27A) in Southampton Village. Turn south onto Halsey Neck Lane.

1) Shinnecock East County Park: Suffolk County Park "green key" needed; can be purchased at the park gate. Drive to south end of Halsey Neck Ln., turn right onto Meadow Lane and continue 3.4 miles to the park entrance. Launch at small beach east of rock revetment.

2a) Narrow, unpaved road that leads to the bay: Southampton Town or Village permit needed. 2.8 miles west of Halsey Neck Lane.

2b) Same as 2a; 2.6 miles west of Halsey Neck Lane.

2c) Narrow, unpaved road that leads to the bay: Southampton Village permit needed. 2.3 miles west of Halsey Neck Lane.

3) Road D: No permit needed. 1.9 miles west of Halsey Neck Lane.

4) Munn Point Preserve: Southampton Town or Village permit needed. 0.9 miles west of Halsey Neck Lane.

5) Boatman's Lane: Southampton Village bay access permit needed. From Montauk Highway (Rte. 27A) turn south onto Halsey Neck Lane. Drive 0.4 mile and turn right onto Boatman's Lane. Drive to end.

6) Oxpasture Road: No permit needed. From Montauk Highway (Rte. 27A) turn south onto Halsey Neck Lane. Drive 1.1 miles and turn right onto Oxpasture Road. Drive to end.

*Ponquogue Bridge Area:*

1) Old Ponquogue Bridge Fishing Pier (a.k.a. Old Bridge Road): No permit needed. From Sunrise Highway, take exit 65 south onto Rte. 24 and turn left at the traffic light onto Montauk Highway. Follow this to the center of the Hampton Bays business district and make a right onto Ponquogue Avenue (0.0 mile). At the "T" intersection, turn left onto Shinnecock Road (1.5 miles) and follow the signs to the beach.

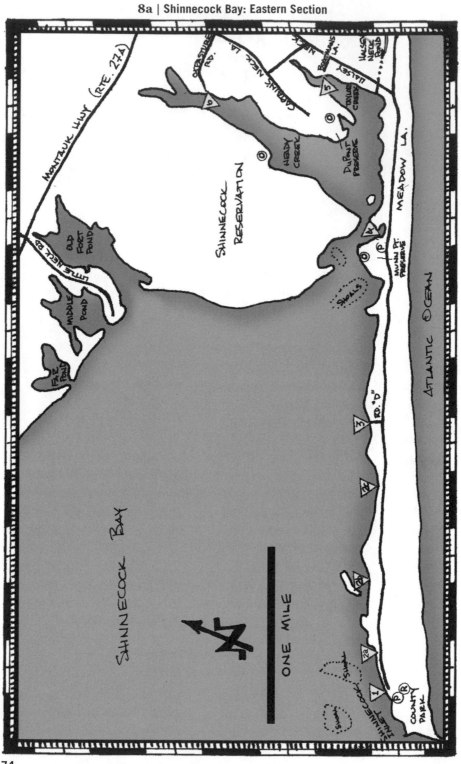

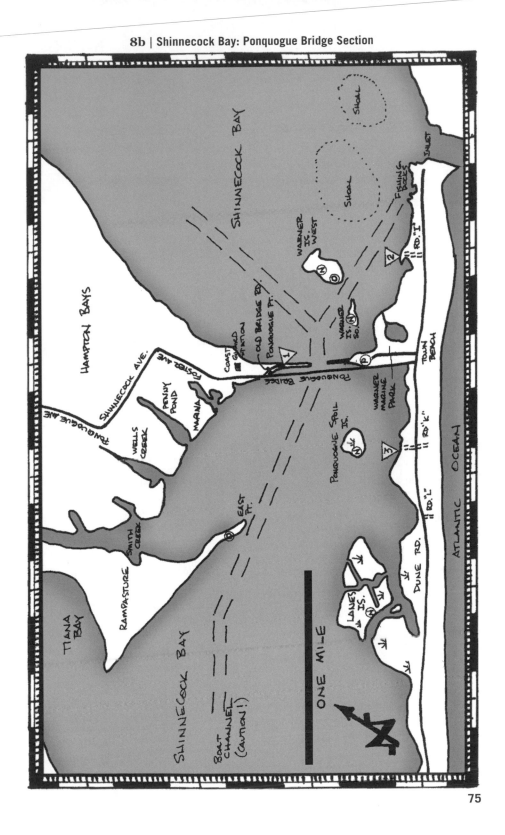

SHINNECOCK BAY

SHOAL

SHOAL

SHOAL

INLET

FISHING DOCKS

RD. "I"

2

WARNER IS. WEST

WARNER IS. SO.

HAMPTON BAYS

COAST GUARD STATION

OLD BRIDGE RD.

PONQUOGUE PT.

SHINNECOCK AVE.

FOSTER AVE.

PONQUOGUE AVE.

PENNY POND

MARINA

WELLS CREEK

PONQUOGUE BRIDGE

P

TOWN BEACH

WARNER MARINE PARK

PONQUOGUE SPOIL IS.

RD. "K"

3

ATLANTIC OCEAN

EAST PT.

SMITH CREEK

RAMPASTURE

TIANA BAY

SHINNECOCK BAY

DUNE RD.

RD. "L"

LANES IS.

ONE MILE

BOAT CHANNEL (CAUTION!)

SHINNECOCK BAY

75

> After the Coast Guard Station (2.4 miles) take the first left (2.6 miles) which leads to The Old Bridge access. Park along the curb.
>
> 2) Road I: No permit needed.
>
> 3) Road K: No permit needed.
>
> 4) The marine park: Southampton Town permit needed.

*Eastern Shinnecock Bay*
*July*

Paddling towards the western horizon and the yellow-orange glow of the setting sun, everything around me slowly drains of color. The marsh grasses to port, the Ponquogue bridge in the far distance, the land mass of Hampton Bays to starboard, and even the string of birds floating on the bay not far ahead—all are transformed into grayish silhouettes.

Something about the latter seemed odd and I stop paddling for a few moments. One of the birds has turned in such a way as to reveal a classic heron profile. This is a group of birds referred to as waders, and I can't recall ever seeing any swimming on the surface of the water as ducks or gulls do. Soon I realize the bird, now close enough to recognize as a Snowy Egret, is standing in a few inches of water, as are the strings of shorebirds and gulls to my left and right!

Although I am several hundred yards north of the bay marsh fringing the Meadow Lane barrier beach, a large shoal area stretches far out into Shinnecock Bay, forcing me, even in my shallow draft kayak, to alter course. I had hoped to hug the Meadow Lane salt marsh but, since it is low tide, that idea is out of the question. This is a lesson that I make note of: plan my trips on Shinnecock Bay to coincide with a high tide.

This trip is an evening exploration of the extreme eastern end of Shinnecock Bay and two of its tributaries: Heady Creek and Taylor Creek. Paddling from the Ox Pasture Road access south along the east shoreline of Heady Creek, a low tide reveals extensive mats of large, plate-sized, green seaweed below my boat. My guess is this may be a type of Sea Lettuce called *Ulva latissima*, common on muddy shores.

The shoreline here has a narrow band of salt marsh, 10 to 30 feet in width, backing up to a variety of woody shrubs and, in places, Phragmites. The marsh seems to consist solely of *Spartina alterniflora*, with none of the upper marsh grasses present. Perhaps the shoreline here is too bold to support a more diverse marsh community. This changes dramatically at the Nature Conservancy's Ruth Wales DuPont Preserve.

The 32-acre preserve boasts extensive salt marshes and an Osprey nest occupied by a single fledgling. Other local nesters are also evident. Most conspicuous is an overly protective Willet that begins noisily buzzing me while I am still 200 feet from shore and its young. The fledglings, in the company of a mature Lesser Yellowlegs, scurry about the exposed mud flats and edges of the Salt Marsh Cordgrass, apparently feeding on small invertebrates unseen to me.

Rounding the south end of Captain's Neck, I cut across Taylor Creek and head directly for the narrow dreen that links the bay with Halsey Neck Pond. The dreen provides a conduit for Alewives to reach freshwater spawning habitat in the spring. It is five to eight feet wide and most likely navigable by canoe or kayak near high tide—but not on this tide—for a good portion of its length to Halsey Neck Lane.

Turning westward, I follow the northern shoreline of the Meadow Lane marshes. These marshes have been the focus of preservation efforts over the past 15 years, with some limited success. As the Group for the South Fork's Environmental Planner, I had been involved in testifying before Village officials against several development proposals here. I wasn't always successful. Much of Meadow Lane's natural environment—its barrier beach, dunes, and salt marsh communities—has been compromised by a scale of residential development that is quite shocking. And it doesn't end with the huge houses: swimming pools, tennis courts, pool houses, and landscaping plans that incorporate sod, topsoil, and underground irrigation systems are part of the mix. The result: every trace of the dune setting that first attracted people to this beautiful spot is obliterated. I really don't understand what possesses people to do this.

Soon after passing the infamous Trupin mansion, I encounter the first of many sand bars and mud flats that are now exposed at low tide. This one actually shows up on the USGS topographic map as an island. Resting on this temporary land sanctuary is a small flock of Semipalmated Plovers. This shorebird nests in the far north, with the most southern nesting sites found in Nova Scotia. According to John Bull's book *Birds of New York*, a few summering nonbreeding individuals of this species are regularly present on Long Island. But expert birder Steve Biasetti later reminds me that, although it is mid-July and it seems that summer has just begun, some of these Plovers may have completed their nesting and rearing young obligations in the far north and already begun to migrate south.

Abeam of the Munn Point Preserve and another active Osprey nest with one fledgling visible, a west wind increases. A series of poles topped with red flags marks a deep water route around a large shoal. I am hoping to continue west to the inlet and the Suffolk County park on its east side, but light is fading and I turn north to return along the shoreline of the Shinnecock Indian Reservation.

A large sand shoal off the southwest corner of the Reservation has a pair of American Oystercatchers feeding on it. I paddle over for a closer look and find the shoal covered with mussels—not the common Ribbed Mussel found in the salt marshes nearby, but the Blue Mussel normally found attached to pilings, rocks, and other hard surfaces. Surprised, I pick up a few clumps of the fingernail-sized mussels to see what they have attached themselves to and find nothing solid. I can pick up the entire mass of shells—some weighing several pounds—off the sandy bottom. The mussels are merely attached to one another, apparently relying on their own mass to hold them in place on the shoal. A closer inspection reveals that the oldest mussels attached themselves to large fragments of clam and whelk shells.

The Shinnecock Reservation has the largest undeveloped shoreline in the eastern portion of Shinnecock Bay and provides a stark contrast to the McMansions looming over Meadow Lane. It is a pleasure to paddle here, with extensive marshes set against a backdrop of forest. Rounding the Reservation's southeast point, I find Roddy Smith and his youngest daughter, Cholena, fishing and exploring the mud flats. Roddy and I share an interest in natural history, as well as a love of the Canadian north, and I stop for a long chat. They have just returned from a visit to Labrador, and I listen to stories of their adventures, recognizing placenames I dream of visiting myself someday.

Our talk is periodically interrupted by an interesting bird flying overhead, or a discovery by Cholena, who shares her father's interest in the natural world. With darkness not far off, we each retrieve our boats and part ways for our respective homes.

*Ponquogue*
*July*

The Ponquogue section of Dune Road is a popular destination for a wide variety of outdoor lovers. I don't get over there very often, but in my visits to the area I have seen surfers, birdwatchers, fishermen, duck hunters, and scuba divers all enjoying their various hobbies.

On this visit, I am joining Hampton Bays resident and long-time paddling friend Rob Battenfeld for an evening trip through the area by kayak. Rob has explored most of Shinnecock Bay by sea kayak, paddling as far west as Moriches Bay, and suggests we rendezvous at the site of the old Ponquogue bridge just south of the Shinnecock Coast Guard station.

This is an excellent choice. The launch site has easily accessible sandy beaches on both sides (east and west) of the dead end road. Since our first destination is one of the Warner Islands (Warner Island West on the accompanying map), we unload gear and launch from the east side of Old Bridge Road.

Before setting out, Rob points out the location of boat channels in the area and offers the same safety advice, in somewhat different words, that Jimmy Minardi had shared with me while cycling the week before. That is, assume that you are invisible. In this case, it means to assume that you and your kayak are invisible to powerboaters and to take particular care when crossing the channels. July and August are popular boating months, and there is a fair amount of powerboat traffic in the area.

Knowing that I wanted to paddle along the edge of the Dune Road marshes and

Diamondback Terrapins reside in Shinnecock and other East End bays. This female came ashore to lay eggs in June.

adjacent low-lying islands, we had planned the trip to coincide with high tide. Tide is a very important factor here; much of the route we want to paddle is exposed mud flat and unnavigable even in our shallow draft kayaks at low tide.

Conditions are perfect. We set off and paddle eastward under clear, sunny skies, and with a light and cool southwesterly breeze. Warner Island West (I have used the names given to the islands in the *Long Island Colonial Waterbird and Piping Plover Survey*) has a thicket of tall shrubs located near its center on its west side, and these are clearly visible from the Old Bridge Road launch site a half-mile away. As we get closer, an Osprey pole just south of the shrubs comes into view. With the aid of binoculars, I note a Double-crested Cormorant and a Herring Gull perched on opposite corners of the platform. Obviously this Osprey nesting structure has not been used this season by the fish hawk for which it was erected.

Within a couple of hundred feet of the island we can see a half-dozen Snowy Egrets perched atop the 10-to-12-foot-high shrubs, watching our approach. This island, along with a dozen other small islands located along the south shore of Shinnecock Bay adjacent to the barrier beach, is an important bird nesting colony. I am surprised to note that this island, as well as the others we visit this trip, is not posted in any way to warn boaters to stay off during the nesting season. Although the nesting season is generally over by late July, we do not land there as a precaution against disturbing late nesters.

Under the watchful eyes of hundreds of noisy gulls and Cormorants, we circle around Warner Island West's north and east sides. Mixed in among the ubiquitous gulls on the shoreline are terns, Oystercatchers, Black Skimmers, and Sanderlings, the latter being recent migrants from nesting areas in the far north.

## Bird Nesting Colonies

One in eight avian species is a colonial nester. Ornithologists have puzzled over the rationale for nesting in large, conspicuous colonies, such as found among the terns and herons. The disadvantage of colonial nesting is fairly obvious: try finding the nest of the colonial Common Tern versus the nest of the solitary Piping Plover. One would think the easy-to-find colonial nesters would be easy targets for predators. Many colonial nesters make up for their conspicuous rookeries by choosing hard to reach sites—for example, small islands, marshes, and cliffs. Some, including the terns, compensate for their vulnerable nesting locations on open beaches by being very aggressive. They will fearlessly swoop down and strike any intruder, no matter how big, thought to be a predator... including biologists studying the colony!

So then, what are the advantages to colonial nesting? Somewhat offsetting the high visibility of colonial nests is the increased ability to detect predators. But food resources seem to be the key factor. Most colonial nesters rely on food resources that are locally abundant, but patchy and not always in the same place—for example, the schools of small fish that seabirds feed on. Research indicates that information sharing is the main advantage of colonial nesting. A group of birds can spread out and search a larger area than one individual can; once a school of fish has been located, the location of the school is shared among birds back at the colony.

Although we call it the fall migration, here it is late July and birds are already showing signs of movement. Several active Osprey nests, having successfully fledged young, are now abandoned. Nesters from the far north, including Sanderlings and Ruddy Turnstones, are showing up on the South Fork in small flocks. Assuming they have been successful in their nesting efforts, they have constructed nests, laid and incubated eggs, and raised young between ice-out in the far north and late July. Amazing! While I am thinking about all this, a flock of Cormorants flying in "V" formation, not unlike Canada Geese except for being completely soundless, passes overhead.

The islands' nesting birds are periodically inventoried every few years as part of the *Long Island Colonial Waterbird and Piping Plover Survey* organized by the New York State Department of Environmental Conservation (NYSDEC). Approximately 100 wildlife professionals and skilled volunteers took part in the 1995 Long Island census, the last year for which I have published data. Twenty-one species were surveyed, including Double-crested Cormorants, gulls, herons, egrets, Glossy Ibis, Oystercatchers, terns, Black Skimmers, and Piping Plovers.

Michelle Alfieri and Ken Meskill of the NYSDEC and Marilyn England of the National Audubon Society surveyed the islands in the Ponquogue area of Shinnecock

Bay. They documented nearly 1,000 nesting pairs of birds on Warner Island West in 1995: 300 pairs of Great black-backed Gulls, 550 pairs of Herring Gulls, 45 pairs of Common Terns, 6 pairs of Oystercatchers, and 2 pairs of Roseate Terns. The island was a new nesting site for Roseates in 1995, a significant finding since the species was listed as "endangered" by the U.S. Fish and Wildlife Service and was the focus of recovery efforts by biologists.

I was surprised that the survey did not find any herons or egrets nesting in the small trees and shrubs on the island. I phoned Eric Salzman, an avid birder residing nearby in East Quogue, for more recent information about the nesting site. Eric has published several articles about birding in this area, and informed me that the main colony of nesting herons and egrets, or heronry, was on Ponquogue Spoil Island up until a few years ago. At that time, for unknown reasons, the heronry relocated to Warner Island West. The heronry transplants included Snowy Egrets, Great Egrets, Black-crowned Night Herons, and Glossy Ibis, and a new species for this area: the Little Blue Heron.

The origin of these low-lying, marshy islands is worth noting, and is a reminder that coastal areas are very dynamic and unstable. Most were formed by storms breaching the dunes on the barrier beach. In some cases, the storm waves carried dune sands into the bay to form overwash fans. In other cases, coastal storms breached the barrier island to form inlets. According to coastal geologist Stephen Leatherman's *The Barrier Island Handbook*, overwash generally results in a widening of the barrier island and the development of extensive salt marshes, while inlets create flood tidal deltas that, over time, develop into salt marsh islands. In both cases, the partially submerged deltas and outwash fans are colonized by intertidal marsh grasses, notably the pioneer Salt Marsh Cordgrass (*Spartina alterniflora*).

The flood tidal deltas are formed by tidal currents carrying sediment from ocean to bay through inlets on a flood tide. These are clearly evident in the vicinity of Shinnecock Inlet and are marked on the accompanying map as shoals. The westernmost of the shoals, although mostly underwater at high tide, supported three Oystercatcher nests in 1995 and is a good spot to look for basking seals in the winter months.

You might wonder how Warner Island South, Warner Island West, Ponquogue Spoil Island, and Lane Island, all once flood delta islands, formed so far from the inlet. The answer can be found in the history of Shinnecock Bay's inlets. Up until the hurricane of 1938, there was no permanent ocean inlet on Shinnecock Bay. In fact, there were no permanent inlets on Long Island's south shore east of the Fire Island inlet until Moriches Bay inlet was opened in 1930. Both Moriches and Shinnecock inlets have been maintained in their 1930 and 1938 positions by way of periodic dredging and, in the 1950s, the construction of stone jetties.

But every so often a storm would breach the barrier beach and a temporary inlet would form, not unlike the inlets that form at Mecox Bay and Sagg and Georgica

Ponds. These inlets would remain open until shoreline currents sealed them off from the ocean. In some cases, as with the inlet that formed in 1938 just south of the Warner Islands and the 1889 inlet that formed south of Ponquogue Spoil Island, they were very short-lived. In others, as with the inlet that formed south of Lanes Island in 1834 and remained open until 1891, they were around for quite awhile.

In any event, all the islands found here line up with old inlets, as noted in the book *Living With Long Island's South Shore*, co-authored by retired Southampton College professor Larry McCormick. Several of the islands (including Ponquogue Spoil Island and Warner Island West) have been recipients of dredge spoil during channel maintenance. In many cases, dredge spoils can be deposited in such a way as to enhance nesting habitat for rare and endangered shorebirds.

Crossing the main boat channel connecting the Shinnecock Inlet with the inter-coastal waterway (the latter heads west towards Moriches Bay and east to the Peconic Bays via the Shinnecock Canal), Rob points out Road I, another good water access point. This area gets a fair bit of boat traffic in the summer months, including the obnoxiously loud muscle boats. Don't assume their skippers know enough to stick to the marked channels.

West of Road I is a large expanse of salt marsh. Among the tall Cordgrass leaves and stems, the heads and necks of quite a few Great Egrets appear. They are busy stalking prey, most likely Mummichogs, who themselves are using the high tide to move through the marsh grasses to capture mosquito larva and other prey.

Passing along the south side of Warner Island South, the island seems much smaller than I expected, and I recheck my map. It is photocopy of the NYSDOT topographic map for the Shinnecock Bay area, with the topographic lines drawn in 1955. Not only was the island significantly larger 50 years ago (approximately 200 by 600 feet), but the map shows another crescent-shaped island closer to Road I that is now completely gone.

I am not certain why the one island disappeared and the other is being washed away, but a possible explanation could be changes at Shinnecock Inlet. The construction of stone jetties in the 1950s, combined with dredging that deepened the inlet and increased tidal flow (and tidal range in the bay near the inlet), could have caused the demise of these low-lying islands.

In any event, the loss of these important nesting islands is a concern of Suffolk County Parks, which owns and manages the islands, as well as local conservationists. In 1995, ornithologist Marilyn England reported 34 nesting pairs of the federally and State endangered Roseate Tern at Warner Island South, along with Oystercatchers, Black Skimmers, and nearly 400 pairs of Common Terns. In 2000, as the island continued to erode away, County Park employees and Town bay constables attempted to shore it up with sand bags and barged-in sand. As described by Nick Gibbons of Suffolk County Parks, the effort was quite labor intensive. Although the effort may have salvaged another nesting season, both species of terns using the site continued to decline and the island continued to erode.

In 2003, Mike Wasilco of the NYSDEC reported that no Common or Roseate Terns successfully nested at Warner Island South. Aside from a couple pairs of Roseates nesting on Lanes Island and Warner Island West, the only sizeable colony of Roseates remains at Great Gull Island east of Plum Island. Both Mike and Nick Gibbons mentioned that there is some discussion of using dredge spoils from future boat channel maintenance to enhance tern nesting habitat on one of the Warner islands.

As depicted on the Soil Conservation Service maps for this area, dredge spoils have been deposited on several of these islands in the past. Most of Ponquogue Spoil Island is dredge spoils (hence the name) laid over tidal marsh, and at least the southern half of Warner Island West is labeled "Fd," for "filled" on the soil map. These spoil deposits on tidal marshes were done prior to the passage of the State's Tidal Wetlands Act in 1973, and it is unlikely they would be permitted today.

Continuing west, Rob and I cut under the fishing pier and the Ponquogue bridge, where the tide is still flooding. Care should be taken to avoid fishing lines while passing under the pier, and to be ready to encounter swift currents and strong eddies while passing under both.

Between the west side of the bridge and Ponquogue Spoil Island is a large area covered with Blue Mussels that are visible at low tide. I am surprised to find the Blue Mussels so abundant here on the firm, but sandy, bottom; I usually encounter this species fixed onto hard, stationary substrates such as pilings and large rocks. Southampton Town Bay Constable Ted Sadleir informed me that large beds of Blue Mussels can be found concentrated near both Moriches and Shinnecock inlets. According to Sadleir, another large bed is located off East Point, and no large beds are found west of Pine Neck Point. He speculates that the higher salinity level near the inlets is a factor.

In a 1985 issue of *The Kingbird*, a quarterly newsletter of the Federation of New York State Bird Clubs, Eric Salzman described an unusual heronry on Ponquogue Spoil Island. (My understanding is that a heronry, or heron rookery, is a nesting area, although some birders also use these terms for areas where herons roost during the non-nesting season.)

Most herons nest in colonies of fairly closely-spaced nests. Suitable habitat for these waterbirds generally include shrubs or trees in which to construct their stick nests, areas somewhat isolated from human activities and, of course, proximity to water. Many heronries are comprised of several species of herons and associated waterbirds. In the case of the Ponquogue Spoil Island heronry that Eric wrote about, Great Egret, Snowy Egret, and Glossy Ibis nests were mixed in among the Black-crowned Night Heron nests.

What made the heronry unusual was the lack of any trees or even tall shrubs. Some herons and egrets will nest as high as 40 feet in the tops of trees. Yet Eric noted many of the flimsy, stick nests were constructed right on the ground, tucked in among the island's dense vegetation: Bittersweet vines, Phragmites, and Poison Ivy. The tallest shrubs on the entire island were those of Salt Spray Rose, or *Rosa Rugosa*.

I had known that the island hosted a heronry, and it was one of the places I was looking forward to visiting on this trip. But I didn't know about the unusual nature of this heronry and, knowing that herons preferred to nest well above the ground, I am quite surprised to be looking over a very low-lying island with no trees at all. From the low vantage point of our sea kayaks, I can't even make out any woody shrubs standing out above the island's fringe of marsh grasses. The tallest plants appear to be Phragmites reeds, certainly incapable of supporting a heron nest.

Hatchling Terrapins spend their first years foraging in the intertidal zone of the salt marsh.

Ponquogue Spoil Island, as the name suggests, has been used in the past as a dredge spoil deposition site. I should point out that the island has two other commonly used names. One is Jackson's Fort Island, which links the island to members of the Jackson family who have been hunting waterfowl from a duck blind on the island's south side for close to 100 years. The other common name, which Eric uses, is Gull Island. This refers to the island's most abundant nesting birds: Great Black-backed Gulls and Herring Gulls. In 1985, these two species of gulls outnumbered the island's nesting pairs of egrets and herons by a tally of 1,000 to 600.

Eric provided some interesting updates on the heronry. Little Blue Herons began nesting there fairly recently; it was not listed as a breeding bird in the Shinnecock Bay area in the 1988 Breeding Bird Atlas. This species, along with a number of other now common "southern" herons and egrets (Yellow-crowned Night Heron, Great Egret, Snowy Egret, and Tricolored Heron) first started nesting in New York State in the 1950s. It's hard to imagine that our local marshes were once devoid of Great and Snowy Egrets.

Eric also mentioned that, a few years ago, most of the heronry seemed to shift east and became established on Warner Island West. There, a stand of Ailanthus (Tree-of-Heaven) provides a place for nesting above ground. As well, Boat-tailed Grackles recently began nesting on Ponquogue Spoil Island and in the marshes along Dune

Road. Another southerner that is expanding its range northward, this huge grackle (much larger than the Common Grackle) first nested on Long Island in the 1980s. The closest nest to Shinnecock Bay listed in 1988 Breeding Bird Atlas was in New York City at Jamaica Bay.

While on the topic of recent immigrants from the south, I should mention the Glossy Ibis. I first saw this quite distinctive-looking bird at Jones Beach in the 1970s, where a colony was nesting in Japanese Black Pines along Ocean Parkway. Into the 1940s, this species only nested in southern Florida. Twenty years later (1961) it was nesting in Jamaica Bay, Queens. In 1970, it made its way to Gardiners Island. They established a nesting colony at Ponquogue Spoil Island in the 1980s.

Leaving the island, Rob and I head south and west, paddling along the edge of a large marsh between Road K and Road L. Here we are finally far enough away from the boat channels that I make a note of the quiet, along with the fact that the marsh is teeming with Great Egrets.

West of Road L we work our way over to Lanes Island, another important bird nesting area, this one having no herons but a large tern colony. The 1995 census reported 824 pairs of Common Terns nesting there, in addition to a fairly large colony (59 pairs) of Roseate Terns, and a handful of Black Skimmer and Oystercatcher nests. The Lanes Island Roseate Tern colony was the third largest on Long Island in 1995.

We explore the interior of Lanes Island by way of a tidal creek that connects with several mosquito control ditches and, at least at high tide, enables one to paddle through to the north side of the island. Along the shallow, muddy bottom, at the time covered by the tide, the huge, webbed tracks of a Great Egret and the tiny, hand-like tracks of a Raccoon are visible.

Continuing westward beyond the island, we find ourselves downwind of a club in the Tiana Beach area, being serenaded by a band playing a very poor rendition of "American Pie." We take it as a signal to start heading back, and turn north for East Point on the Rampasture peninsula. Many years ago I helped erect an Osprey pole on a small but picturesque Peconic Land Trust preserve there, and I am thinking it will be worth visiting on the return paddle. We are not disappointed.

The Osprey nest has not been occupied this season, but the sliver of a preserve is a delight to paddle by. The north side of the point, with an exposure to the northeast, is experiencing a fair bit of erosion as evidenced by the toppled trees and shrubs at the water's edge. This evening though, the north side is nicely sheltered from the southwesterly wind and chop on the bay, and we stop to drift and chat about faraway places to explore by kayak. As the sun dips low on the western horizon, Rob and I watch a small flock of Ruddy Turnstones forage on the point's pebble beach, prompting us to consider dinner plans before returning to our cars at Ponquogue Point. ╳

# 9 | SEBONAC CREEK

*North Sea, Town of Southampton*

DISTANCE: 6.5 miles R/T.

ACCESS: 1) Scallop Pond Road: No Permit needed. From Rte. 27 turn north (a left if eastbound) onto North Sea Road. Continue straight through the Noyac Road intersection (2.7 miles), and make a left onto Scallop Pond Road (3.2 miles). Drive straight across Scott Road where Scallop Pond Road continues as a narrow, unpaved and unmarked road for 0.5 rough miles to a beautiful launch site.

2) Sebonac Inlet Road bridge: No permit needed. From Rte. 27 turn north onto Magee Street (at traffic light and Sunoco station). At stop sign turn left onto Sebonac Road (0.2 mile). Take second right onto Sebonac Inlet Road (1.2 miles) and follow to the water (on right). Park on shoulder along guardrail (1.8 miles). Use one of the narrow sandy paths through the marsh grasses to launch.

3) Sebonac Inlet: No permit needed. Continue to end of Sebonac Inlet Road (see#2 above). Launch from beach on either side of bulkhead section. (NOTE: this area has strong tidal current.)

There are four other Southampton Town roads that dead-end on the Sebonac Creek estuary; all provide water access suitable for launching a canoe or kayak. Directions can be worked out from the accompanying map:

4) Barker Island Road.
5) West Neck Lane.
6) West Neck Point Road.
7) Island Creek Road.

*September*

My favorite paddling area in Southampton? The Sebonac Creek estuary in North Sea. The three-mile-long waterway is a series of tidal creeks (Sebonac, Little Sebonac, West Neck, Island) connecting Scallop Pond at the north end with Bullhead Bay at the south and emptying into Great Peconic Bay at Sebonac Inlet. The maze of creeks and embayments is easier to navigate than the maze of roadways which lead to it. Have a good road map on hand before you set out.

Even the launch site at Scallop Pond is a spectacular setting. Salt marshes dotted with small forested hummocks stretch away to the south and east, while small farm fields and meadows interspersed with thick woods lie to the north and west. In no

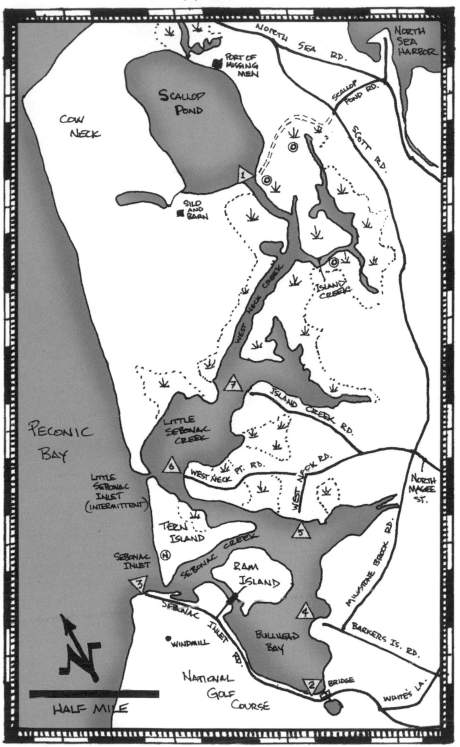

hurry to launch and paddle away from this beautiful spot, I scan the waters of Scallop Pond and the marshes of West Neck Creek for wildlife.

I am not disappointed. Lingering summer residents mingle with migrants from nesting grounds further north, affording me a look at an astonishing variety of waterfowl and wading birds. Among the mix are egrets, herons, terns, Black Duck, Canada Geese, Common Mergansers, Double-crested Cormorants, Common Goldeneye and Bufflehead.

Across the creek the raucous behavior of a flock of Common Crows draws my attention and, with the aid of binoculars, I am rewarded with a fairly unusual sighting: a Barn Owl. The owl ignores the harassment but the crows are relentless, forcing the owl to take flight. This only seems to enrage the crows even more. Their calls become louder as the flock follows the owl over the tree tops and out of view.

After launching, I paddle along the east side of Scallop Pond and past the only pondfront dwelling, the odd-looking Port of Missing Men that was built in the mid-1920s. The structure's most interesting aspect is best viewed from the water where it's entire pondfront side, constructed to resemble the stern of a ship, is visible. The original owner, Henry Huddleston Rogers Jr. of Standard Oil fame and fortune, also owned 1,200 acres in the area. The land and building were managed as a hunting preserve where friends and acquaintances, some very well-known public figures, could go "missing" for a long weekend.

Through the woods bordering the west side of the pond, some of the fields and meadows managed for deer and game birds are visible. Also visible is a large barn and silo. The name Cow Neck is derived from the cow head and neck shape of this peninsula (turn the map to view it from north to south). But the neck also contained a small dairy herd. In 1954, Peter Salm, the grandson of H.H. Rogers, bought Richard G. Hendrickson's herd of 30 milkers from the Lumber Lane farm in Bridgehampton. According to Mr. Hendrickson, this dairy operation outlasted the last commercial dairy farm on the South Fork operated by Sayre Baldwin.

The Cow Neck property, a 600-acre gem of tidal marshes, freshwater ponds and swamps, forest, and fields, with over two miles of beach fronting Peconic Bay, was high on the acquisition lists of two very different interest groups. The U.S. Fish and Wildlife Service and New York State Department of Environmental Conservation saw its potential as a permanent greenbelt for wildlife, while golf course developers saw its "green" potential in the form of fairways and revenue. In the mid-1990s it was purchased by the owner of Robins Island, a conservation-minded individual who has kept it pretty much as it has been since the early 1900s: a hunting preserve.

Exiting the pond and entering the narrows of West Neck Creek, the wooded shoreline gives way to extensive marshland. There are also some tidal sand flats at this confluence where, on a high tide in May and June, Horseshoe Crabs congregate to lay eggs. Most of the marshes and forests on the east side of the creek, all the way to

Island Creek Road, have been protected through the efforts of the Nature Conservancy, the Peconic Land Trust, the Town of Southampton, and conservation-minded landowners such as the Ellistons, Salms, and Berglunds.

At Little Sebonac Creek, the first clusters of homes come into view on the left. Straight ahead is the windmill and clubhouse at National Golf Links. The creek widens to a quarter-mile here. Keep to the more scenic Cow Neck side and look for the tiny inlet connecting Little Sebonac with Peconic Bay and separating Tern Island from Cow Neck. Depending on the tide and the condition of the bay beach, this inlet may or may not be open. If open, shoot through and into the bay for a view of Robins Island to the north, and continue paddling south along the bay beach. Keep in mind that this stretch of bay beach is private and often inhabited by nesting terns and Piping Plovers. During the nesting season (late spring and summer) take care to avoid disturbing the birds.

The current at Sebonac Inlet can be quite strong. If you arrive during an incoming tide, enjoy the ride. If not, take advantage of the nearshore eddy, a counter current that allows you to paddle effortlessly at least as far as the narrowest point in the inlet. Once there you have two options. One, being sure to keep the boat parallel to the current and close to shore where the current is weakest, paddle as hard as you can. Two, in shallow water close to shore, get out and walk it through the toughest section. The latter is a modification of "lining" the boat, a technique (with lines attached to bow and stern) often used by canoeists to negotiate difficult rapids, either going up or downstream, instead of portaging around them.

Once inside Sebonac Creek, look for the narrow waterway separating Ram Island and Sebonac Neck. You will pass under a small bridge and into Bullhead Bay. National Golf course is visible on the west side of the bay. In 1650 this site was occupied by a Native American village whose residents, the Shinnecocks, also paddled the local waterways to get around.

In 1902, an excavation of the village site was undertaken by Mark Harrington to provide insights into the design and layout of the wigwams, diet, and hunting and farming implements. Two large pieces of a whale's jaw were uncovered, as well as the remains of a potter's workshop. In her book *In Old Southampton*, author Abigail Fithian Halsey writes that while cutting a road through Sebonac Neck in 1923 to provide access to the future golf course, several Native American skeletons were unearthed in the vicinity of the creek at Bullhead Bay. No mention was made of their ultimate fate.

For the return trip to Scallop Pond, leave Ram Island to port and head directly for Little Sebonac Creek. Take some time to explore the eastern reaches of Little Sebonac and Island Creek en route back to the car. And, before leaving the serenity of this beautiful backwater, be sure to prepare yourself mentally for re-entry into the frantic Hamptons scene. ✕

## Horseshoe Crab (*Limulus polyphemus*)

In my favorite book about the beach, *The Wild Edge: Life and Lore of the Great Atlantic Beaches*, author Philip Kopper describes the Horseshoe Crab as "a beast that deserves far higher esteem than it usually receives along our shores." This much maligned but harmless creature has been around for 200 million years, prompting some to refer to it by the contradictory phrase "living fossil."

Perhaps an explanation of this bizarre-looking organism's anatomy and behavior will illicit some interest and admiration among readers. The dome-like, horseshoe-shaped shell is designed to protect the more vulnerable thinner-shelled, moving parts found underneath. It is shaped such that a strong current forces the crab down as it moves along the bottom in search of prey, and it offers lift when the crab is swimming, upside down, in the water column.

The protective shell's design is a liability when the crab finds itself upside down, since its legs can not reach around to right itself. This is a position the crab might find itself in when venturing into wave-tossed shallows. That's where the long, hinged tail goes to work. This menacing appendage is used solely as a lever to right itself. Having watched many perform this arduous maneuver, I can't help but wonder why a flattened tail tip didn't evolve at some point over the past 200 million years!

The largest pair of the Horseshoe Crab's eyes, located on the upper sides of its shell, has been studied by engineers and determined to be the most efficient light-gathering design possible. These compound eyes detect patterns of polarized light in the sky, enabling them to navigate celestially during their migration to and from offshore wintering grounds. The smaller pair of simple eyes located on either side of the midline of the shell is extremely sensitive to ultraviolet light from the moon. These work in conjunction with a biological clock to trigger the shoreward migration for egg-laying in spring.

All my reference books describe six pairs of leg-like appendages on the Horseshoe Crab's undersides. But a close look reveals seven, most tipped with sharp, and harmless, pincers. The aft-most two pairs are the exceptions. The pair furthest towards the rear near the book gills are not easily discernible and I haven't found any information regarding their function. The next pair are the largest and are tipped with a series of paddles that act as snowshoes or ski pole baskets when moving over soft sand and mud. They are also used to propel the crab through the water when it is swimming upside down, and act as shovels for digging nests and burying itself. The most forward set of legs is noticeably shorter. These are the feeding legs that pass food items, such as worms and thumbnail-sized clams, into the mouth. The mouth is a nondescript opening where the walking legs converge. The bristle-covered legs grind up the shells and meat, requiring the Horseshoe Crab to eat on the run.

In male Horseshoe Crabs, the second set of legs is tipped by specialized structures that resemble boxing gloves. This obvious feature makes distinguishing males from females, at least those over three years in age, quite easy. These are used solely for grabbing onto the aft end of a female that is ready to lay eggs, although it is not uncommon to see a second male hanging onto the first, forming a three-car train of crabs. Despite not being in the best position to fertilize eggs, as many as four other males may hang on to one another or the sides of the female in an attempt to pass their genetic information onto a future generation. Another distinguishing feature between the sexes is size. Females are much larger than the males.

The Horseshoe Crab mating ritual commences in May and continues through June. This can be observed during any high tide, but the largest numbers of crabs congregate to spawn on the spring high tides associated with new and full moons. With as many as 10,000 BB-sized, light-green eggs packed inside her shell and at least one mate in tow, a female follows a rising tide towards a sandy beach. Near the high tide line, she begins to excavate a slight depression, deposits 1,000 eggs, and drags her mate across the nest to release his sperm and fertilize the clutch. This is repeated up to 10 times per season.

Those that aren't consumed by hungry shorebirds, Mud Snails, or other predators will hatch in two weeks and swim out into the estuary on the next spring tide. They resemble miniature Horseshoe Crabs in every aspect except the tail, which is missing. During their first year, they will shed their hard exoskeleton five or six times, growing 20 percent with each molt. After 7 to 10 years and 17 molts they are fully grown and no longer shed their shells. The now permanent shell collects a wide assortment of organisms over its remaining 10 years of life, including Barnacles, algae, and Slipper Shells.

# 10 | NORTH SEA HARBOR

*North Sea, Town of Southampton*

DISTANCE: A circumnavigation of the harbor is 3 miles. Davis Creek adds 2 miles (R/T), the narrow cove leading to the Alewife Dreen is 1 mile out and back, and Fish Cove has another 1 mile of navigable shoreline for a total of 7 miles of shoreline to explore.

ACCESS: 1) Conscience Point Road: No permit needed. From Rte. 27 in Southampton Village, turn north onto North Sea Road (0.0 mile), continue straight past Noyac Road (2.7 miles) to next right (3.2 miles) onto Conscience Point Road. Park and launch where it dead-ends on the water.

*March*

The month of March often brings quirky weather, and this one is no exception. Not long after Skunk Cabbage flowered, Spring Peepers began calling from flooded swamps, and Ospreys were sighted circling over our bays and ponds, a heavy, wet snowfall put us back into the grip of winter. The grip was short-lived and followed by several consecutive warm and sunny days, one of which coaxed me into my kayak for a paddle around beautiful and historic North Sea Harbor.

The harbor is a fairly protected body of water, although in places a half-mile of fetch can pose a challenge for paddlers in a strong wind. Its four appendages (Fish Cove, Davis Creek, the Alewife Dreen cove, and a small tidal creek in the Conscience Point Wildlife Refuge) are well sheltered and worth exploring even on a calm day. Although not a pristine embayment, with several clusters of very dense development along its shoreline, much of the harbor is rimmed by high quality salt marsh and is home to a wide assortment of wildlife. In fact, the entire northeastern corner of North Sea Harbor borders Conscience Point National Wildlife Refuge, a pretty mosaic of salt marsh, maritime grassland, and forest.

In addition to its ecological assets, the harbor boasts one of the most important historical sites in the region. In June 1640, Conscience Point, as noted on the monument at its northern tip, was the landing site for a group of English settlers sailing from Lynn, Massachusetts to establish the first English settlement in New York State (or the second in the State, as some in Southold would argue). According to William Halsey's *Sketches From Local History*, one of the adventurous group, upon setting foot on *terra firma*, exclaimed, "For conscience sake, I'm on dry land once more!," giving rise to the place name Conscience Point.

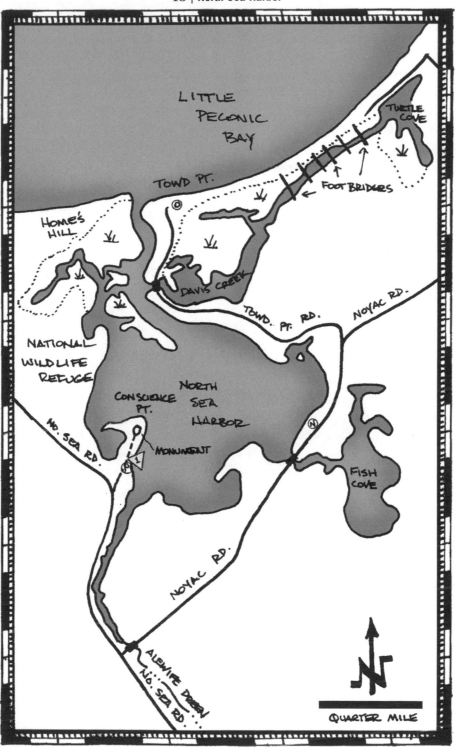

The actual settlement, called Old Town, was located four miles south of the harbor (present day Southampton Village) in an area of particularly rich and fertile soils being cultivated at the time by the Shinnecock Indians. North Sea Harbor became the settlement's seaport, an officially designated Port of Entry complete with a Customs House and the township's first tavern.

Before launching from the point, I watch a Greater Yellowlegs searching an exposed mudflat for food. A generalist among the shorebirds, it uses its long, stout bill to capture small fish, crabs, snails, insects, and worms in the shallows of the harbor and adjacent intertidal zone. Wintering as far south as Tierra del Fuego and nesting in the muskeg and tundra of Canada, this constantly bobbing bird is one of our many transient visitors, stopping to feed in eastern Long Island's productive estuaries during migration. Although they don't nest in this area, I often see them throughout the breeding season. Perhaps these are adolescent birds that are not quite mature enough for nesting and rearing young.

Paddling west to the shoreline of the Conscience Point National Wildlife Refuge, I pass a flock of Black Duck and several pairs of Canada Geese in a small embayment. According to the U.S. Fish and Wildlife Service, North Sea Harbor and the Sebonac Creek estuary (nearby to the west) are important overwintering and nesting areas for Black Duck, with winter densities among the highest on Long Island. Horned Grebes, Buffleheads, and Red-Breasted Mergansers are also common here during the winter months.

The 60-acre refuge was established in 1971 through the donation of the property by Stanley Howard to the federal government. Strictly a wildlife sanctuary, it is not open to the public. The only practical way to view the area is by boat.

In addition to its waterfowl nesting and shorebird feeding habitat, the refuge contains a maritime grassland, a plant community that is becoming rare on Long Island. Grasslands are comprised of early successional plants that, over time, are naturally replaced with shrubs and trees through a process called ecological succession. In order to maintain and enlarge the grassland area, the USFWS periodically removes woody plants and burns portions of the refuge.

Refuge managers hope that these management practices will attract grassland dependent birds such as the Grasshopper Sparrow, Savannah Sparrow, Eastern Meadowlark, and Bobolink. It is also excellent habitat for American Woodcock. In addition to the native grasses, the refuge is home to two rare plants, Bushy Rockrose and Nantucket Shadbush. The latter is very difficult to distinguish from the more common Shadbush (*Amelanchier canadensis*). Its presence along the LIPA powerline in Shinnecock Hills makes me think it doesn't mind occasional cutting.

West of a long, narrow island of marsh grasses that separates the refuge from the harbor's boat channel is a low sandy bluff rimmed with Eastern Red Cedars and Black Cherry. Near the top of the bluff is a Red Fox den. This diminutive member of

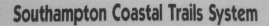

### Southampton Coastal Trails System

#### Conscience Point Historic Site

Dedicated in memory of Southampton Colonial Society President Robert Keene

Conscience Point is the approximate landing place of the first English colonist who arrived here in June of 1640. The Shinnecock Indians lived around this harbor for many centuries before the arrival of the English who subsequently settled in the vicinity of the present Southampton Village. Both the early settlers and the Native Americans benefited from the productivity of the marsh-bordered land and harbor.

Conscience Point is owned by the Southampton Historical Museum. The trail leads to a commemorative monument placed here in 1910. In 2000, the Museum and the Town of Southampton completed a project to restore this location to a more natural condition and to conserve its resources for the future.

North Sea Harbor includes historic Conscience Point.

the dog family rarely enters the confines of its den, preferring to rest in the open where it can better sense danger. Dens are used by females for a short period in late spring when the young are born and nursed. According to my reference books, as well as one of my graduate school mentors who once hunted foxes in southern New Hampshire for a living, foxes do not excavate their own dens. Rather, they retrofit a natural cavity or an abandoned Woodchuck den. This is definitely not true on the South Fork, where our sandy soil causes dens to collapse after a few years, but also makes for easy digging.

Just around the bend, four Great Egrets, one of many summer residents who recently arrived from their winter haunts further south, bask in the leafless boughs of a large oak. Turning into a small tidal creek, I note the perfect imprints of a Great Blue Heron's four-toes, an incredibly huge track, on the creek's sandy bottom. The heron is just ahead, moving slowly in search of small fish and crabs, neither of which is very abundant at this time of year. In fact, I have not seen a single finfish or crab at this point, just the ubiquitous Ribbed Mussels and Mud Snails that line the sides and bottom of the creek.

Off to my right are the light-colored sands of Homes Hill. This unusual forested hillside, looming 100 feet above the refuge and sea, is covered with windblown beach sands. It is one of the little gemstones among North Sea's jewels, and will hopefully be added to the hamlet's list of permanently protected open spaces.

Exiting the creek and leaving the refuge astern, I enter a narrow channel that I hope separates two small islands of salt marsh and provides a shortcut to Davis Creek on the opposite side of the harbor. Luckily it doesn't dead-end and I am soon crossing the main channel that connects the harbor to Peconic Bay, and then passing under the barnacle-encrusted Towd Point Road bridge. I paddle as far north into the Davis Creek marsh as I can to observe the Towd Point Osprey tower. The Ospreys have just recently returned from their overwintering areas as far south as the Amazon basin, and I am pleasantly surprised to see this nest already occupied by a pair.

The Osprey's diet is almost exclusively fish, which it snatches with its feet and taloned toes. This fishing technique limits it to catching fish swimming within two feet of the water's surface, and the Osprey's arrival is a sign that other, less visible, migrations are also underway—fish moving from their deep, offshore winter haunts into the shallow margins of the estuary. One such migration, that of the anadro-

## Alewife (*Alosa pseudoharengus*)

The Alewife is a type of river herring, 10–12 inches in length, found from Newfoundland to South Carolina. An anadromous species—meaning one that migrates from salt water to freshwater to spawn—Alewives congregate at the mouths of the rivers and brooks they will ascend as early as late February. Although adults can detect their natal waters, there is much mixing of populations on the continental shelf where they overwinter, and some will stray to different spawning sites. Most make the trip upstream under the cover of darkness, with peak spawning activity taking place after dark.

There are over a dozen Alewife runs on the East End, the most well known being the Alewife Dreen that links Big Fresh Pond with North Sea Harbor. The spawning run is triggered when water temperature reaches approximately 50°F. After a short stay of about five days in freshwater where they spawn, the adults head back to sea. At least 50% of the adults will not survive the rigors of spawning and the gauntlet of predators (Ospreys, herons, egrets, Raccoons, man) patrolling the shallow spawning areas. And only 0.02% of the eggs laid will produce 3–4-inch-long juveniles that will make it downstream to the sea the following fall. However, each female lays 60,000 to 200,000 eggs, so the 0.02% survival rate yields a not insignificant 1,200–4,000 juveniles per female.

This fascinating creature is an important ecological link in the food chain between its prey (mostly large zooplankton) and a wide variety of avian and aquatic piscivores. It also provides an important link between freshwater and marine environments. As NYSDEC fisheries biologist Byron Young points out, "Everything loves to eat Alewives. Its presence enhances the prey base of both freshwater and marine ecosystems. Largemouth bass, pickerel, and yellow perch feed on the young Alewives from late spring through the summer months, while striped bass, bluefish, and seals, to name a few, feast on them year-round in the marine environment."

mous Alewife from the bay to spawning areas in the upper, freshwater reaches of tidal creeks, is so closely aligned with the arrival of Ospreys that there may be an evolutionary connection between the two species.

Davis Creek is intersected by at least a half-dozen wooden footbridges that provide creekside homeowners with access to the bay. A canoe or kayak can easily slip under them. Although the paddle eastward to Turtle Cove is an enjoyable and scenic traverse with beautiful salt marshes on the creek's north side and the cove's south, I decide to head directly to the Alewife Dreen this trip. Seeing the Ospreys has piqued my curiosity about the Alewife run, and I hope to glimpse a school congregating in the shallow dreen.

En route I pass two small flocks of overwinterers who have not yet left for their northern nesting grounds in the arctic tundra and boreal forest. Unlike the Osprey or heron, neither the Bufflehead, with its striking, white head patches, nor the Long-Tailed Duck, with its unusual, tail feathers, have a problem catching fish in even our deepest bays. Both are excellent divers with the latter documented at depths of 200 feet.

Crossing the middle of the harbor, I can see the beach that once hosted a noisy colony of nesting terns, and on the northern flank of the moraine in the distance is the North Sea landfill. A southwesterly breeze has picked up and I am glad to tuck into the narrows of the Alewife Dreen. Although quite protected, the paddling experience is greatly diminished by the densely developed shoreline. Nearing the culvert at Noyac Road, I note the first schools of fish in the shallows. They are all less than three inches in length and most likely some type of killifish (*Fundulus*) species. There is no sign of the Alewives, but I later learn from Howard Reisman, a marine biologist at Southampton College who lives nearby, that the run had indeed begun.

Heading back to Conscience Point, I reflect on the fact that the signs of spring are most evident in our changing fauna. While the landscape surrounding the harbor still has a strong winter tone, and it will be quite some time before the marsh and forests green up, it is an interesting time to be on the water. March provides an opportunity to bid farewell to our winter wildlife guests and greet the newly arrived migratory transients and summer breeders, all intriguing creatures. ✕

# 11 | JESSUP NECK

*Noyac, Town of Southampton*

DISTANCE:  4 miles R/T.

ACCESS:  1) Cedar Point Lane: No permit needed. Cedar Point Lane intersects Noyac Road 0.6 mile east of the easy-to-find entrance to Morton National Wildlife Refuge and 1.5 miles west of Long Beach Road. It is very close to the intersection of Millstone Road and Noyac Road. Cedar Point Lane dead-ends on Noyac Creek.

2) Noyac Bay Avenue: No permit needed. Westbound on Noyac Road, take the second right after Trout Pond (1.1 miles west of Long Beach Road) onto Mill Road (eastbound on Noyac Road, this is a left turn 1.0 mile from Morton National Wildlife Refuge). Go to end and turn left onto Noyac Bay Avenue. Follow this around bend to water (Noyac Bay) and park.

*September*

No more than three hundred yards wide and nearly two miles in length, Jessup Neck is a long ribbon of land undergoing continual metamorphoses which, unlike our own, result in measurable increases in length and decreases in girth over time. The change has been slow but dramatic. The three conical hills of glacial deposits, called kames, that comprise the bulk of Jessup Neck today were once two islands (two kames formed a northern island, one a southern island). Over the course of many thousands of years, wind, tide, and littoral currents redistributed some of their material into a series of interconnected spits, called tombolos, that harbor salt ponds, marshes, and lagoons. There is no better way to see and sense this process than by paddling along the shoreline of the peninsula.

An Osprey perched atop the nest on Clam Island watches as I organize my boat, binoculars, and maps at the Cedar Point Lane launch ramp. Schools of small Mummichogs (*Fundulus heteroclitus*) and Striped Killifish (*Fundulus majalis*) swirl about me in the shallow water, the sudden movement of my kayak causing a few to dart away and strand themselves on the sandy shore. Across the small embayment known as Noyac Creek, a small flock of Canada Geese drifts along the shoreline of Morton National Wildlife Refuge. Donated to the U.S. Fish and Wildlife Service in 1954 by Elizabeth Morton, this popular 187-acre preserve is one of only eight National Wildlife Refuges on all of Long Island.

Paddling west towards the creek's inlet, the Osprey lets loose its classic piercing call as I pass close by. This seems to attract the attention of another Osprey perched

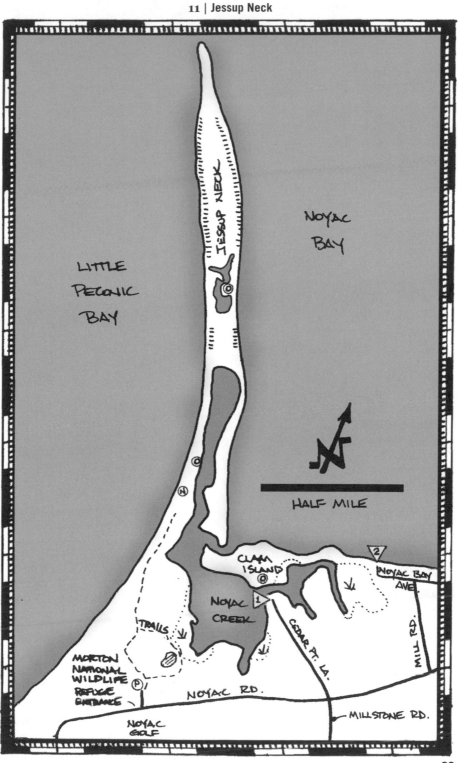

LITTLE PECONIC BAY

JESSUP NECK

NOYAC BAY

HALF MILE

CLAM ISLAND

NOYAC CREEK

NOYAC BAY AVE.

TRAILS

MORTON NATIONAL WILDLIFE REFUGE ENTRANCE

CEDAR PT. LA.

MILL RD.

NOYAC RD.

MILLSTONE RD.

NOYAC GOLF

nearby, which flies over with a bloody flounder-shaped fish in its talons to join its agitated colleague on the nest. With binoculars, I take a close look at the pair to see if one or both might be class of 2000 fledglings. This nest had been occupied this breeding season and produced one young. These are both adults, possibly not even the occupants of the nest but migrants from nesting areas further north heading to their overwintering areas in the Caribbean and South America.

Approaching the west end of Clam Island County Park, another piscivore, the Great Blue Heron, stalks the shoreline for a meal. Despite the name, a visit to Clam Island does not have to involve a boat or a swim. A quarter-mile-long tombolo connects, although very tenuously on a spring high tide, this 20-acre preserve to the mainland of Noyac.

This small gem was purchased by Suffolk County in 1988 after years of lobbying by Group for the South Fork, the Noyac Civic Council, and the Property Owners Association of Noyac Harbor. The effort involved a campaign, targeted at the U. S. Army Corps of Engineers and the NYS Department of Environmental Conservation, to oppose a development plan which included a bridge and raised roadbed for auto access, and a 200-foot-long catwalk into Noyac Bay. First proposed for preservation by County Legislator Tony Bullock, the acquisition plan was finally pulled together under Fred Theile's County tenure, surviving some bickering among County Legislators on another matter in which the island's purchase was temporarily held hostage. In the end, the good guys prevailed.

Rounding the west end of Clam Island, I head for the inlet and enter Noyac Bay, deciding to circumnavigate the neck in a counterclockwise direction to take advantage of the southeasterly wind. A recent storm has littered the low-lying spit north of the inlet with Green Fleece (*Codium fragile*). Picking up a few specimens, I note that each is anchored to a stone and the stone is host to as many as a half-dozen Slipper Shells (*Crepidula fornicata*), each arranged tightly one atop the other. Also known as the Boat Shell because of its shape and half-decked bottom, this gastropod is the most common shell on many of our bay beaches.

The beach here and all along the east side of Jessup Neck is quite stony and noticeably devoid of beachgrass. From the inlet north to the beginning of the bluffs, the stony spit is sparsely vegetated with Eastern Red Cedar, Beach Plum, and Poison Ivy. One very low section of the spit is lacking any woody growth due to frequent overwash caused by easterly winds, which tend to blow hard out here.

Abeam of the bluffs the shoreline and vegetation changes abruptly, with Groundsel bush growing at the high tide line and the bluffs themselves topped with a mature oak forest. The entire wildlife refuge is second growth forest with an unusual mix of ornamental, non-native plants, reflecting a long and interesting history of agriculture dating back to the 1600s. Originally named Farrington Point for John Farrington, one of the founders of the South Hampton Colony, the peninsula took its current

## Common Slipper Shell (*Crepidula fornicata*)

The Slipper or Boat Shell is the most common shell found on many of our bay beaches. The life cycle of this gastropod is quite interesting, and somewhat bizarre. Fertilized females lay up to 10,000 eggs packaged in 50 interconnected capsules that they glue onto the rock to which they are attached. This takes place twice yearly. After hatching, the larvae spend a month adrift as zooplankton before settling and taking up permanent residence on rocks or other securely anchored Slipper Shells, adhering via the strong sucking action of its muscular foot.

Once settled, the shell grows to make a tight fit on the substrate. After two years, most animals lose the very limited mobility they had and become completely sessile. Food particles from the water are trapped on its cilia and mucous coated gills; the catch is gathered every four minutes or so by twisting its mouth from one side to the other. What food isn't immediately eaten is stored in a pouch and saved for later consumption.

Slipper Shells live five to ten years, and it is not uncommon to find successive generations stacked, one atop the other, up to ten high. Within each stack of shells, the younger and smaller Slipper Shells are obviously found on top and the larger, older ones on the bottom. All Slipper Shells start out as males. Those that land on unoccupied rocks can transform into females within two months.

For those that land atop a stack of other Slipper Shell, life is more complex. At the top of the stack are several generations of males in various stages of sexual maturity, at the bottom is the mature female. In between are hermaphrodites, individuals undergoing a sex change from male to female. The final metamorphosis from male to female is held in check by pheromones released from the stack's reigning female, and will not occur until that female, the stack's anchor, dies.

Or so the story goes. Think about it. The female is the one holding the stack to the rock. She dies and the stack topples over. Even if the stack landed on a substrate that did not clog their feeding mechanisms, how does the female-to-be reposition herself on another hard surface? She can't move. Does she hang onto the shell of the previous—now deceased—female to protect her vulnerable, soft underside? I have yet to hear an explanation of this often described but seemingly impossible event.

name from another of the newcomers from Lynn, Massachusetts who first settled in this area, John Jessup. Jessup was deeded the neck in 1679 and, through the ensuing 275 years, ownership was transferred to only two other families.

Jessup's daughter, Abigail, was buried on the east side of the neck in 1724. On a canoe outing with Richard G. Hendrickson in 1994, we looked for the gravestone but could not locate it.

In 1800, Isaac Osborn acquired the land and began experimenting with a variety of crops and livestock, including mulberry trees for raising silkworms and the first shorthorn cattle and merino sheep introduced to Long Island. During this time, the entire area was cleared and either under cultivation or used for pasturing livestock. Even the salt marsh was periodically mowed. These grasses, collectively called Salt Hay, were used as winter fodder for the cattle and sheep.

Continuing northward, the bluffs diminish and reveal another low section of the neck, this one harboring a small pond, young Red Cedars, and a natural Osprey nest in a short snag. Just beyond this pretty spot is a another kame with a maximum elevation of 50 feet above mean sea level. The face of the steep sandy bluff here is riddled with deer tracks and a keen eye can pick out a fox den and some Belted Kingfisher holes just below the top edge. The bluff here is obviously eroding. Many of the large oaks have most of their roots exposed and will someday topple down the bluff face.

Continuing northward, the tall bluff diminishes and the mature oak forest gives way to a young woodland of early successional, shade-intolerant species such as Black Cherry and Eastern Red Cedar. According to Bridgehampton resident Richard Hendrickson, this northern reach of Jessup Neck was host to an international canoe regatta at the turn of the century. Paddlers from the U.S. and Canada, and their boats, were dropped off by steamship and camped near the point, where a well and hand pump provided fresh water. Participants demonstrated their skills in races and other competitions in Noyac Bay.

Jessup Neck's northern tip is a long, narrow, barren spit that reaches far out towards the North Fork. Since it is mid-September, I ignore the "No Boat Landing: Bird Nesting Area" sign and portage the 100-foot-wide spit separating Noyac and Little Peconic Bays. A closer inspection of the stony spit reveals quite a large quantity of empty shells, mostly Slipper Shells, and some hardy plants: a fleshy, succulent plant called Sea Rocket (*Cakile edentula*) and a spiny plant called Common Glasswort (*Salsola kali*).

Heading south along the west shoreline of the neck, several striking differences from the eastern side are apparent. One is the presence of a sandy beach and Beachgrass, in some places quite dense, along the shore. A portion of Beachgrass' scientific name, *Ammophila breviligulata*, translates as "sand loving," a reference to the fact that it grows best in a medium that few plants thrive in: pure sand. It also grows most robust where there is regular sand deposition; the process of being partially buried by windblown sand stimulates the growth of buds in its stems.

The presence of sand and Beachgrass here, and the lack of both on the east side, would indicate that the west side is accreting and the east side is eroding. Another contrast is found in the bluff top vegetation. Oaks are few and those that can be found are quite stunted in size, rarely reaching heights greater than 15 feet. There are many more low growing plants here on the west side, a variety of vines and Northern Bayberry shrubs dominate. Exposure to the prevailing southwest wind during the growing season may be limiting plant growth via desiccation and salt deposition.

Adjacent to the low area where a pond nestles between kame sections, a tiny, intermittent inlet can be found. The brackish pond that the inlet links to is not visible from the bay, and the inlet itself may not be very prominent in all seasons and years. It appears that seawater only flows into the pond periodically during extreme high tides or storms, and the brackish pond water flows out only when heavy rains overtop the small waterbody.

Paddling past the southernmost of the kames, I reach a long section of narrow beach, another tombolo, that extends for over a half-mile to the Noyac mainland. This area is an important tern and Plover nesting site, and from April through July should be avoided. I portage over the tombolo and into the quiet salt lagoon fringed with salt marsh grasses and Sea Lavender. The latter's delicate purple flowers are now in bloom.

Paddling south, toward Noyac Creek and the launch site at Cedar Point Lane, I witness a huge mass of Fiddler Crabs moving in unison on the bare, wet sands of the intertidal zone. The crabs must number in the thousands. Although I've seen this phenomenon several times before, I am always surprised that no predators take advantage on the easy meal. Describing this to a few baymen, they nod knowingly of the scene, but cannot offer any explanations for this particular behavior. ✗

# 12 | GENET CREEK

DISTANCE: 2.5 miles R/T.

ACCESS: There is no convenient public access for launching a canoe or kayak directly in the creek. The closest public access is 0.3 miles to the east of the creek's inlet on Shelter Island Sound.

1) Rte. 114–South Ferry: No permit needed. Follow Rte. 114 north through North Haven to the South Ferry terminal. Park in the lot on the left (west) side of the road and launch from the sandy beach on the west side of the dock, staying well clear of the ferry operation.

*April*

After a long winter off the water, a warm, sunny morning in early April got me thinking about paddling. The forecasted very light winds for the entire day prompted me into action, brushing oak leaves out of the cockpit of my kayak, sliding my paddle out of the garage rafters, and rummaging around for other gear that had been stowed away months ago. By mid-morning I was en route to North Haven to poke around a beautiful little tidal waterway called Genet Creek.

A paddle around the well-protected creek involves launching into and paddling along a fairly exposed stretch of water. Although it is only a third-of-a-mile paddle to the creek's inlet, this section of Shelter Island Sound has strong tidal currents and a long fetch to the west and northwest. Fortunately the wind is not a factor to contend with today, and the worst of a foul tidal current can easily be avoided by hugging the shoreline.

From the sandy beach just west of the ferry dock, I head westward. Despite the spring-like weather, the water temperature of Shelter Island Sound is around 40°F. A mishap resulting in a swim at that temperature is a dangerous situation. Closely following the contours of North Haven's northern coastline, my course not only keeps me out of the strong ebb current but in shallow water that I could stand up in.

A quarter-mile west of the ferry, a rock jetty forces me further out from shore and momentarily into the swift current. The sudden change from still water to swift current involves crossing an eddy line, a feature evident to the experienced eye. Be prepared for a sudden sideways pull on your boat as it noses across one of these.

Clearing the rocks, I turn back towards shore where a pair of Great Black-backed Gulls is foraging among the flotsam and jetsam left behind by the receding tide.

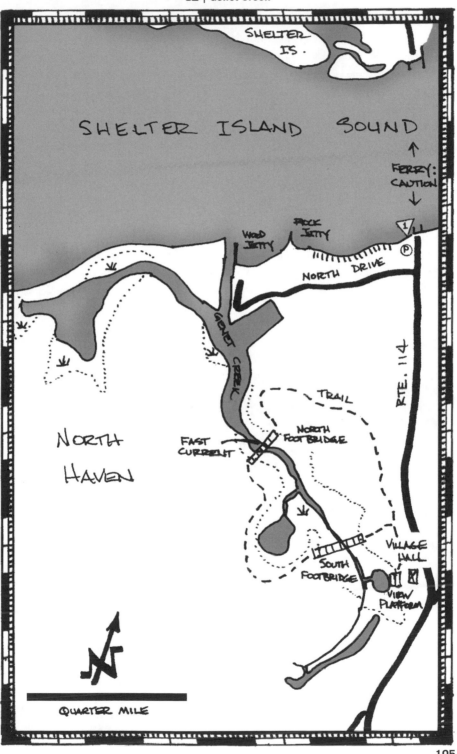

Although common and rarely given a second look by most, this large gull is an amazing flier and the mature adults have quite a strikingly handsome plumage.

A wooden jetty marks the entrance to Genet Creek. A large sandy shoal has migrated around the end of the western jetty and built up on the inlet's western side. The presence of the shoal, together with the lack of one outside of the eastern jetty, would indicate that net littoral drift along the northern shore of North Haven is eastward, most likely driven by northwesterly winds. Under natural conditions, littoral drift causes inlets to migrate, sometimes creating serpentine waterways and perhaps briefly sealing them shut by way of a narrow sandbar. Looking at an aerial photograph, it is not hard to imagine Genet Creek's inlet being further to the west many years ago.

Turning into the inlet, I am surprised to find the current generated by the outgoing tide much less here than outside. Where the creek widens and branches to the left and right the current is barely noticeable. To the left (east) is a man-made basin for docking and mooring boats; to the right (west) is a natural channel that may once have been the original route of the creek to Shelter Island Sound. However, an

---

### Great Black-backed Gull (*Larus mariuns*) and Herring Gull (*Larus argentatus*)

The Great Black-backed Gull and the Herring Gull are so commonly seen in our area that they are often taken for granted, dismissed as "sea gulls" without a second look. This is unfortunate, as they are truly magnificent fliers and, in their adult plumage, handsome creatures. They are also opportunistic and adaptable, and their foraging antics alone can provide hours of interesting and sometimes comical entertainment.

While lifeguarding at Jones Beach State Park over many summers I witnessed some amazing feeding frenzies involving gulls and the carefully wrapped lunches of unsuspecting beachgoers who momentarily abandoned their blankets for a swim. Whole sandwiches, paper or plastic wrap and all, would disappear in several quick gulps. I once watched an entire chicken leg go the same way. It was a struggle, and at one point seemed improbable, but the gull, a Herring Gull in this case, somehow managed to pull it off.

All food items not completely ingested were fair game to other gulls, including items protruding from bills. This often resulted in incredible aerial chases complete with rolls, dives and quick bursts of speed. After a Herring Gull landed on my grill and took flight with a quarter chicken in its toes, I found myself in one of the chase scenes. My dinner was a bit too heavy for the gull to gain altitude or maneuver well, and soft sand beach sprints were a specialty of mine back then. Realizing I was gaining and nearly within reach, the gull conceded defeat and dropped its prize. Although at most a 50-yard sprint down the beach, it remains one of my most memorable races.

undated Town of East Hampton Bicentennial–Historic Map shows the large lagoon at the western end of this fork as a pond unconnected to the creek.

Although much of the creek's shoreline has retained its scenic beauty through the recent building boom, a couple of large homes loom over the waterway. Genet Creek courses through what was once the Stock Farm. The 400-acre farm included areas of mature forest, as well as the marshes adjacent to the creek. A proposal to subdivide the property was bitterly contested in the 1970s with Village officials, environmental organizations and the community in general raising concerns about building in the floodplain, clearing impacts on the creek, habitat fragmentation, and the impact of the development on the Village's fragile water supply.

Despite the opposition and concerns, 133 residential lots were eventually approved. The subdivision layout, even for that time, was very poorly designed. Large building lots needlessly fragmented wildlife habitat, buildings and lawns were permitted quite close to the creek, and wetland buffer areas were so narrow in places, as is evident here, as to be of questionable value.

I was surprised to learn that these ubiquitous gulls are relatively recent nesters here on Long Island. Both nested further north: Great Black-backed Gulls in the Canadian maritimes and Herring Gulls from Alaska across the length of Canada and south into northeastern United States. The Herring Gull was nearly extirpated from New York State as a result of egg collecting and hunting in the 1800s. By 1900, the only remaining nesting populations were those established on remote lakes in the Adirondacks. At that time, they did not nest on the coast anywhere south of Maine.

The first nesting pair of Herring Gulls on Long Island was found at Orient Point in 1931. The population expanded rapidly. By 1985, 24,000 nesting pairs were documented on Long Island, with the largest single colony (located at Plum Island) totaling 7,000 pairs. The Long Island nesting population has declined since to a low of 9,500 pairs (1993). Some attribute the population increase and expanded range to new sources of food in the form of open garbage dumps, and the more recent population decline to more stringent landfill management practices as well as landfill closures on Long Island.

The Great Black-backed Gull story is similar. They did not nest south of the Canadian maritimes until 1930. In 1942, local naturalist Roy Wilcox recorded a nest on Cartwright Island in Gardiners Bay. As with the Herring Gull, the Great Black-backed Gull population exploded. Over the decade between 1985–1995, 52 colonies were documented on Long Island with an average of 7,100 nesting pairs per year. In 1995, the Gardiners Island colony of 3,420 nesting pairs was the State's largest; it alone accounted for nearly half the total number for New York State. Today, both species are found nesting as far south as North Carolina.

Inside the protected waters of the tidal creek, the shoreline vegetation is dominated by salt marsh grasses, *Spartina alterniflora* and *S. patens* and, lower in the intertidal zone, a group of olive-brown seaweeds (*Fucus* spp.) commonly referred to as Bladder Wrack or Rockweed. Under the right conditions, the *Spartinas* can colonize sand and silt substrates, eventually creating the classic spongy, marsh peat from their own dead leaves. The peat provides the perfect habitat for the Fiddler Crab, who is not making an appearance despite the mild weather and falling tide.

The *Spartina* root systems provide a relatively stable point of attachment for another ubiquitous marsh organism, the Ribbed Mussel, via its hair-like byssal threads. In the absence of rocks in the inter- and subtidal zone, its shell, in turn, provides a suitable point of attachment for the rockweed's holdfast.

As the creek narrows and swings to the left, the northern of two footbridges comes into view. These are part of a nature trail system which loops around the creek and adjacent forest. Directly beneath the bridge are large boulders; stay in the middle of the creek to avoid running aground on them. The current here races around the boulders and funnels through the narrow channel with some force, but can usually be overcome with a couple of hard strokes. Get up some steam on the approach and keep your boat pointed straight into the current until clear of the bridge.

The rock material was placed here many years ago, most likely to allow wagon carts to cross the creek. The crossing was located not only where the creek is very narrow but where the distance across the adjacent marsh to uplands is also quite short. Rockweed and barnacles cover many of the boulders. Except for high tide when the rocks are completely covered, the water rushing through here creates the soothing sounds of a babbling brook.

Beyond the bridge the creek continues to narrow and lose depth while the marsh widens considerably against a beautiful forest landscape. The winter-brown marsh grasses are just beginning to show a hint of green low down on their stems. Another sign of spring is the abundant, one-inch-long Shore Shrimp (*Palaemonetes* spp.), that dart for cover among the grasses as my boat approaches. In the shallower vector control ditches, I spot a few small fish, most likely Striped Killifish or Mummichogs (*Fundulus* spp.) who have spent the winter months buried in the soft mud of the creek and marsh. The dearth of small fish may explain the absence of herons, egrets, and other common marsh piscivores.

With the right tide, it is possible to paddle to the south footbridge, and maybe even the small pond with the wildlife viewing platform near Village Hall, but I decide to leave the main channel and paddle into a large and very shallow salt pond midway between the bridges. A Red-tailed Hawk circles quietly overhead, while a Red-headed Woodpecker "churrs" and drums in the nearby woods. Putting my paddle down, I sit back and enjoy the warm spring sun and the sights and sounds of Genet Creek before heading home. ✕

# 13 | SAG HARBOR'S COVES

*Sag Harbor, Town of Southampton*

DISTANCE: This labyrinth of coves and creeks has over 10 miles of shoreline to explore.

ACCESS: There are a dozen access points that are suitable for launching a canoe or kayak in the Sag Harbor area. Three are listed here.

1) Long Wharf: Time limit on parking in summer. Launch from sandy beach in front of the windmill.

2) Bay Street launch ramp: Check parking signs in the area for restrictions.

3) Long Beach Road: No permit needed. Park on the wide paved shoulder at the north end of Long Beach Road (Noyac Bay side). Carry across the road to launch in Sag Harbor Cove.

*January*

In a normal January, warm and sunny weather might be referred to as a "January Thaw." But, this January, an exceptionally warm November and December didn't create anything to thaw. The unseasonable temperatures prompted me to consider kayaking. The early morning sky was clear and still, and the forecast called for the thermometer to hit the 50°F mark. It looked to be a good day for a paddle.

I decided to paddle a loop through a very sheltered series of coves, creeks, and ponds in Sag Harbor. Despite its dense development and bulkheaded shoreline, I enjoy paddling the backwaters of my favorite village. My trips there have always included sightings of a wide variety of waterfowl and shorebirds throughout the year. In summer, I have counted over 30 thumb-sized Diamondback Terrapin heads protruding from the surface of the water. Even in the summer season, this small estuary has very little boat traffic.

After securing the kayak to the car, I run through a brief equipment list in my head: boat and paddle. Believe it or not, more than once I've arrived at the launch site without a paddle. Then the ghost of Mr. Murphy, eternal pessimist and author of Murphy's Law, interrupts my thoughts with lots of questions: "Water temperature?" "Paddling alone?" "In the event of a capsize, how long would it take to swim to shore?" "How many minutes before hypothermia sets in?" Hmmm. Back into the garage to get my wetsuit, neoprene booties and gloves, and a lifejacket.

I launch from the sandy beach near the Long Wharf windmill. Several patches of Salt Marsh Cordgrass (*Spartina alterniflora*) grow along the shoreline. Well adapted to the stresses of the intertidal zone where temperatures and salinity can fluctuate dramatically over a six-hour period, even this hardy pioneer plant of the salt marsh has its limits. Here, the generous fetch to the north creates enough wave action to constrain marsh development.

Crossing under the Rte. 114 bridge, keep an eye out for powerboats even in the middle of winter. The previous week I had waited for a large boat towing a section of dock to pass by. The channel here cuts through a tombolo that once connected North Haven to Sag Harbor. I follow the southern shore of North Haven, once known as Hog Neck, westward toward the Long Beach tombolo—a crescent of low-lying, sandy beach that links North Haven with morainal deposits at Bay Point and Noyac.

On the east side of the tombolo, protected from the wind-driven waves on Noyac Bay, an extensive salt marsh was able to develop. Unfortunately, most of the original salt marsh here is gone, having been filled to create parking and Long Beach Road. But tucked in the northern corner of this arm of the cove is the prettiest section of salt marsh in the entire Sag Harbor Cove area.

A nearby culvert under Long Beach Road is navigable at mid-tide (no clearance at high) and connects through to a small tidal lagoon at Short Beach. This enables paddlers bound for Noyac Bay to avoid carrying across Long Beach Road, although a short portage across the beach between bay and lagoon is still necessary. I turn south and follow the shoreline of Bay Point into the Big Narrows. The light wind has freshened and turned more westerly and, although the temperature has warmed to 50°F, I feel the wind chill factor in my hands. Reminded that neoprene gloves are not very wind-proof, I head for the lee afforded by Long Beach, and cruise comfortably along its Phragmites-lined shoreline.

The intertidal zone on the Sag Harbor side of Long Beach is dominated by Phragmites, a plant of questionable ecological value. A restoration project undertaken by Southampton Town can be seen near the entrance to Paynes Creek. There, an area of old fill was excavated down to the intertidal zone and marsh grasses were planted. The aggressive and invasive Phragmites has moved back in and, if left unchecked, may overwhelm the *Spartina* in the end. This is a good example of the difficulties inherent in marsh restoration and why salt marshes should be protected.

The loss of highly productive salt marsh grasses in these coves has been extensive. In addition to filling of the Long Beach marsh, much of Sag Harbor Village was built on salt marsh and freshwater wetlands. I note that landward of some bulkheads, *Spartina* grasses have reestablished themselves. Perhaps over time with the resiliency of nature, good stewardship, and enforcement of wetland protection regulations, the ecological recovery of this small estuary might continue. Today though, these coves have the distinction of registering some of the worst water quality values in the entire Peconic Estuary.

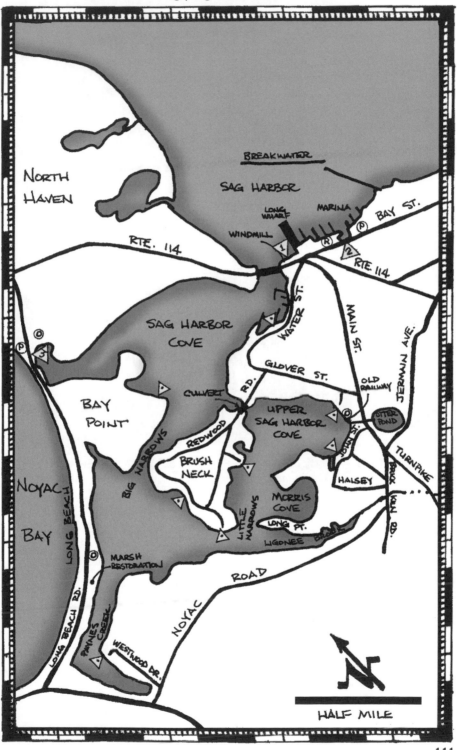

## Diamondback Terrapin (*Malaclemys terrapin*)

Diamondback Terrapins are true survivors. Their meat has been considered a delicacy dating back to pre-colonial times. In fact, "terrapin" is an Algonquin word for "edible turtle." From the 1880s through the 1920s terrapin meat became such an extremely popular gourmet food item—some would say a food fad—that local populations here on Long Island were nearly exterminated. They were ultimately saved not by conservation efforts, but by the economic impact of the Great Depression on the terrapin meat market.

The Diamondback Terrapin population has rebounded well. On a calm sunny day, their thumb-sized heads can be seen poking up from the waters of most of our bays and harbors. It's a shame they are not more visible, as the shell and skin markings are quite beautiful. Although it is still harvested for its meat, New York State enacted conservation measures in 1990 in the form of size and season restrictions. Still, there is some concern about harvest numbers and the accidental by-catch of terrapins in crab pots, where they usually drown.

The Diamondback Terrapin is our only resident turtle which is designed to live in the estuary. It has several unique adaptations that enable it to survive long periods in full seawater (34% salinity), including skin that has a very low permeability to water and a powerful salt gland that excretes excessive sodium chloride from its body. Still, they need to offset salt buildup in body fluids. They can drink up to 15% of their body weight in freshwater in 10 minutes when it is available, even if the water is the thinnest of films on marsh peat and mud.

Even with these adaptations, it cannot survive indefinitely in full seawater, and so it is most often found in the less saline waters of our estuaries. Although this habitat type is very common throughout the terrapin's range (Cape Cod to Texas), the estuaries themselves occur as thin, discontinuous bands along the coast. This has limited gene flow among populations and resulted in an unusual degree of subspeciation. Currently, scientists recognize seven distinct subspecies.

Other than seeing their heads sticking out of the water, we are most likely to encounter female Diamondback Terrapins when they come ashore to lay eggs in May and June. Those that are not consumed by predators hatch in August and September. As with our other local turtles, Diamondback Terrapin eggs generally suffer very high predation rates, with as few as 3% of the eggs hatching in some years.

While it is tempting to think that boosting those paltry egg and hatchling survivorship figures will make the overall population more robust and secure, studies have shown that protecting adults from human impacts (e.g. roadkills and habitat loss) is the best long term conservation strategy. Feeding on a largely carnivorous diet of crabs, snails, mussels, and worms, males reach maturity within three years. Fully-grown females, which are 30 percent larger than males (nine inches in length), require eight years to mature.

The life history of the terrapin was missing a key chapter for many years: little was known about the hatchlings. Recent research revealed some surprises, at least to me. Upon leaving the nest, hatchlings do not head for water but the nearest vegetation. Their first years of life are spent beneath mats of *Spartina* grasses that form the wrack line in the marsh, where they forage for small invertebrates that also inhabit this shifting and constantly changing microenvironment. Researchers who released hatchlings into the water reported that they immediately swam to shore and burrowed into the flotsam and jetsam at the high tide line.

With the wind at my back, it's a quick paddle over to the Little Narrows. Crossing Morris Cove to Bluff Point, I pause to watch a flock of Bufflehead and Red-breasted Mergansers take flight. Both are winter visitors from the far north. The former preys on small shellfish and crustaceans while the latter, an excellent underwater swimmer, feeds on fish. At the outlet to Otter Pond, a Northern Flicker works on a large White Oak while a small flock of Canada Geese keeps a close watch on me. The incoming tide sucks my boat through a narrow opening once spanned by a railway connecting Long Wharf and the main LIRR line at Bridgehampton. This rail link was completed in 1870 and abandoned in 1939. Today, a long stretch of the railway serves as a trail through the Long Pond greenbelt.

Remnants of the railway embankment are quite visible here today. Its lower reaches serve as an egg-laying area for Horseshoe Crabs; higher and drier portions are used for the same purpose by Diamondback Terrapins. Its highest point sports an Osprey nesting tower.

While working at the Group for the South Fork in the 1990s, I was able to get permission to erect three Osprey nesting poles in this area. This one on the railway embankment, one on Long Beach at the confluence of Paynes Creek and Sag Harbor Cove, and one in the pretty stretch of salt marsh mentioned earlier. All three have seen some Osprey activity, but as of 2004 only the Paynes Creek nest had produced young.

I ride the incoming tide right under the Main Street bridge and into Otter Pond where an odd assortment of waterfowl, some not to be found in my Peterson Field Guide, congregates. Heading back out against the tide is a bit tricky, and I am

The easily overlooked but plentiful Ribbed Mussel, a keystone species of the salt marsh, seen attached to Cordgrass and Rockweed.

thankful that I don't have a nice fiberglass boat as I scrape against the barnacle-covered rocks on the east side of the bridge. This is only passable at or very near high tide.

Back in Upper Sag Harbor Cove I head for the Redwood Drive bridge, hoping to slip through and avoid the one-and-a-half-mile paddle around Brush Neck. Near the bridge, I interrupt a Great Blue Heron stalking for a meal in the shallows, and wonder how easy it is to find fish in less than two feet of water at this time of year. I hadn't noticed the usual flashes of Silversides and Mummichogs as I was paddling along through the very clear water. Another piscivore, the Belted Kingfisher, takes flight from a nearby tree, so there must be some fish around.

My notes claim that this bridge is passable at low and high tide. But high tide leaves only two feet between the water and roof of the bridge, and I opt against the awkward contortions required to slide under. Back on the water after a short portage, I put my binoculars away and paddle hard for the windmill, my car and a hot cup of coffee in the village. ✕

# 14 | LONG POND

DISTANCE: Circumnavigating the pond's shoreline is a 1.25-mile-long paddle.

ACCESS: 1) Sayre's Park, Snake Hollow Road: No permit needed. From Rte. 27 in Bridgehampton, turn north onto Snake Hollow Road (the first road east of the Bridgehampton Commons Shopping Center). Cross the railroad tracks and make the first left onto an unpaved drive that runs along the southern edge of the Hamptons Horse Classic grounds (0.0 mile). Continue straight for 0.2 miles and onto a faint dirt road/grass strip to a sign announcing Town's rules and regulations for the park (0.4 mile). Carry your boat down the steep hill to the launch area.

*August*

Bridgehampton's well-known weatherman, Richard G. Hendrickson, has been after me to canoe Long Pond for many years. Not the Long Pond of the Long Pond Greenbelt which stretches from Sag Harbor to Sagaponack, but the South Fork's lesser-known Long Pond which lies in the middle of western Bridgehampton's farmbelt.

I finally got around to exploring the pond on an unusually cool, overcast day. A short detour was made to the Hendrickson homestead to give Richard one last chance to drop the hundred interesting things he is involved in and join me. That was unsuccessful, so I set out in my kayak from the pond's access point for a solo paddle.

Long Pond is the largest of a series of kettlehole ponds oriented northwest-to-southeast between Paul's Lane and the southern flank of the terminal moraine. Kellis, Goldfish, Haines, and Short's Ponds—and a very small, unnamed pond visible on the north side of the highway just west of the Bridgehampton Commons shopping center—make up the rest. Geologists sometimes call these strings of small lakes or ponds "*pater noster* lakes," supposedly because they resemble a string of rosary beads. Whatever. *Pater noster* is a Latin phrase that literally translates as "our father" but usually refers to the Lord's Prayer, which begins "Our Father, who art in heaven." (I was an altar boy long before I became a naturalist.)

At one time the string of ponds numbered just six, and Long Pond was quite a bit longer. The construction of the LIRR across the southern third of Long Pond created a seventh pond, aptly named Little Long, and made Long Pond 1,000 feet shorter. Another change occurred more recently. Long Pond was tucked in among farmfields for several hundred years. Today, a significant portion of its landscape includes large houses and lawns. Still, much of the shoreline, particularly along the east side and at the south end, is comprised of tall Black Willows, Red Maples, and Pepperidge trees, giving it a natural, wild-looking appearance that is a joy to paddle along.

Shoving off from the access point, I head west and follow along the edge of the steep embankment that leads up through the woods to the railroad tracks. I pull up at an American Beech grove and go ashore in hopes of crossing over to nearby Little Long Pond. It has been a dozen years since I was last there, and I am looking forward to revisiting the stand of spectacular Pepperidge trees that grace its western shore. But access to the tracks is blocked by a formidable wall of vine-covered shrubs, so I abandon the idea and retreat to the kayak.

Pondward of the swamp trees that border the waterway are many Buttonbush shrubs, and most are in bloom. Buttonbush is one of the few shrubs that can tolerate long periods of immersion in standing water. Its blooms are attractive sources of nectar for many butterflies, and a number of Cabbage Whites drive that point home.

Working up the west side and past a lawn and dock, I tuck into a narrow channel separating a small island of wetland shrubs (West Island) from the shore. The surface of the pond here is covered with Duckweed, and the long branches from another grove of American Beech create a closed canopy of leaves overhead. Several branches arch downward within reach, revealing the spiny husks of beechnuts. This important mast item appears to be fully formed and nearly ripe.

A quick inventory of the island's vegetation turns up over a dozen native wetland shrubs in various stages of reproductive development. Buttonbush, Swamp Azalea, Sweet Pepperbush, Water Willow, and Swamp Rose are still flowering, while Chokeberry and Elderberry dangle small fruit from their branches. This is a very beautiful spot.

Up at the north end of the pond I am able to paddle in among the willows and get a close look at their strange roots that encircle the lower trunk like a grass skirt. A muskrat takes advantage of the cover created by the willows' broken branches and swims by. According to Hendrickson, an ice house once stood just west of here, as well as a magnificent stand of Pepperidge trees. Both are gone now. The latter was sacrificed, illegally, by the creator of a miniature private golf course.

The route back along the east shoreline is very scenic and offers excellent wildlife viewing opportunities, particularly the stretch south of the wooded point. By now the sun has come out and Painted Turtles are basking. Kingbirds and Tree Swallows catch unseen insects on the wing while an Osprey circles high over the pond.

Paddling into the shrub swamp that links the East Island with shore, I catch sight of a Green Heron perched motionless on a dead willow limb. Noisy rustling overhead is a Gray Squirrel busily feeding on Pepperidge berries. And over at the East Island a small flock of Red-Winged Blackbirds harasses a Red-tailed Hawk until it takes flight from a large snag and leaves the area. Look for the large stick nest of the Red-tailed Hawk in a Tupelo at the point north of East Island.

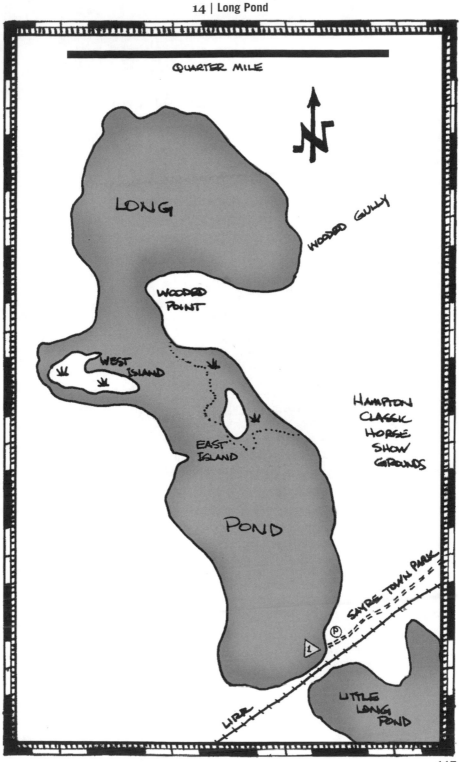

QUARTER MILE

N

LONG

WOODED GULLY

WOODED POINT

WEST ISLAND

HAMPTON CLASSIC HORSE SHOW GROUNDS

EAST ISLAND

POND

SAYRE TOWN PARK

P

1

LIRR

LITTLE LONG POND

This whole section of the pond borders the Hamptons Classic Horse Show property, If not already in place, a conservation easement on the wooded shoreline would be worth pursuing in the future. Although Long Pond was a priority protection area as part of the Kellis Pond greenbelt and listed in the 1980 Southampton Master Plan, little was accomplished towards that goal. Yet, with good stewardship practices by adjacent landowners, and strict enforcement of wetland protection laws by Town staff and officials, Long Pond will remain a beautiful place to visit in the future. ✕

### Osprey (*Pandion haliaetus*)

It is no surprise that the Osprey is one of the most popular wildlife species on the East End. Its six-foot wingspan, habit of hunting in broad daylight over open water, and large, highly-visible nest all combine to make it the most easily recognized bird of prey in our area.

It is not uncommon, particularly among paddlers, to witness an Osprey circle high overhead, hover for a moment, and then tuck its wings as it dives head first towards the water. Adjusting itself at the last moment to hit the water feet first, its momentum sometimes carries it completely underwater. Back at the surface, it unfolds its wings and struggles to get airborne again. More often than not, it rises from the water empty-taloned.

A successful plunge is evident in the form of a wriggling fish in its talons. Once airborne, the Osprey will reposition its feet such that the head of the fish faces forward while flying, apparently making its load more aerodynamic for the trip back to the nest or a favorite dining perch. Fish are the main prey of the Osprey, so much so that it is also known as the Fish Hawk. Its arrival here in mid-March is closely synchronized with the movement of Alewives from their deep water overwintering sites to the shallows of bays and tidal creeks and the start of the spring spawning run.

The Osprey has a few unique adaptations for catching and hanging onto fish. Its front talons are the most flexible of any raptor, and can turn completely backwards. And the rough pads on the undersides of its feet and toes have spines for holding onto slippery fish. Despite its preference for fish, it is sometimes seen hunting over land, and occasionally catches other types of prey.

On their Atkins-style diet, the fledglings grow quickly, reaching adult size by late July. At this point, it's not easy to distinguish the adults from the young by size alone. With the aid of binoculars, look for a distinctive flecked or dappled color on the topside of the wings, marking the young-of-the-year, as opposed to the uniform chocolate brown of the parents.

In August, Ospreys begin heading south to their overwintering areas in Florida, the Caribbean, and as far as the Amazon basin. I've always wondered why this fish-lover leaves so early, just before the big fall run of Bluefish, Striped Bass, Herring, and Silversides on the East End. Must be better fishing in the south.

# 15 | MILL POND

*Water Mill, Town of Southampton*

DISTANCE:  2.5 miles (circumnavigation).

ACCESS:   1) Old Mill Road: No permit needed. From Rte. 27 in Water Mill, turn north onto Old Mill Road. Pass the Water Mill Museum and continue over the railroad tracks. Access to the pond is an unmarked area on the right where the water is visible through a break in the thick shrubs, 0.4 mile from Rte. 27.

*July*

I love poring over maps. Not road maps, but detailed topographical maps showing kettleholes ridges, marshes, and streams. I'll study a map before setting off on a hike or paddle, pull it out dozens of times in the field, and stare at it again back home after the outing. To me, maps are fascinating for what they reveal and what they hide. Will that steep-sided knoll offer a view over the bay? Is there a vernal pond at the bottom of that deep kettlehole? Can I navigate my canoe through that shallow marsh and intermittent stream?

Studying the USGS topographical map of the Mill Pond area before setting out for a paddle there, I noted one inlet draining the so-called Seven Ponds and two outlets passing under Old Mill Road. The eastern outlet flows over or through a dam depending on whether the mill sluice way is open. Constructed in 1644, the dam and mill, from which the hamlet Water Mill gets its name, is part of a museum today. I have followed this outlet by canoe from the pond, carefully portaging over the LIRR tracks and embankment (the culvert being too small for a canoe), crossing a very small pond to the north side of Old Mill Road (the road is built over the dam) portaging across the road and, with the permission of an adjacent property owner, put in on the east side of Mill Creek and continued on under Montauk Highway and into Mecox Bay.

The presence of a western outlet surprised me. Since both outlets eventually meet and drain into Mill Creek, the land mass between them, including the Berkowski farm, would have once been an island. I searched but could not locate any culverts leading out from the pond and under Old Mill Road in the vicinity of the pond access. Nearby resident Marlene Haresign informed me that the swamp located between Old Mill Road and Upper Seven Ponds Road was excavated in 1960 to create a pond—perhaps that work sealed off the western outlet.

Well, enough about history and maps. Let's get paddling! The pond access is a quiet and unassuming spot, easily missed when driving by. Tall shrubs and small trees hide all but a narrow sliver of water from the passing motorist. The first quarter-mile of paddling is through a very unpond-like setting, following a beautiful, narrow corridor lined with an assortment of wetland trees, shrubs, herbs, and ferns. This is my favorite section of the pond. Soon after launching, you will realize that the waterway bends off to the left and right; take either direction as both will soon merge back together on the far side of a small island. Scattered over the waterway near the launch point are the large round leaves of the Sweet-scented Water Lily (*Nymphaea odorata*), whose white petaled flowers are just beginning to open. There is also a large sign planted in the water announcing that this is a nature preserve owned by the Southampton Trustees.

The island, crowded with small Tupelo (*Nyssa sylvatica*) and Red Maple (*Acer rubrum*) trees, is rimmed with a dense thicket of wetland shrubs that provides excellent cover for nesting waterfowl. Even from my kayak I can pick out many of the shrub species by their telltale fruit or flowers. Swamp Azalea's flowers are past prime but a few fragrant white flowers still hang on. Sweet Pepperbush hasn't bloomed yet but last year's peppercorn-like seed capsules are visible. Chokeberry's fruit is dry and shriveled, while that of the Highbush Blueberry is just beginning to ripen. A rose bush covered with pink blossoms is probably Swamp Rose (*Rosa palustris*). Forming a mat along the edges of the waterway is an arching, woody stemmed plant with leaves arranged in whorls of three. Called Swamp Loosestrife or Water Willow (*Decodon verticillatus*), its magenta flowers are about to unfold.

Peter Corwith, a Southampton Town Trustee, avid fisherman, and lifelong resident of Mill Pond who is now deceased, was a wealth of information about the pond's history and wildlife. At the edge of a short embankment adjacent to a landscaped residential property, I once found a clump of Cranberry vines (*Vaccinium macrocarpum*). According to Peter, this corner of the pond, including what is now the Town Trustee swamp off to the east, had been part of a commercial cranberry operation many years ago.

Peter's father, Eric Corwith, purchased the wetland area from the Benedict family and in 1954 dug the channel that I am now paddling through. He finished it off with a waterway cul-de-sac, creating the island near the put in. The dredge spoil was deposited on the western edge of the marsh and became house lots. The remaining wetlands were deeded to the Town Trustees as a nature preserve. Thus it is Eric Corwith I have to thank for creating my favorite stretch of paddling on Mill Pond.

Continuing down the channel, watch for Painted Turtles basking on the edge of the swamp and listen for the "ker-chunk!" of Green Frogs and "bo-ker-ree" of Red-winged Blackbirds. As the channel opens up into the main pond, an Osprey nest atop a tall metal pole that Corwith set up with the Group for the South Fork is visible. Further along to the northwest, an adult Osprey perched in a tall Tupelo is busily feeding on a freshly caught fish, while off in the distance three other Ospreys

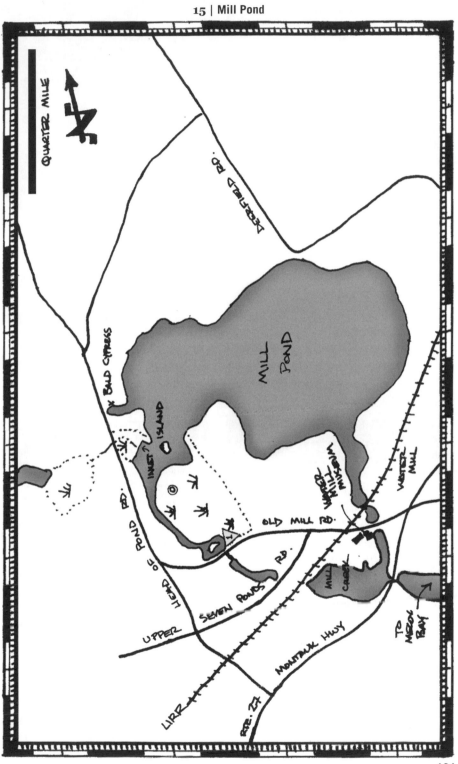

## Osprey Nesting Poles

A pair of Ospreys, clearly agitated by our presence, circled overhead while Kurt Billing and I finished repairing the dilapidated nesting platform near Sebonac Creek. Most of our East End Ospreys were back from their winter haunts far to the south, and many had already begun sprucing up their old nests. Every so often one of the pair would let out a piercing, "Chir-chir-chir," seemingly an impatient cry directed at our slow and clumsy efforts. I did sympathize with the anxious birds; somehow we missed noting the platform-less pole in our annual review of the 50-plus Osprey nests on the South Fork.

Fortunately, there are quite a few people keeping an eye out for the Ospreys, and several phone calls to the Group for the South Fork alerted me to the problem. We would have the nest platform and pole repaired in plenty of time for the birds to have a successful nesting season, but perched precariously atop a 15-foot ladder with a chainsaw in hand, I was not about to be chastised into hurrying up.

The idea of erecting artificial nesting structures for Ospreys probably originated from observations of the bird's ingenuity in choosing nest sites. It readily takes to any structure near water that can support a large nest of sticks, including channel markers and the cross pieces atop utility poles. Many of the first artificial nesting structures erected were probably done to attract Ospreys away from potentially hazardous situations.

Putting up Osprey poles became a popular annual activity among environmentalists on the East End in the 1980s. At that time, the Osprey population was finally showing signs of recovering from the harmful effects of DDT on its reproduction. Many felt that the recovery could be sped up by attracting birds to secure nesting sites—poles installed with raccoon-proof predator guards— in areas where human disturbance would be minimal. Today there are over 150 man-made Osprey nesting poles on the East End.

Ospreys normally nest in large snags (standing dead trees) near the water. Every spring they add another layer of nesting material, and in this activity they also demonstrate some ingenuity and adaptability, occasionally placing some strange pieces of rubbish among the usual sticks and seaweed. Over the years, the weight of the nest becomes substantial, and it is not uncommon for the supporting branches to give way and come tumbling down, along with the entire nest and, unfortunately, its contents of eggs or chicks.

Well-sited and maintained artificial nesting structures reduce this annual loss, increase nesting success and productivity, and contribute to the overall recovery of our Osprey population. Be aware that poorly sited poles may add to the problem, and leave this work to knowledgeable natural resource managers.

circle over the pond, calling out periodically. I watch several dives; two come up empty-taloned but a third is rewarded with a meal (one of the smallest fish I've ever seen an Osprey catch).

Approaching another island that is mysteriously absent from my topographical map but found on my nautical chart of the area, I first catch the strong scent of defecating piscivores and then see the white-washed vegetation. The culprits are just around the corner: twenty Great Egrets and three Double-crested Cormorants perched in the small island's trees. Peter Corwith was able to shed some light on the unmapped island. He estimates that sometime in the early 1900s a storm dislodged this piece of real estate from the southeast corner of the pond and blew it over into the shallows here where, over time, it has become fairly well anchored.

Crossing over to the west shoreline, I paddle under the overhanging branches of a large grove of Tupelos and make my way around a corner into a small cove. Among the Tupelos on the south side of the cove are quite a few roosting Black-crowned Night Herons, fidgeting and obviously nervous at my intrusion. On the north side is a cluster of 10 large snags, well worked over by woodpeckers and other cavity nesters.

Nearby, an odd looking conifer catches my eye. Its green needles seem somewhat sparse and recently leafed-out. A deciduous conifer? Yes. This is one of three locations I know of on the South Fork for the Bald Cypress (*Taxodium distichum*): here at Mill Pond, Long Pond (Long Pond Greenbelt), and behind the Springs General Store on Accabonac Harbor. I am fairly certain these are all transplants from down south. The northern limit of this species is Delaware. I've since learned the origin of the ones at Mill Pond; they were dug up as saplings in Florida and transplanted here by the Squires family sometime around 1955–1960.

With darkness approaching, I start the return trip with one more stop in mind: the pond's inlet. I've seen the small stream from Head of Pond Road, and after several searches back and forth along the thickly vegetated shore where I know the inlet meets the pond, I realize that there isn't enough water flow now to locate it. Peter Corwith also had some interesting information about the inlet. Realizing they needed more water pressure to run the mill, a team set out to connect, by ditch, several of the Seven Ponds to Mill Pond. So the inlet, as with much of the pond and its adjacent landscape, has been significantly altered by man over the past several hundred years. Still it is an interesting waterway to explore and observe nature. ⟋

# 16 | MECOX BAY

*Water Mill, Town of Southampton*

DISTANCE: The bay and its creeks and coves offer over 16 miles of shoreline to explore.

ACCESS: 1) Scott Cameron Beach: Southampton Town permit needed between May 15 and Labor Day. From Rte. 27 east of Water Mill turn south onto Mecox Road (just east of the Milk Pail farmstand). Continue 2.0 miles and turn right onto Job's Lane, which becomes Dune Road after crossing a small bridge and making a sharp right. Continue to Town parking lot at end. Access is on northwest side of lot.

2) Job's Lane: Southampton Town permit needed between May 15 and Labor Day. From Rte. 27 east of Water Mill turn south onto Mecox Road (just east of the Milk Pail farmstand). Continue 2.0 miles and turn right onto Job's Lane. Drive 1.0 mile to small bridge over Sam's Creek and drop boats. Park in nearby lot.

3) Horsemill Lane: No permit needed. From Rte. 27 east of Water Mill turn south onto Mecox Road (just east of the Milk Pail farmstand). Continue 1.7 miles, turn right onto Horsemill Lane and drive to end.

4) Mecox Bay Lane: No permit needed. From Rte. 27 east of Water Mill turn south onto Mecox Road (just east of the Milk Pail farmstand). Continue 1.2 miles and turn right onto Mecox Bay Lane. Drive to end.

5) Bay Avenue: No permit needed. From Rte. 27 east of Water Mill and 0.3 mile east of Scuttlehole Road, turn south onto Bay Avenue and continue to launch site at end.

6) Cove Road: No permit needed. From Rte. 27 east of Water Mill, turn south onto Rose Hill (just west of the Hess station). Cove Road is the second left and ends on Hayground Cove.

7) Rose Hill Road: Southampton Town Ramp permit needed. From Rte. 27 east of Water Mill, turn south onto Rose Hill (just west of the Hess station). Access is the third left that leads to Hayground Cove.

8) Crescent Avenue: No permit needed. From Rte. 27 at the green in Water Mill (across from the Post Office), turn south onto Halsey Lane. Crescent Avenue is the second right and ends on the bay.

9) Mohawk Avenue: No permit needed. From Rte. 27 at the green in Water Mill (across from the Post Office), turn south onto Halsey Lane. Mohawk Avenue is the first right and ends on the bay.

10) Flying Point Road: Southampton Town permit needed for parking along bulkhead and between May 15 and Labor Day for parking at Fly-

ing Point Beach. From the traffic light at Rte. 27 and Hampton Road (Rte. 27A) west of Water Mill, head south on Flying Point Road for 1.7 miles. Look for the access point at the south end of the bulkhead. Flying Point Beach parking lot is 0.2 mile further.

NOTES:    Mecox Bay is one of the salt ponds that is periodically opened to the ocean, at which time it becomes tidal. Under those conditions, near low tide, the entrance to some of the bay's coves may be too shallow to cross, even in a canoe or kayak, and an extensive shoal area on the bay side of the gut may be exposed.

*July*

With over 1,200 acres of surface water and a dozen finger-like coves and creeks radiating out from the main, square-shaped bay, a paddler could spend an entire day exploring Mecox Bay's shoreline. We didn't have that much time. Meeting after work at the Sam's Creek access on Jobs Lane, we plan on covering a good portion of the eastern side of the bay and set off.

Soon we are at the sand bar that separates Sam's Creek from the bay. When the water is low, I've had to get out and portage over the spit. But today we are able to squeak through a small channel that hugs the Dune Road marsh, and we are out on the bay. It's windier than I had expected, and as we turn northward along the bay's east shoreline we feel the full force of the southwesterly wind. The combination of wind, shallow water, and long fetch makes for a choppy sea and wet paddle here but, at least for now, we stubbornly stick to our plan.

Single file, our kayaks squeeze through a narrow opening in the Phragmites and slide over a shallow spit into the calm, coffee-colored water of Swan Creek. Well protected from the wind and chop on Mecox Bay, the boats glide silently around a blind corner where both paddlers and Great Egrets are startled by the sudden appearance of each other. The egrets, fishing from the edge of an old duck blind, take flight and perch in a short pine tree a safe distance away.

As the creek widens, we unconsciously position ourselves four abreast and alternately paddle and chat while the light breeze pushes us northeasterly towards the upper reaches of the creek. As the creek both narrows and decreases in depth, we find ourselves herding a school of large Carp, some with dorsal fins protruding several inches above the water. Sensing the shallows ahead, the fish seem to panic. Many leap clear out of the water with a startling splash and one actually hurdles the bow of a kayak. Others turn back towards the raft of kayaks and deeper water, banging hard into the sides of our boats in the confusion and creating a moment of panic among some of us as well.

Back on the main body of the bay, we look at the wind-generated white caps, reconsider our route, and paddle south toward the lee of the dunes and barrier spit. There, continuing westward and hugging the Phragmites-lined shore, we somehow miss the Nature Conservancy preserve wedged in among the marsh-front houses.

South of the marsh, a home fronting the ocean and perilously close to being in the ocean was the site of an interesting attempt to arrest coastal erosion (estimated to average one foot per year here) in the late 1990s. Temporary steel bulkheading was installed in the surf zone to enable huge, sand-filled geodesic tubes to be arranged in the shape of a dune. As winter storms worked away at the edges of the project, it became clear that the idea had some fatal flaws, despite the consultant's accusations that the tubes were sabotaged.

Nearing the location of the bay's temporary inlet, also referred to as the gut, we are forced far to the north to avoid grounding out on the extensive shoal there. Even though the gut is closed, as it has been for some time, the few inches of water covering the shoals is not enough to allow our shallow draft kayaks to slide over.

When the gut is open, the bay level can drop two feet. A 1970 study of Mecox's water quality by James Lackey estimated the bay's average depth at four feet. A two foot drop might greatly limit access to some of the bay's coves and creeks, something to keep in mind before untying your boat and carrying it down to the water.

If the gut is open and water level is very low, you might want to forget about paddling and head down to the beach with your binoculars. When the shoals are high and dry they become a mecca for shorebirds and birdwatchers. Steve Biasetti of the Group for the South Fork points out that the Mecox mudflats (or sandflats) attract some species of shorebirds that won't be seen anywhere else on the South Fork.

Clearing the shoals, we turn south again towards a marsh growing along the north side of the barrier spit. Great Blue Herons, Great Egrets, Snowy Egrets, and Black-crowned Night Herons eye us warily from their roosting and feeding areas. A small break in the Phragmites-choked shoreline is occupied by *Spartina alterniflora*, or Cordgrass, the pioneer plant of the salt marsh.

Further west we duck under a water main fastened under the Flying Point Road bridge and coast into the serene waters of Channel Pond, whose southern shoreline has an interesting assortment of wetland flora including Groundselbush, Salt Hay, and a striking, triangular-stemmed plant with the distinction of having some of the most confusing common names in the botanical world: Three-square, Chairmakers Rush, and Sword Grass (*Scirpus americanus*). Despite the latter two names, the triangular stem gives it "edges" and identifies it as a sedge ("sedges have edges"), adding to the confusion for beginner botanists trying to distinguish among the grasses, sedges, and rushes. East Hampton Natural Resource Director Larry Penny has reported the Black-spotted Stickleback (a small fish) residing here, the only naturally occurring population in New York State.

After watching an acrobatic show performed by a flock of Barn Swallows, we return to the bay and head north to Burnett Creek. Two delightful children hail us from the Flying Point bulkhead, complimenting us on our colorful kayaks and filling us in on the details of their stay with their grandparents, who are close by. Grandma is all business, never looking up as we drift by. She slowly retrieves a line that drags a chicken neck across the bay bottom, her eyes glued to the progress of her bait and the creatures that follow it. Gramps stands by with a long handled net, waiting for orders from the boss. "Now!" Grampa lunges forward with the net but comes up empty, prompting an earful of comments and some dramatic eyeball-rolling from his partner. The youngsters seem to find their grandparents' hunter-gatherer antics quite amusing, yet proudly boast of their evening catch of Blue Crabs.

With dusk coming on, we turn our kayaks into the narrow opening of Burnett Creek and paddle toward the setting sun. An Osprey circles overhead, positions its wings for a dive and splashes out of view. A moment later it comes up wet but fishless. Among the creek's trees and shrubs are quite a few herons and egrets hunkering down for the night. In the shadows cast by shoreline trees, a large creature slowly rolls about on the surface. A closer look reveals a huge pair of Snapping Turtles locked in a courtship embrace. Later, at home, I check my references for the courtship and mating dates of this common and widespread turtle species and learn that surprisingly few have witnessed this event.

At Cobb Road, the creek passes through a culvert that is not navigable. In the twilight, we turn our backs to Venus and a crescent moon now clearly visible in the western sky, and begin a pleasant downwind paddle back to Sam's Creek.

Returning the next afternoon to explore the bay's northern coves and creeks, I launch from Bay Avenue, once the site of the Mecox Bay Yacht Club. The southwesterly sea breeze is blowing hard again, forming steep, breaking waves and wet paddling conditions in this corner of the bay.

Tucking my map and clipboard out of the way of the continuous spray being thrown up and over the kayak, I head for the narrow entrance to Hayground Cove. There, a shallow bar and long, partially vegetated sand spit separating the cove from the bay forms the Wading Place, where one can walk—or, more accurately, wade—from one side of the cove to the other. For many years this route was used to get from the Water Mill Commons to Sagaponack via Halsey Lane and Bay Avenue, and may predate those roads as a Shinnecock trail.

Sliding over the Wading Place, I leave the wind-blown chop astern and turn downwind to the northeast, making quick progress towards the entrance of Calf Creek. An arm of Hayground running northeasterly to Mecox Road, Calf Creek is shown on USGS topographical maps as a narrow waterway in the bottom of a long swale that runs all the way to Kellis Pond, making it the outlet of the kettlehole pond.

## Salt Pond Sandflats

A long midsummer opening, or let, of the oceanfront salt ponds is relished by birders. According to Hugh McGuinness, one of the East End's most avid birders, Mecox Bay, Georgica Pond, and Sagg Pond are important resting and feeding areas for shorebirds from late July through September, and the presence of large expanses of sandflats created by a let greatly enhances their feeding and resting opportunities during the fall migration.

Steve Biasetti at the Group for the South Fork points out that the Mecox sandflats attract some species of shorebirds that won't be seen anywhere else on the East End. During one recent summer when Mecox had been open for an unusually long time, Hugh and Steve counted up to 1,000 sandpipers and Plovers, hundreds of terns (Royal, Common, Roseate, Least, and Fosters), and as many as 100 recently fledged federally endangered Least Terns.

Many people refer to these as mudflats, but they are largely composed of sand. They are similar to flood tide deltas found at most permanent inlets, but wind also plays a role in their formation. It carries sand off the unvegetated beach in the vicinity of the gut and deposits it in the pond.

The various bill shapes and lengths of the shorebirds are specifically designed for probing for the many burrowing organisms found in sandflats. Although the terns do not forage there, these isolated areas seem to provide secure resting areas for them. Bear this in mind when paddling nearby, and keep far enough away so as not to disturb the resting and feeding birds.

I've never seen water in the upper end of the swale between Newlight Lane and Kellis, but it shouldn't take too much of a rise in the water table to cause the pond, at 13 feet above sea level, to spill over its banks and into the swale. In *Memorials of Old Bridgehampton*, published in 1916, author James Adams writes that the pond did drain into Mecox through this swale. In fact, it appears that the flow was once quite substantial. Researchers who published *Water Mill: Celebrating Community* in 1996 report that "permission was granted to establish a water mill on Calf Creek in 1740 and again in 1742 near where it empties out of Kellis Pond. The records indicate a mill was operating on Calf Creek in 1790."

A recent conversation with Richard G. Hendrickson of Bridgehampton shed some light on the dramatic change this creek bed seems to have undergone. He remembers the creek flowing out of Kellis following a reasonable rainfall. But, along with the pond water and rainfall, a large amount of the South Fork's prime agricultural soils washed into the swale. Several hundred years of soil erosion seems to have filled the swale to the point where it no longer functions as an outlet or creek.

Making my way up into the eastern end of Calf Creek, I count nine jet skis tied up to docks and piers. Fortunately, only one of these pesky craft is out and about; either ignoring or oblivious to the 5 mile per hour posted speed here, it whines in and out of the creek over the course of several minutes. Hearing nothing, seeing nothing, knowing nothing, the skier whines on to another part of the bay.

The shoreline vegetation here begins to reflect a less saline environment, and the coffee-colored water takes on a green sheen, not surprisingly reminiscent of the bright green waters I've seen in Kellis Pond. Nearing Mecox Road, the creek forks at a point of land that serves as a formal garden for a creek-side house, with a wood and steel footbridge connecting the two. Before backtracking, scan the overhanging branches of the tall willows and Tupelos here for herons and egrets.

Back on Hayground Cove, I follow its eastern shoreline north toward the highway, passing a well-placed but uninhabited Osprey pole en route. The waterfront vegetation here consists almost entirely of Phragmites. At its northeastern corner, the cove narrows dramatically and shoals up while the water loses its turbidity, becoming crystal clear and highlighting a firm, stony bottom. Pushing the limits of my shoal-draft boat, I ease into a completely different world: a small stream bed with a closed canopy forest of large Swamp Maples and Tupelos. Peering into the adjacent woods, a beautiful and lush assortment of ferns and mosses carpet the forest floor, beckoning one to stop and linger. Although no evidence is visible from the creek, I am in the vicinity of the old St. James Hotel, an area with a long history of habitation by the Shinnecocks that predates the hotel and English settlement. The creek is one of several important prerequisites for a Shinnecock encampment: nearby sources of fresh water, wood, and food, the latter being the fish resources found in the bay.

Continuing counterclockwise around the cove, I paddle past the condos that occupy the former Bellini duck farm site, closed in 1972, and turn south at a cattail marsh nearly within sight of Montauk Highway. With a few exceptions, those being bulkheads and lawns, the western shoreline from here to Wading Place has much more plant diversity than the Phragmites-choked eastern shore. In addition to a freshwater *Spartina*, Three-square (*Scirpus americanus*) is quite abundant. The latter is tolerant of the whole range of salinities in addition to being able to withstand some wave action; a perfect combination of tolerances for the Mecox shoreline. I also pass by another Osprey pole, this one occupied by two adults and two fully grown young.

Approaching Wading Place again, this time from the west side, I note that the sand spit shown on my map is now a small island. The sun is getting low on the horizon as I re-enter the main part of the bay, and I paddle hard for Mill Creek, my destination. Even so, I opt for a short foray into Mud Creek, where I watch a pair of Muskrats busy foraging among the submerged vegetation. One swam off with a large plant trailing from its mouth, possibly returning to a nearby bank den to feed its young.

Entering the southern end of Mill Creek, the second most common type of shoreline found in the pond dominates: bulkheads and lawns. Although clearly acceptable to the several dozen Canada geese foraging on the lush, emerald green monoculture, bulkheads and lawns often replace ecologically important and diverse wetland zones, including the nearshore area of emergent vegetation and the upland buffer zone. These areas provide important feeding, roosting, nesting, and spawning habitat for fish, birds, reptiles, and mammals. One of the longest stretches of bulk-heading and lawn on the entire bay, the Villa Maria property, had been considered for wetland restoration work. If completed, it could serve as a catalyst for similar projects on Mecox.

The striking structure found there, now called the Siena Spirituality Center at Villa Maria, dates back to 1887 when it was constructed as a wooden-exterior Queen Anne-style mansion. Around 1910, possibly to make the structure more fire-resistant, the wooden exterior was replaced with cement and stone.

Paddling under Montauk Highway, the Mill Creek shoreline changes abruptly from a suburban tone to a wilder, less orderly setting of thick vegetation and trees. Six Black-crowned Night Herons are spaced at intervals in branches overhanging the water, while a Belted Kingfisher and Osprey dive for fish in the fading light.

On this stretch of water is the water mill for which the hamlet is named. Built in 1644, the mill was originally located further upstream on the north side of the railway. It was moved to its present site in 1746. Now part of a museum owned by the Ladies Auxiliary of Water Mill, it is well worth a visit.

As on the previous evening, Venus and a sliver of a moon are visible in the western sky. I have one more place to visit, the Nature Conservancy preserve near Meyers Pond, before returning to my car at Bay Avenue. The preserve is a small peninsula that always turns up something interesting. My last visit was in early March to check the condition of its Osprey pole. As I walked along the shore in the midst of a late winter snowstorm, I counted 50 Great Blue Herons tucked in among the branches of the preserve's small trees.

What this visit lacked in numbers it made up for in variety. Perched in the trees and shrubs, settled in for the night, were Great Egrets, Snowy Egrets, Great Blue Herons, Black-crowned Night Herons and Green Herons. ✗

# 17 | SAGG POND

*Sagaponack, Town of Southampton*

DISTANCE: 4 miles R/T from Sagaponack Road.

ACCESS:  1) Sagaponack Road: No permit needed. From Rte. 27 in Bridge-hampton turn south onto Ocean Avenue (at flagpole and traffic light). Take the second left and travel 0.8 mile along Sagaponack Road to a small white concrete bridge. Cross bridge and park on right (south) shoulder. Launch site is a narrow path near the southeast corner of the bridge. (CAUTION: beware of fast-moving traffic).

2) Bridge Lane: No permit needed. Continue south on Ocean Avenue as above, past Sagaponack Road and turn at the third left onto Bridge Lane. Cross bridge and park on the shoulder. The access is on the southeast side of the bridge.

3) Sagg Main Beach: Pay for beach parking from 9am–5pm in summer months. From Rte. 27, turn south at traffic light onto Sagg Main Street. Continue to end at ocean beach and turn right into the parking lot. The access is a path through the Phragmites on the right (north side of the lot).

NOTES:  Sagg Pond is one of the salt ponds that is periodically open to the ocean, at which time its water level is lowered and it becomes tidal. Near low tide it is necessary to follow the pond's sinuous channel around the shoals at its south end.

*July*

Situated at the end of a chain of kettlehole ponds that extend south from Sag Harbor, Sagg Pond is one of our particularly interesting and unusual waterbodies that—either naturally via storms and rising water levels or artificially via a backhoe—periodically empties into the Atlantic Ocean, an event known locally as a "let." (I use the term "salt ponds" to describe these intermittently tidal waterbodies.)

The sand bar that normally separates the pond from the ocean, a leaky dike at best, is not visible from my vantage point on the Sagaponack Road bridge. But it has clearly breached, as the pond level has dropped four feet overnight. What is less clear is whether or not there is enough water to float my canoe through the upper section of the pond.

There is plenty of water at the put in near the southeast corner of the bridge. Even in high water conditions, this section of the pond resembles a creek, with a slight current flowing out from the swamp on the north side of the bridge. There, Solomon's

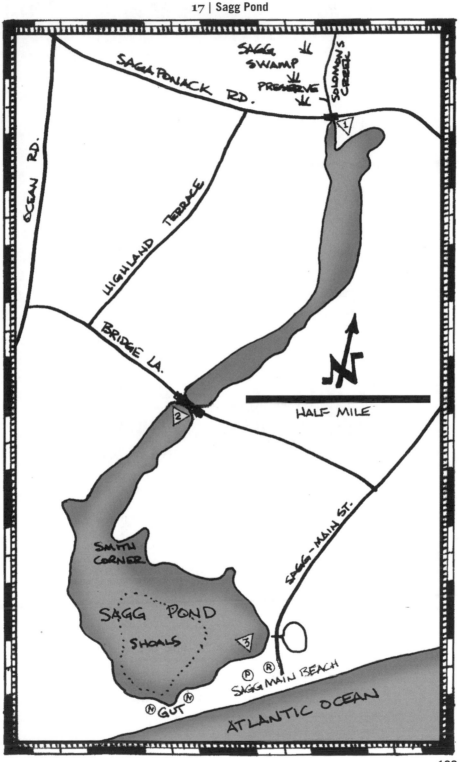

The ocean beach at the end of Sagg Pond is a popular
destination for paddlers to enjoy a picnic.

Creek winds its way through the Nature Conservancy's Sagg Swamp Preserve, a 100-acre forested wetland that extends nearly to Montauk Highway. In terms of surface water flow, the swamp is considered the headwaters of the pond, but much of the swamp's water supply is actually groundwater flow from as far away as the morainal woodlands south of Crooked Pond, one and a half miles further to the north.

As I survey the situation from the Sagg Road bridge, several dark shapes dart up the channel and disappear into the darkness under the bridge. The size of these aquatic creatures astounds me. Hoping for a better look, I cross to the Sagg Swamp side of the bridge.

There, facing upstream in the shadows of the Swamp Maples and Arrowwood bordering the narrow creek, are three large carp, each exceeding eighteen inches in length with a dorsal fin protruding from the water. These freshwater behemoths seem out of place here. Perhaps they were forced into these cramped quarters by the rising salinity levels in the lower reaches of Sagg Pond. Or they may have been migrating into the upper freshwater shallows to spawn.

I am checking out the conditions for the Group for the South Fork's annual Sagg Pond paddle and beach barbecue later this evening. I know we can launch from Bridge Lane in low water, but that would mean missing out on one of the prettiest stretches of the waterway, the wooded shoreline at the north end. So I decide to launch at the Sagg Road bridge to see how difficult the shallows really are.

Letting the current push me along, I scan the stately Tupelo and Black Willow trees bordering the both sides of the pond. A half-dozen Black-crowned Night Herons, three Snowy Egrets, and a Great Blue Heron roost among the branches overhanging the water, unfazed by the canoe. Not so the Belted Kingfisher. The striking, crested, blue and white bird darts from its hidden perch with a noisy rattle-call.

Two hundred yards from the bridge the pond widens dramatically and I run aground. The channel has disappeared and the water now runs in a thin sheet over a broad expanse of muddy pond bottom. Fortunately, my plastic canoe slides easily over the shallows and, by using my paddle like a pole, I manage to continue south toward the ocean beach.

Within 100 feet of having to resort to poling, the pond deepens and I can resume paddling. The eastern shore is now completely rimmed by a monoculture of Reedgrass, or Phragmites, which towers six to ten feet above the canoe and is so thick as to obscure any view of the adjacent farm fields. Its long, thin, brittle stem is topped by a beautiful plume-like inflorescence—not an unattractive sight, particularly when set in motion by a light ocean breeze and the late afternoon sunlight. It's no wonder that some are dismayed to learn that this plant is the bane of many wetland ecologists who have devoted their careers to eradicating it.

No longer confined to a narrow channel, I opt to explore the western shore where a wide variety of plants are found, including a small patch of cattails and Threesquare Rush. Both provide excellent food resources for waterfowl, shorebirds, and Muskrats that inhabit the pond. There is also a *Spartina* here, possibly the freshwater species, *S. pectinata.*

By the time the Bridge Lane bridge comes into view, Phragmites dominates both sides of the pond. On the bridge are several fishermen trying their luck for Whitefish and White Perch. Eels and Blue Crabs are also harvested from the pond. Eels are caught in pots, similar to a lobster trap. I've noticed a few high and dry along the way. Blue Crabs are caught with chicken necks, a small net, and a good feel for pulling the crabs within netting reach.

Between the bridge and Smith's Corner I enjoy a rare sight: there are at least six Ospreys hunting for fish. They circle, dive, plunge feet first into the pond, struggle to get airborne, and repeat the performance. One takes a particularly dramatic plunge and disappears completely underwater for a second before surfacing empty-taloned.

Catching Blue Crabs is a popular summer activity
enjoyed by all ages.

The word must be out. No matter how many Ospreys fly off to the north with a fish in their talons, more appear to take their place and there are never fewer than six in the sky overhead.

Other piscivores have joined the fray. A small group of Cormorants swim and dive in formation. Least and Common Terns hover close to the surface, diving beak-first. A Black Skimmer silently glides by, flying inches above the water, with its odd beak barely touching the pond. It appears that the let has stimulated both post-spawning adult and juvenile fish to congregate at the pond's south end to await the next outgoing tide and a trip to the sea.

When open to the ocean near low tide, the lower section of the pond has some large areas of shoals that are tricky to negotiate. The exposed mudflats are teeming with all sorts of shorebirds probing their bills in search of worms and small mollusks. It's tempting to take a direct course to the ocean beach, but I know from past experience that even a shallow draft kayak will soon be hard aground, and far from terra firma.

The channel swings due east before circling back to the gut. Feeling my way among the shoals, at one point it seems that I am paddling away from my destination. But my roundabout route soon leads to the main channel where an outgoing tide pulls me towards the ocean.

A section of the beach is roped off to protect a tern nesting colony, and possibly a nest of the endangered Piping Plover. I look for a landing well away from the fencing and, once ashore, head for the gut. It is nearly low tide. Soon the incoming tide will send pulses of sea water through the narrow gut and into the pond, filling it ever so slightly but enough to make my return trip easier. For now, I am content to sit near this fascinating place where the ocean meets the pond, and be mesmerized by all the water in motion. ✕

## Salt Ponds

Mecox Bay, Sagg Pond, Georgica Pond, and Oyster Pond are unusual waterbodies in that they are intermittently tidal. Collectively they are referred to by a wide variety of names, but I have yet to find one that accurately reflects their unique condition, so I have chosen the simplest among the lot: salt pond.

A sandy beach, one to several hundred feet wide, separates these ponds from the sea and provides a porous but effective dam behind which pond levels can rise as much as four to six feet above mean sea level. All four ponds have freshwater creeks flowing into them, but much of their freshwater inflow is underground via groundwater.

Either naturally via a high spring tide, big surf, and high water levels in the pond or, in the case of the oceanfront ponds, artificially via a back hoe (Oyster Pond is only opened by Mother Nature), these waterbodies periodically empty into the Atlantic Ocean or Block Island Sound.

This "let" is quite a spectacular thing to witness. Working from the ocean towards the pond, a small trench is dug. It doesn't have to be very wide but a certain depth is key in getting the bay water to flow out to sea.

Sound simple? That last scoop holding the bay water in place can be tricky. Once it starts to flow, watch out! The back hoe operator makes sure of his path of retreat, and veteran onlookers back up. The newly created ditch quickly transforms into a raging river that seems to have a mind of its own. The success of the let in terms of tidal exchange and the duration of the opening depends largely on sea conditions, and they can change dramatically over the course of a single day.

Normally, if that word can be applied to coastal dynamics, the opening eventually seals itself via littoral drift and sand deposition. "Eventually" can be overnight, days or weeks. In 2001, Mecox Bay was let on June 5 and "eventually" was three months later, when an early September hurricane storm surge finally plugged the inlet.

Think about the ecological ramifications of periodic lets. With a flood tide, the current in the new inlet reverses itself and the highly saline sea waters enter the bay. The abrupt change in salinity is a stress that few plants and animals can easily cope with. Unlike the regular, twice daily flood and ebb tides, there is little in the way of a pattern for organisms to acclimate to. And then there's the dilemma posed by the several foot drop in pond water levels: aquatic plants left high and dry, fish and crabs having to relocate from once inundated areas, and relatively immobile shellfish left behind on now exposed mud flats.

The management of the salt ponds is a source of much spirited debate. Maintenance of salinity levels suitable for the growth of Oysters is a management priority for Mecox Bay. In addition to salinity, other management issues considered are the height of the bay relative to local flooding, water quality (particularly coliform bacteria counts) and the yearly cycles of fish that come in to the bay to spawn.

Don't open the gut soon enough and there are complaints of flooded basements, cesspools, farm fields, and tern nesting areas. Open the gut too long and there are complaints about the bouquet of exposed mud flats, poor boating and swimming, and a lack of Ospreys and herons.

In the hot seat are the Town Trustees. These elected officials are charged with managing this resource for the benefit and well-being of all Town residents. That means trying to consider the interests of recreational fishermen, birders, crabbers, baymen, boaters, swimmers, and bayfront property owners. In other words, it's often a "Mission Impossible" situation.

# III | EAST HAMPTON TOWN

# 18 | GEORGICA POND

DISTANCE: 2.5 miles (R/T) from the Montauk Highway access to the ocean beach. Six creeks and coves provide 6.5 miles of shoreline to explore.

ACCESS: 1) Montauk Highway Rest Area: No permit needed. Located on the south side of Rte. 27 just east of the Wainscott commercial district and Wainscott Stone Road.

2) Cove Hollow Road: No permit needed. Traveling east on Rte. 27 through Wainscott, take the first right *after* the rest area and Stephen Hands Path onto Georgica Road. Stay on this for 0.7 mile and make the next right after Cove Hollow Farm Road onto an unnamed road that appears to be an extension of Cove Hollow Road. Park at the end of the road. The route out to Georgica Cove involves paddling a narrow slot through a thick stand of Phragmites.

NOTES: Georgica Pond is periodically "let" at which time it is open to the ocean at its southern end, subject to ocean tides, and generally has very low water. Under these conditions, use the highway access point. Launching there may involve walking your boat for a short distance through shallows to deeper water.

If you visit Georgica Pond for a paddle, please respect the privacy of waterfront residents, and help keep the highway launch site clean.

Since 2003, a particularly aggressive Mute Swan has been terrorizing paddlers near the Rte. 27 launch site, and is back for the 2005 season.

*August*

Georgica Pond and most of its six coves and creeks are named for individuals who lived nearby long enough to be intimately associated with each particular stretch of water. In the case of the pond, the individual happened to be a Native American named Jeorgkee. Then, as now, he wouldn't have had to wander very far from the pond to obtain all his basic needs: freshwater, firewood, venison, ducks and geese, shellfish, finfish, and fertile soils classified as among the best agricultural soils in the country for growing crops.

This productive waterbody is one of three unusual coastal salt ponds on the south shore of Long Island; unusual in that salinity and water levels can change dramatically in a very short period of time. Under certain conditions, natural or man-made, the narrow sandy beach separating the pond from the Atlantic Ocean can breach, causing the pond to lose more than half its water to the ocean and creating an inlet that transforms the once-enclosed waterbody into a tidal estuary. Over time, a span that may be days or months, littoral currents reseal the breach.

My kayak glides effortlessly over the still waters of Talmage Creek, named for a nineteenth-century Town Trustee, as I approach the main body of the pond. The shoreline vegetation of willows and Red Maples gives way to an upland forest of Pitch Pines and oaks, reflecting a subtle change in the pond's shoreline topography, as I paddle southward.

My progress is watched quietly by a dozen Double-crested Cormorants perched in the large Pitch Pines on the pond's western shore. The birds shift and grunt nervously as I paddle by them, and directly under some, but they don't take flight. They are very reluctant to leave their well-oriented night roosts that face east and the early morning sun's warming rays.

Although the cormorants congregate in the pond to ply its fish-rich waters, they do not nest here. Shunning the rich and famous residents of Georgica Pond, the cormorants have established their nesting colony in the treetops of Homes Pond, situated on the very exclusive and much more secluded Gardiners Island, 10 miles away.

Approaching Burnt Point, I steer the kayak away from the shore to give the shallows there wide berth. In the 1800s, the only routes to the East Hampton Village market for Wainscott farmers was either Montauk Highway or along the beach. Neither option was desirable. The highway was a toll road, and the beach route involved, as it does today, travelling over soft sand. The former irritated the thrifty farmers, and the latter didn't work well with the narrow wooden wheels with which their wagons were clad.

The farmers decided to build a causeway of sand and silt across the pond at its narrowest point, from Burnt Point to the east shore where Briar Patch Road would have extended. Considering the tools and equipment at hand in those days, it was quite an ambitious undertaking. When completed sometime in the late 1870s, the local press hailed it as "a stupendous piece of amateur engineering." With fluctuating water levels and wave action, the causeway required constant maintenance. It lasted only a few years, eventually washing away. Some remnants of the causeway in the form of wooden posts and planks are still visible on both sides of the pond today, and the location of the causeway itself can be traced across the shallow water on aerial photographs.

Further south I cross the mouths of Goose Creek and Eel Cove where two of the pond's most knowledgeable residents lived. Donald Petrie, a self-appointed "Pond Watcher," has chronicled physical and biological changes over many years in an attempt to understand the pond's dynamics, interrelationships and cycles. Jim McCaffrey, who passed away in the winter of 2005 while this book was being writ-

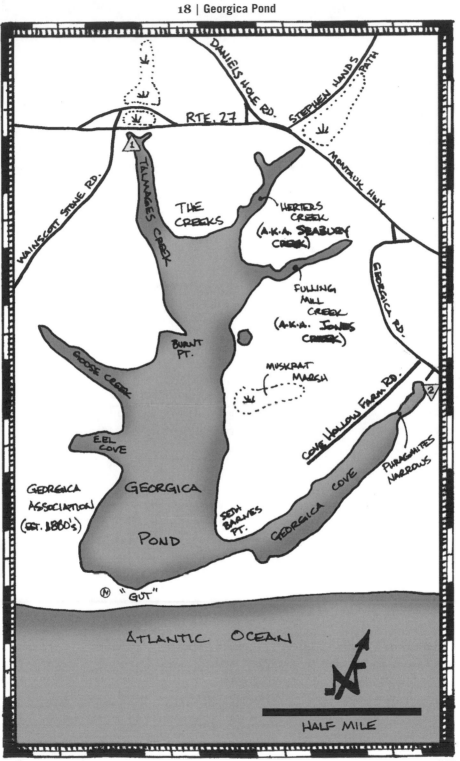

ten, was an elected Town Trustee charged with the pond's management and well-being for the benefit of all Town residents, a responsibility that involved juggling many competing and conflicting interests.

Perusing one of Petrie's annual *Pond Watcher* newsletters, I learned that soon after a gale had opened the pond to the ocean, several people reported seeing a whale in the pond. It was assumed that the whale escaped before the gut closed, as there were no additional whale sightings. That was in December 1992. Seven months later, in July of 1993, an eye-watering stench was traced to a thick stand of Phragmites in one of the pond's coves. There, partially buried in silt, was the carcass of a 16-foot-long Minke whale.

Approaching the ocean beach, the breaking surf is now visible over the duneless, unvegetated area that marks the gut. Monarch butterflies drift across my bow at regular intervals, slowly but steadily making their way south to their overwintering areas. Poorly camouflaged, these strikingly beautiful insects rely on potential predators knowing that they are harmful to eat. Feeding on milkweed plants as larvae, the monarch absorbs toxins that render it very distasteful and poisonous. As a winged adult, it derives nourishment from the nectar of various goldenrod species, Seaside Goldenrod being the common species along our South Fork beaches and presently in bloom.

Swinging north for the return paddle, I pass by Seth Barnes Point and the narrow entrance to Georgica Cove, also known as Siny's Cove. A flock of cormorants is working a school of fish up ahead, swimming and diving in formation to limit the fish's ability to dart away and escape. From Muskrat Marsh to Jones' Creek, the freshwater swamp tree, Blackgum or Tupelo, forms nice stands along the shoreline. Although it is still August, their leaves have already begun to take on their deep scarlet autumn colors.

It is still early, so I decide to make a short detour up into Jones' Creek, named for the late 1800s proprietor of the land from the creek south to Briar Patch Road. I hope to find some basking turtles and enjoy the different feel of paddling in this narrow stretch of water. A Great Blue Heron stalks the shallows up ahead. No turtles, but a worthwhile side trip nonetheless. As I head back to the main body of the pond, a loud crash attracts my attention and three deer bolt from the woods off to the right. Without hesitation, they leap into the creek only 75 feet ahead of me, wade the short distance to the opposite shore, and disappear noisily in the forest. Well, that was worth the detour!

Back in the main pond, I bypass Seabury Creek, named for Judge Samuel Seabury, once the owner of the land that is now Georgica Close. Judge Seabury was the special prosecutor who, in 1932, was involved in fighting corruption in New York City and was instrumental in ousting its mayor, Jimmy Walker, from office.

The point of land separating Seabury and Talmage Creeks is appropriately named

The Creeks. The 64-acre estate was once owned by Alfonso Ossorio, an artist whose works included an evergreen sculpture garden and a collection of exotic trees arranged on the property. Personally, I find the pond's natural landscape much more aesthetically pleasing, but perhaps that is a taste developed over many years of studying the natural environment.

To his credit, Mr. Ossorio donated portions of the property to the Nature Conservancy. On the other side of the equation are a long concrete bulkhead and a rather garish waterfront house that destroyed valuable wetlands.

Back at Talmage Creek, a bayman is checking his Eel traps, or pots. Georgica Pond still supports a viable commercial fishery. In fact, I've been told that one of the Lester clan made a living solely from the fishery resources found here: a variety of fin fish, Eels, Blue Crabs, and bait fish. Taking advantage of the distraction provided by the bayman, I quickly paddle towards the launch site and avoid a confrontation with a somewhat territorial Mute Swan that has recently developed a nasty habit of terrorizing paddlers in Talmage Creek. Take note! ✕

## Mute Swan (*Cygnus olor*)

Although one of the most recognizable, conspicuous and popular members of our local fauna, many people know surprisingly little about the Mute Swan. With an eight-foot wingspan and average weight of twenty-five pounds, this majestic animal is probably the largest our resident birds. Native to Europe and Asia, it was brought to the United States in the early 1900s by way of a 1910 introduction near Rhinebeck in the Hudson River valley and a pair released in 1912 right here at Lake Agawam in Southampton Village. Celebrated in art and prose, Mute Swans were imported to grace waterfront estates.

Over the past century they have spread throughout much of the eastern United States and Canada. As is often the case with introduced species, wildlife biologists are beginning to see its potential harm to both native waterfowl and aquatic vegetation. The swan's long neck (it can reach one and a half meters below the water's surface to graze plants) and large appetite are cause for concern that it might overgraze and uproot ecologically valuable aquatic plants, such as Eelgrass. That, in turn, could disrupt the fauna associated with underwater plant communities, everything from tiny zooplankton, to fish species, crabs, and other waterfowl. Biologists also noted the swan's behavior towards other waterfowl in its nesting or feeding territories: no match for the huge birds, our smaller native waterfowl are easily driven off and at times killed by the fiercely aggressive Mute Swans.

A Mute Swan, displaying its aggressive, arched-wing posture, approaches a paddler.

As a result, the Fish and Wildlife Departments of several states have implemented programs to slow the growth of swan populations. This usually involves some method of insuring that the eggs do not hatch, such as shaking the eggs (egg addling) or coating them with a light oil. Mute Swans are ready to breed in their third spring, and although there are reports that they can live up to fifty years of age, most studies found their average lifespan to be approximately seven years. In theory, if all the nests could be located, after seven or eight years this strategy would eventually result in a population decline. But in most cases this strategy has slowed population growth, not reversed it.

Mute Swans' behavior towards paddlers varies greatly depending on the individual, time of year, and proximity of nests and young. Most problems can be avoided by giving them wide berth during the nesting season or when young are nearby. Extremely aggressive behavior is unusual, and is often a sign that the swans are being fed. Be aware that an encounter with an aggressive swan can take the fun out of a paddling outing, and bones at their wing wrist can pack a dangerous punch.

*Please do not feed swans!*

# 19 | NORTHWEST HARBOR

*Northwest, Town of East Hampton*

DISTANCE: A circumnavigation of the harbor and Northwest Creek is 10 miles.

ACCESS: 1) Northwest Landing Road: No permit needed. From Rte. 114, turn onto Swamp Road (2.2 miles from Long Wharf in Sag Harbor), travel another 2.0 miles and turn left onto Northwest Landing Road. Continue 0.5 mile to end and a County-owned boat ramp and parking area along the bulkhead.

2) Barcelona Neck State Preserve: No permit needed. Entrance to preserve and "Sag Harbor Golf Course" is off Rte. 114. (From East Hampton Village, entrance is first right after Swamp Road; from Sag Harbor Village, entrance is a left turn at 0.9 mile from the Mobil Station). Follow the paved road for 0.6 mile through the golf course to the clubhouse. Turn right and proceed straight on narrow unpaved road past garage. At fork (0.7 mile) bear left and continue to dead-end near the Northwest Creek inlet (1.8 miles).

3) Mile Hill Road: East Hampton Town permit needed. From Rte. 114, travel along Swamp Road past Northwest Landing Road and make the next left turn onto Phoebe Scoy Road. Follow to end and turn left onto Mile Hill Road, which dead-ends on the water.

For the following, see directions under the Alewife Brook Chapter:

4) Alewife Brook Road.

5) Cedar Point County Park.

*September*

Northwest Harbor is surrounded by an impressive collection of greenbelt preserves. On its northern side is the 600-acre Cedar Point County Park, its eastern shoreline borders the 500-acre Grace Estate Town Preserve, to the south is Barcelona State Preserve and Northwest County Park, totaling 850 acres, and off to the northwest is the crown jewel of the harbor, the Nature Conservancy's 2,100-acre Mashomack Preserve. In addition to large stretches of undeveloped shoreline, Northwest Harbor is rich in historic and ecological resources. All this, plus a variety of small but navigable creeks, makes a perfect setting for a canoe or kayak excursion.

Heading out from Northwest Landing Road one September day, I decide to take advantage of the calm conditions and paddle immediately for the inlet, leaving the exploration of Northwest Creek's upper reaches for later. Traveling westward through the creek's mooring area, I note that each mooring buoy is occupied by an immature Common Tern which, despite my close approach, does not take flight. Perhaps they are anticipating their upcoming migration, a long journey where resting perches may be few and far between.

To my right is Stratton's Beach, a narrow peninsula separating the creek from the harbor. This County Parkland is actively managed to enhance its shorebird nesting habitat, and is monitored each year by the Long Island Colonial Waterbird and Piping Plover Survey team. Among its windswept dune grasses are the striking, bright yellow flower heads of Seaside Goldenrod, now in full bloom. Dancing among them, stopping briefly for a drink of its sweet nectar, are a number of Monarch Butterflies making slow but steady progress southward towards their choice wintering grounds in the mountains of southern Mexico, a seemingly impossible journey for such a delicate creature.

Riding the outgoing tide through the inlet is a simple matter in my shallow draft boat; deeper craft need to exercise caution in navigating the ever-changing channel. Each change of tide creates a of tug-of-war between the creek and harbor, with the result being the development of a sandy shoal, or delta, on both sides of the inlet. The source of these sand deposits is the bluff at Barcelona Neck, to the west, and the mechanism of transport is a wind-driven shoreline current called littoral drift that, in the case of Northwest Harbor, favors a counterclockwise gyre. The result is an eastward trending spit on the west side of this inlet and at Barnes Meadow, a northward trending spit at Alewife Brook, and a westward trending one at Cedar Point.

Once out in the harbor, I follow its eastern shoreline to the outlet of the tidal creek that meanders through Barnes Meadow. I've never tried to paddle up this narrow, unnamed creek and the tide is too low to attempt it now, but I pause to enjoy two Snowy Egrets and the fall colors in this beautiful marsh before continuing on.

Not much further ahead another narrow channel intersects the shoreline. This one is fixed more permanently with bulkhead and jetty material, part of an abandoned marina project just south of Mile Hill Road and the old Camp Saint Regis property. Beyond Mile Hill Road I start looking for the stand of Common Reedgrass, or Phragmites, and a small grove of Tree-of-heaven, also known as Ailanthus, that mark the Grace Estate Preserve.

This is a great place to stop for a short hike. The tall-stemmed Phragmites, with its feathery, plume-like inflorescence that waves in the slightest breeze, is easy to pick out from a distance. These mark the seaward edge of a small pond, one of many on the South Fork named Fresh Pond, and the eastern terminus of Whalebone Landing Road, an unpaved Town Trustee road dating back several hundred years and now part of the preserve's trail system. Just inside the forest here, under a large Basswood tree, is a picnic area.

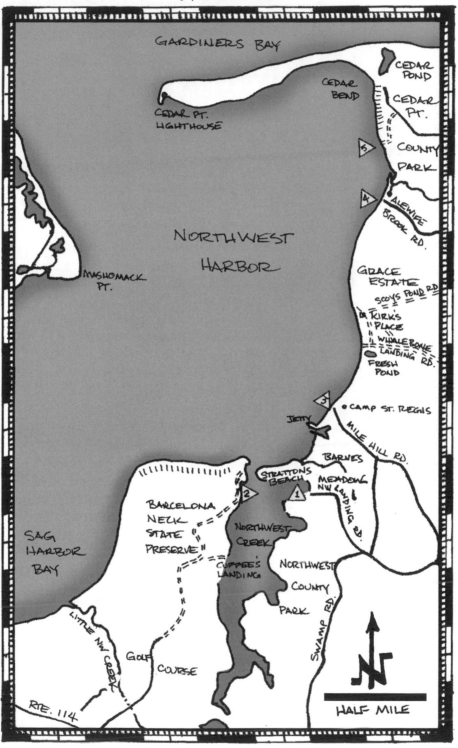

GARDINERS BAY

CEDAR POND

CEDAR BEND

CEDAR PT.

CEDAR PT. LIGHTHOUSE

COUNTY PARK

5

4

ALEWIFE BROOK RD.

NORTHWEST HARBOR

GRACE ESTATE

SCOYS POND RD

DR. KIRK'S PLACE

WHALEBONE LANDING RD.

FRESH POND

MASHOMACK PT.

3

● CAMP ST. REGIS

JETTY

MILE HILL RD.

BARNES

STRATTONS BEACH

MEADOW

NW LANDING RD.

2

1

BARCELONA NECK STATE PRESERVE

NORTHWEST CREEK

SAG HARBOR BAY

CUFFEE'S LANDING

NORTHWEST COUNTY PARK

SWAMP RD.

LITTLE NW CREEK

GOLF COURSE

RTE. 114

NW

HALF MILE

## The Long Island Colonial Waterbird and Piping Plover Survey

Colonial waterbirds are water-dependant birds that often nest in close proximity to one another, sometimes forming a dense cluster of hundreds of nests called a colony. These include Black Skimmers and Double-crested Cormorants, as well as several species of herons, egrets, terns, and gulls. Surveys of nesting areas on Long Island began in 1983, prompted by concern over dwindling habitat for colonial waterbirds and the federally endangered Piping Plover. Data collected includes location, number of nests, number of young fledged, and potential problems (e.g. predators, human disturbance, changes in vegetation) for each site. Many of the sites are protected with string fencing as well.

This important work is carried out by the New York State Department of Environmental Conservation with assistance from the Nature Conservancy, Audubon Society, the Federation of New York State Bird Clubs, Town and County Natural Resource staff, and a small army of dedicated volunteers.

As stated in one of the recent survey reports, recreational use of coastal areas is a major challenge in the effort to protect nesting and feeding areas. Please do not disturb these important nesting areas. Paddlers can play an important stewardship role in the protection of these nesting areas by reporting problems to the appropriate agency (see "Contacts" in Appendix 1).

The Northwest area was East Hampton's main port from 1653 until the first wharf was built at Sag Harbor in 1761. Whalebone Landing Road derives its name from the whale oil and whalebone that were carted from whaling stations on the ocean beach at Sagaponack and Mecox to shipping wharfs at Northwest. There, along with furs and horses, they were loaded on ships bound for England and the West Indies; ships bound for the West Indies would return with holds full of rum and molasses. Some historic maps locate the wharfs here, others place them further north at Cedar Bend. No one has been able to accurately pin down the location.

Three hundred yards further north is Kirk's Place and another old woods road, called Scoys Pond Road, that intersects the harbor. Several large Basswood trees and the stone foundations of a house, an ice shed, and a barn mark the old homestead of Josiah Kirk, an "obstinate Irishman" according to Harry Sleight, editor of the early *Town Trustee Journals*, who farmed here on 390 acres of land in the late 1800s.

Apparently he was best known for his 11-year court battle to keep his fellow townsmen from gathering Eelgrass that washed ashore on his property. In that day, Eelgrass was a valuable commodity used for insulation, fertilizer, and cattle bedding. The following is from his obituary in a 1901 issue of the *East Hampton Star*:

"With the death of Josiah Kirk at the age of 83 years, which occurred at the Suffolk County Almshouse at Yaphank, Oct.21, a man once prominent at the East End and in the County courts passed away. Mr. Kirk settled at Northwest about 30 years ago, and his farm was one of the finest in this section, well stocked with choice herds of animals, high stepping and spirited horses in particular, being well remembered. Mr. Kirk's dwelling at Northwest faced the bay, but a short distance from the beach, and his fertile acres bordered on the water for a long distance. It was on this strip of beach that the controversy arose which resulted in the famous East Hampton seaweed litigation which was waged for a number of years and which finally wrecked him financially. The case was tried many times, and appealed and re-appealed, Kirk losing in most instances, until his once fine property fell into decay and his princely fortune went to pay the costs of court proceedings and to the lawyers."

Paddling north, I pass a string of waterfront homes and an Osprey nest before reaching Alewife Brook Road, Cedar Point County Park, and Alewife Brook. The latter is one of the prettiest tidal creeks on the East End. Like many small tidal brooks in this area, its narrow entrance is easy to miss if paddling too far from shore. If in doubt, follow the line of the unsightly cyclone fencing, one of several questionable management practices at this County facility, that ends at the creek's mouth.

The meanders of Alewife Brook, navigable at all tidal phases, will test the skills, and in the case of tandem craft, the friendship, of paddlers. This trip is described fully in the next chapter.

As mentioned earlier, Northwest was once the main port of call for ships of commerce trading in the area. Now largely forested and relatively far removed from the Town's commercial districts, this area was once completely cleared for farms and pastureland. It also boasted the Town's first school. Although much of Northwest's early history has been well documented, there is little agreement as to the exact location of its main port, or landing area.

One of several likely candidates is an area known as Cedar Bend. Even current nautical charts show this area to have deep water right up close to shore—13 feet at low tide. This was also the location of an old fish processing plant that, in the late 1800s, rendered Menhaden into valuable fish oil and fertilizer used by local farmers.

From Cedar Bend, the paddle westward along the inside of Cedar Point is a pleasant one provided its not duck hunting season and the Point's in-ground duck blinds are unmanned. The large building at the western tip of Cedar Point is the old lighthouse. Built in 1839 to guide the growing fleet of ships, including a prosperous whaling fleet, into Northwest and Sag Harbors, it originally sat atop Cedar Island, with the point located further to the east. Time and coastal processes have worked their magic and bridged the gap between island and point, so that today they are one and the same. The once-inhabited lighthouse is now empty but the focus of histori-

Group for the South Fork and Town Natural Resources Department staff, along with volunteers, construct an Osprey nesting structure on Northwest Harbor.

cal restoration efforts. Its navigation function has been turned over to the modern, unmanned, navigational light atop a nearby steel tower.

From the light, it is a short hop across open water to Gibson's Beach on the east side of Mashomack Point. The three-quarters-of-a-mile paddle involves crossing a strong current, and the set should be accounted for before heading off. A sharp lookout for powerboats is also well-advised. Don't assume they will spot a small, low-in-the-water craft and, even if they do, keep in mind that the helmsman may lack both common sense and an understanding of the rules of the road.

From the southern tip of Mashomack, another open water crossing, this one a mile long, takes you to Barcelona Point. The tall, sandy bluffs on Barcelona Neck's northern shore are readily recognizable landmarks. This feature apparently resembles the approach to the port of Barcelona, Spain, which was also regularly visited by whaling ships in the 1800s, hence the name. An earlier name for the peninsula was Russell's Neck, derived from the Russell family who farmed there in the late 1700s.

Once back at the inlet to Northwest Creek, take some time to explore the creek's upper reaches: a scenic, quiet backwater surrounded by extensive salt marshes and teeming with wildlife. ✕

# 20 | ALEWIFE BROOK

*Northwest, Town of East Hampton*

DISTANCE: 2 miles R/T.

ACCESS: All access points are in or adjacent to Cedar Point County Park. From Rte. 27 east of Wainscott, turn north onto Stephen Hands Path and follow the signs for Cedar Point County Park at all the following intersections: Rte. 114 (straight); Old Northwest Road (left); Northwest Road (right); Alewife Brook Road (left). Directions below are from the intersection of Alewife Brook Rd. and Cedar Point Rd. (park entrance).

1) Alewife Brook Road: East Hampton permit needed at ramp (you could park on the road shoulder back from the ramp and adjacent to County Parkland). Continue straight on Alewife Brook Road past the park entrance to the water.

2) Alewife Pond: No permit needed; pay County Park fee. From Alewife Brook Road (0.0 mile) turn right onto Cedar Point Road and through the park entrance to a small parking area on the right at 0.5 mile. Access to the pond is a carry down an unpaved road to the left.

3) Northwest Harbor: No permit needed; pay County Park fee. From Alewife Brook Road (0.0 mile) turn right onto Cedar Point Road and through the park entrance to a stop sign and Park Police building (1.2 miles). Turn left onto a dirt road and follow "Kayak and Canoe Rentals" sign at intersections and turns for another 0.2 mile to parking area. Carry down road on left to beach.

NOTES: Cedar Point County Park has overnight camping facilities and kayak rentals available during the summer season. The park number is (631) 852-7620.

*September*

Although only three quarters of a mile in length, factoring in all its twists and turns, Alewife Brook manages to pack a lot of scenic beauty into a small area. It is one of my favorite paddles, and a pretty waterway that I never tire of visiting. The brook's scenic beauty stems from the fact that it is tucked into a quiet corner of Cedar Point County Park, well-buffered from both residential development and the park's own poorly designed and laid out facilities.

I prefer using the access point at the end of Alewife Brook Road. Although the brook itself is quite well-protected from wind and waves, this access point is not.

Strong winds blowing from any point southwest clockwise through north can make the short paddle to the brook a rough one.

The entrance to the small brook, as with most tidal inlets, is marked by sandy shoals that, even in a canoe or kayak, are difficult to clear at low tide. At mid to low tide, resist the temptation to turn towards the brook's narrow opening too soon. Stay well outside and give the southern shoal wide clearance.

I find the lower 200 yards of Alewife Brook a fascinating study of coastal processes on a miniature scale. Since a previous visit in early spring, there have been many changes. The sand spit on the inlet's south side has lengthened considerably northward, a section of cyclone fence has toppled into the brook (removal of this eyesore from the park is long overdue), the small island of marsh grasses inside the brook is much larger, and a section of the barrier beach separating the brook from the bay has been breached. All are evidence of the dynamic nature of our coast.

A word of advice for paddlers negotiating the brook's tight bends at low tide: deeper water is generally found to the outside of sharp bends. Taking the shorter route often results in running aground. The brook can be paddled regardless of the tidal direction. If bucking the tide, take advantage of eddies created as the current comes around a bend in the brook. And keep in mind that the current is stronger on the outside, as opposed to the inside, of a bend.

When the water is exceptionally clear, it's fun to drift slowly with the tide, noting changes in water depth and marine fauna. On this visit the section of metal fencing laying in the brook has trapped Eelgrass and other detritus, creating a micro-environment for hundreds of Grass Shrimp and Mummichogs. Some of the shrimp are so big and fat that, at first, I mistake them for small fish. A careful look reveals that some are actually larger than what are most likely young-of-the-year Mummichogs.

At the first big bend, just upstream of the marsh island, the bottom of the brook drops out of sight. Pushed by the current up against the marsh on the outer bend of the brook, I note that the shoreline is no longer sand but a pliable bank of spongy peat. Unlike the sand, which can only maintain a maximum angle of incline of about 40° before it begins to slump and slide, the peat forms a vertical wall here.

The peat wall is pockmarked with golf ball-sized holes created by Fiddler Crabs and topped with marsh grasses. Well-anchored and partially buried at the base of the grass stems are Ribbed Mussels. The edge of the brook is swarming with schools of small fish. Smooth, sleek Atlantic Silversides, some four inches in length, are ready for their annual migration out to sea. Their stockier and hardier neighbors, the Striped Killifish and Mummichogs, are year-round residents of the brook and adjacent marsh. Hopefully there are some young-of-the-year Alewives in the mix, migrating down from the freshwater portions of this waterway where they hatched three months ago.

A bit further upstream, the adjacent oak forest closes in on both sides of the brook and the peat edge gives way to a steep bank of sand and gravel held together by

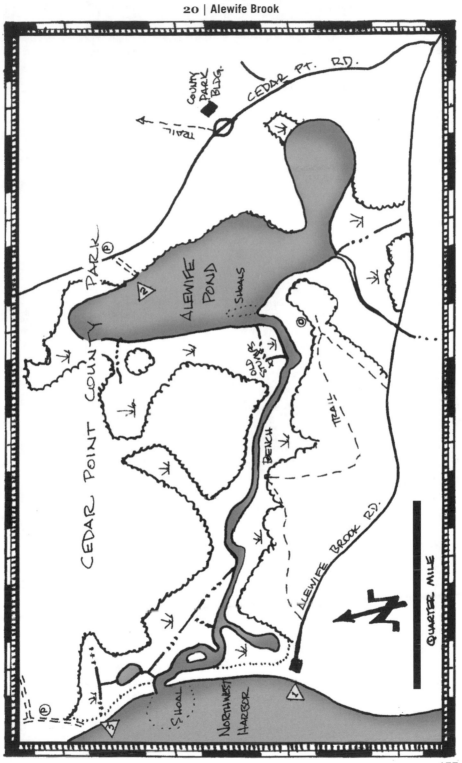

exposed roots. No matter the time of year, I am always greeted here by a Belted King-fisher, who announces itself by way of a loud rattling call and a fly over. Today is no exception, although the flight and rattle appears to be directed at another kingfisher, perhaps an intruder being chased off a choice fishing ground.

Kingfishers don't necessarily nest in their fishing territories, but their distinctive nest burrows are visible in the steep banks bordering this section of the brook. They excavate quite substantial horizontal tunnels, about five feet deep, with their long, stout bills and tiny, partially webbed feet. The bill and feet are really designed for their main occupation, catching fish, which the kingfisher does by plunging bill-first into the water. The webbed feet likely aid it in getting airborne again after the dive.

## Fiddler Crab (*Uca* spp.)

Paddling along the edge of most salt marshes, you will undoubtedly notice the irregular, pockmarked surface of exposed sections of peat. The golf-ball to quarter-sized holes and divots are the handiwork of one of the most numerous, and important, year-round residents of the salt marsh: the Fiddler Crab.

The most distinguishing feature of the Fiddler Crab is the large claw from which it gets its name. The resemblance to a fiddle is... well, you be the judge. The grossly oversized appendage comprises up to 50% of its body weight and is only found on mature males. They wave it around in territorial and courtship displays as if to say, "Yo, check it out. Ladies welcome; guys proceed at your own risk!"

Surprisingly, none of my references mention their pretty shells. These vary considerably, but many are absolutely beautiful shades and patterns of purple. There are three species here, separated by minor shell characteristics and to some degree by habitat. Sand (*U. pugilator*) and Mud Fiddlers (*U. pugnax*) are found in their respective namesake substrates within the intertidal zone, although I've noted much overlap in their populations here. The Brackish-water Fiddler (*U. minax*) is found in the upper reaches of the marsh where groundwater seepage is significant.

Fiddlers are air-breathing crabs with gills and a lung, but their primitive lung only works as long as it's kept moist, preventing them from wandering far from water. They are active in daylight around low tide, when they venture out of the protection of their burrows to feed. Specialized spoon-like feeding structures on the first pair of legs (one leg in the case of mature males) scrape the nutritious film of algae and bacteria off the surface off the sand and mud. Nonfood portions of the sediment are rolled into tiny pellets and cast out of the way. These small pellets, as well as larger pellets formed while excavating burrows, and the burrows themselves, are evidence of Fiddler Crab activity.

A female Fiddler Crab with a mass of hundreds of eggs attached to its abdomen (*credit: Laurie Tamber*).

The process of feeding and digging serves an important ecological role in the marsh: aerating the soil and facilitating peat decomposition. This benefits marsh plants, particularly *Spartina alterniflora*, and has earned the Fiddler Crab the nickname "Earthworm of the Salt Marsh."

As the tide rises, crabs retreat to their burrows and become inactive through the high tide cycle. The burrows are one-to-three feet long. Those constructed in the marsh peat and among the Cordgrass roots are quite sturdy; those in sand less so. To prevent a collapse with the incoming tide, the Sand Fiddler must retreat in time to plug up the entrance. The air trapped within provides enough pressure to maintain the chamber.

Mating occurs in the burrows. The male leaves and reseals the burrow, leaving the female inside for two weeks to incubate the spongy mass of tiny black eggs that are wedged beneath her abdomen. When ready to hatch, the female emerges and releases the larvae into the water, where they live for two months as part of the estuary's zooplankton community before transforming into small versions of the adult crabs and settling in the marsh.

A male Fiddler Crab with its characteristic over-sized claw.

A bench on the right marks a good place to stop and stretch your legs. The trail here links with East Hampton's extensive trail network, including the Northwest Path and Paumanok Path, enabling one to explore some excellent preserves by foot in this corner of East Hampton. To give you an idea of the hiking possibilities, one can walk from here to Montauk Point on marked trails!

Just before the brook joins Alewife Pond there is a tall Osprey tower on the right. The nest's occupants left for the Caribbean, or perhaps the Amazon River basin, last month. In their absence, a Red-Tailed Hawk perches there to scan the marsh, much to the annoyance of a flock of Crows. On the opposite side of the brook from the tower is a wide ditch that is navigable near high tide. Turning into it, note several old, partially submerged stumps in the ditch—most likely the remnants of Eastern Red Cedars, but perhaps the rarer Atlantic White Cedar—from many years ago when sea level was lower.

You can continue through the ditch, turning right and following it to the outlet of Alewife Pond. Today the pond is quiet, a few Double-crested Cormorants ply the waters at its southern end and a Great Egret and Great Blue Heron work opposite sides of the main pond near the north end. Alewife Brook continues through a thick stand of Phragmites at the pond's inlet near its southwest corner. In high water it can be paddled as far as Alewife Brook Road, where you might surprise a Muskrat in the evening. Beyond the road, the brook is a narrow dreen that drains Scoy's Pond in the Grace Estate Preserve, a very pretty freshwater pond and another nice place to visit. ✕

# 21 | GOOSE CREEK

*Three Mile Harbor, East Hampton*

DISTANCE: Providing you minimize bracktracking from dead ends, the Goose Creek maze is a mile-long paddle from the east to west inlet. From Maidstone Beach, through Goose Creek, and back by way of the harbor is a 2.5-mile trip.

ACCESS: Goose Creek is located at the north end of Three Mile Harbor on the Sammy's Beach peninsula. The creek is within easy reach of over a dozen water access points spread around the harbor. The closest of these, at the harbor's north end, are listed below:

1) Maidstone Park: East Hampton Town permit needed. From Montauk Highway in East Hampton Village, turn onto North Main Street (passing a windmill on your right), continue straight through a traffic light (Cedar Street). Bear left at a fork (North Main becomes Three Mile Harbor Road here) and follow this for 4.4 miles, turning left onto Flaggy Hole Road (follow "Beach" sign). Continue 0.3 mile and turn left onto Maidstone Park Road. Follow this to ballfields (it becomes a one-way road), beach parking, and rest rooms. Park near harbor inlet where a sandy beach provides a good launch site (1.0 mile from Three Mile Harbor Road).

2) Gann Road: East Hampton Town permit needed. Same as above to Three Mile Harbor Road. Gann Road is a left turn 4.1 miles from Cedar Street. Go to end. Park in lot on left side of boat ramp.

3) Sammy's Beach Road: East Hampton Town permit needed. Negotiating the roads in East Hampton's Northwest area is more challenging than paddling the Goose Creek maze. Here's the simplest, but not most direct, route. From Rte. 27 east of Wainscott, turn north onto Stephen Hands Path. Follow the signs for Cedar Point County Park at all intersections (straight through Rte. 114, left onto Old Northwest Road, right onto Northwest Road) until you reach Alewife Brook Road. Turn right onto Alewife Brook Road; at stop sign turn left onto Old House Landing Road. Turn right onto Sammy's Beach Road and follow this winding road to the end. At the last sharp bend to the left, a wide dirt path on the right leads to a nice launch site on the harbor.

NOTES: Should your trip coincide with dinnertime, you can enjoy a fine meal and sunset at Bostwick's Restaurant adjacent to the Gann Road launch site.

*August*

Standing up in my canoe, I scan the marsh ahead and realize that the ever-narrowing route I am following turns sharply to the east before petering out into salt marsh grasses. Clearly not navigable, I back up to an area where I can spin my 16-foot boat around and paddle toward a likely passage obscured by another hairpin turn. I am approximately halfway through a maze of small tidal lagoons, narrow, twisting creeks, and even narrower but straight mosquito ditches, all somewhat interconnected, at least at high tide. The entire labyrinth of channels and lagoons, known as Goose Creek, is surrounded by *Spartina* grasses, forming an elongated triangle of salt marsh.

Although nearly 100 acres in size and spanning three quarters of a mile in length as the crow flies, Goose Creek is easily overlooked. As with all salt marshes, protection from wind-driven waves is key to the establishment of Saltmarsh Cordgrass (*Spartina alterniflora*), the marsh's pioneer plant. In this case, the marsh is protected from the northerlies by the formidable coastal dunes of Sammy's Beach, which separates Three Mile Harbor from Gardiners Bay and was recently reconfigured as part of a harbor-dredging project. On the marsh's east side, the limited fetch is protected by Dayton's Island, while its southern and western flank is protected by a very thin but effective sliver of sand mimicking, in form and function, a coastal barrier beach.

Launching from Maidstone Park, I cross the inlet and follow the shoreline of Sammy's Beach southward, entering Goose Creek by way of its eastern inlet. According to the Suffolk County Five Town topographical map of the area, created in the 1970s, there should be two navigable inlets here at the eastern end of the marsh. However, the southern of the two openings now dead-ends less than a quarter-mile in. This seems to be the result of a slow northeasterly migration of the narrow belt of sand that separates the marsh from the harbor, a coastal process resembling barrier beach rollover. This interesting phenomenon, along with many other coastal processes, is well described by geologist Stephen Leatherman in *The Barrier Island Handbook*. The end result, or more accurately the current situation as of this writing, is that a section of the southern channel has filled with sand and now sports a growth of American Beachgrass (*Ammophila breviligulata*) instead of Cordgrass.

The creek first hugs the upland of Sammy's Beach, squeezing between it and a small unnamed island of upland shrubs, before making a sharp left turn and following the western side of the same island. Rounding this turn, I stop and step onto a firm part of the marsh to scout the route ahead, in the process flushing a colorful, male Ringneck Pheasant. The pheasant makes a beeline through the Salt Hay towards the more substantial vegetated cover of the small island. It appears he has found a hideaway, safe for the time being, from the area's exploding Red Fox population.

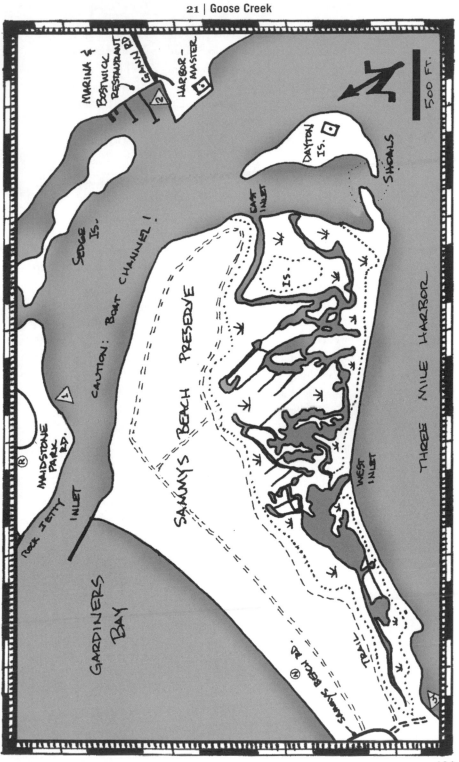

Large schools of Atlantic Silversides and smaller groups of Striped Killifish scatter at the approach of my canoe, while the yellow-billed Great Egrets and smaller, black-billed Snowy Egrets eye me warily before resuming their hunt. Standing once again to scout ahead, I am thankful that I brought along my canoe rather than my sea kayak. The passage now swings south and runs parallel to the harbor shoreline, with the harbor's waters a mere canoe length away. Here, in June of 1998, I noticed another opening between the creek and the harbor that was navigable by canoe, at least on a high tide.

It is hard to believe that this creek was once negotiated by bayman Milt Miller, skippering a boat that drew four feet. Over his seven decades on these local waters, the one constant he observed in the marine environment was change: change in the inanimate physical environment as well as dramatic fluctuations in shellfish and fin-fish stocks. The latter, according to Milt, don't always correspond to the textbook descriptions. As an example he cited several years of excellent scallop harvests during periods of greatly diminished Eelgrass beds.

Sprinkled over the sea of green marsh grasses are the delicate purple-pink flowers of Sea Lavender (*Limonium nashii*) and the even smaller, rice-shaped, white Cordgrass flowers. Nearing the western inlet of Goose Creek, all sorts of winged wildlife show themselves. Among them are noisy flocks of Willets, the unmistakable, bright orange-beaked Oystercatchers, a solitary Great Blue Heron, and several Short-billed Dowitchers. The water is unusually clear for mid-August and the schools of Silversides and deeper-bellied Bunker are easily distinguishable. The Bunker are particularly thick; schools of two-to-four-inch-long fish move like clouds through the water.

Goose Creek is somewhat unusual in that it has two widely separated inlets. Passing through the western one, a large Striper bolts out of the shallows into the deeper harbor waters. The sandy beach on either side of this inlet, contrasting with the peat-sided inlet at the creek's eastern end, attracts scores of Horseshoe Crabs on a spring high tide in May and June. During those months the females, with males in tow, dig small depressions into which they deposit thousands of tiny blue-green eggs.

Leaving the creek, I turn eastward and paddle along Three Mile Harbor's shoreline. At several points the clear, shallow water reveals a dark patch of peat, remnants of the Goose Creek salt marsh and evidence that the adjacent miniature barrier beach has shifted to the north. Approaching Dayton's Island, the tide is still quite high and I decide to try the inside passage over a large mudflat which is high and dry at low tide. A flock of terns is positioned on the sandy spits that define the narrow opening between the island and the Sammy's Beach peninsula. These appear to be a mix of immature and adult Common Terns, but at this time of year any number of at least eight species can be in the area. These normally raucous and energetic birds are unusually quiet and reluctant to take flight as I approach: they have probably just finished gorging themselves on the abundant baitfish in the area.

Both Sammy's Beach and Dayton's Island were the centers of recent, and somewhat unusual, environmental controversies. In 1998, many people were outraged to see bulldozers creating a huge sand dike to contain inlet dredge spoil in the Sammy's Beach Nature Preserve. The work had somehow gotten the approval of East Hampton Town's notoriously pro-environment officials—and haunted one of them, a Town Supervisor well-known for her environmental record, in the next election. Along with an army of local volunteers, the area was eventually replanted and restored.

In 2004 the Town Board acquired Dayton's Island. Despite the community's long history of open space purchases, some questioned the open space value of this already developed piece of Hampton real estate and its very hefty price tag. It will be interesting to see what happens with this island preserve in the future. ✕

### Why Protect Horseshoe Crabs?

Horseshoe Crabs have played an important role in scientific research. A study of their compound eyes determined how optic nerves transmit photo-electric impulses, and was part of the research into the mechanics of human eyes that was awarded a Nobel prize in 1967. Because their blood will not support the growth of bacteria, it is used to test the cleanliness of manufactured drugs, human blood serum, pacemakers and other foreign objects implanted in the human body. The key blood compound, lysate, can be collected without harming the crab.

Horseshoe Crabs are also harvested for use as bait in Eel and conch traps. This practice is the subject of much debate, particularly in Delaware Bay where their most important role is the food value of their eggs to migratory shorebirds. During the three to four weeks that mark the peak of Horseshoe Crab egg laying in the bay, researchers have documented the arrival and departure of 500,000 to 1.5 million shorebirds. Sanderlings, Red Knots, and Ruddy Turnstones consume as many as 9,000 eggs per bird per day during this stopover, doubling their body weight over a two week period. The ultimate fate of over a half-dozen shorebird species rests largely on the health and productivity of the Horseshoe Crab. As such, this "living fossil" plays a critical role on a global stage.

# 22 | ACCABONAC HARBOR

*Springs, Town of East Hampton*

DISTANCE:   A circumnavigation of the harbor's shoreline is a 6.5-mile trip. The loop described below is just under 4 miles long and includes a mile-long section in Gardiners Bay. A nice 1.5-mile loop can be made from Landing Lane to include the Merrill Lake Preserve—around Sage and Wood Tick Islands, and through Hellgate.

ACCESS:   There are many access points to Accabonac Harbor, but my favorite is Landing Lane at its south end.

1) Landing Lane: No permit needed.* From Rte. 27 in East Hampton Village, turn north onto Accabonac Road at the traffic light across from the Post Office. Stay on Accabonac Road until it ends, approximately 2.0 miles, and turn left onto Old Stone Highway. Landing Lane is the first right.

*IMPORTANT: Park on the shoulder of the paved section of the road, where a permit is not needed. Parking near the launch ramp requires an East Hampton Town permit.

*June*

It is one of those moody June days when the warm, moist air settles over the cooler harbor waters in a fine mist. Not quite a fog, but disorienting nonetheless. Every so often a light breeze pushes aside the thin gray veil of mist to reveal wooded hummocks and large expanses of salt meadow at the water's edge. As my canoe crosses into some invisible but carefully guarded territory, the marsh's vocal residents break the harbor's stillness with their calls. A Belted Kingfisher scolds me with its rattle-like chatter as it abandons a favorite fishing perch. A Willet, hidden from view among the marsh grasses, bursts into flight, its sudden appearance as startling as its loud, frantic cries. And somewhere high overhead the piercing chirp of an Osprey can be heard.

I had covered at least a half-mile of shoreline without a house, bulkhead or dock in sight, and am pleasantly reminded of the wild marshes of coastal Maine where I once taught at the Hurricane Island Outward Bound School. Yet I am paddling in Accabonac Harbor—Bonac Crick to those who know it well—in the heart of one of the most densely populated hamlets in the Town of East Hampton: the Springs.

Accabonac Harbor is a shallow embayment separated from Gardiners Bay by two sand spits or barrier beaches, Cape Gardiner (which terminates with Gerard Point) and Louse Point. These low barrier beaches shelter the harbor from wind-driven waves, although not necessarily from the wind itself, providing a safe paddling area

HALF MILE

for beginners. The harbor's calm waters also provide ideal conditions for the development of salt marsh vegetation that rims virtually the entire harbor, and forms quite extensive meadows in several places.

Bay water enters and exits the harbor via a dredged channel between the points, and more recently by way of a box culvert installed in 2005 at the "old gutway" on Cape Gardiner. The salt water mixes with fresh water that seeps into the harbor by way of groundwater flow. At low tide these groundwater seeps are visible in the form of tiny rivulets in the sandy intertidal zone, particularly along the southern and western shorelines of the harbor where groundwater flow in greatest. Wind and tide mix fresh and salt waters, creating a low salinity environment that is ideal for the spawning and growth of many varieties of finfish and shellfish. These in turn provide an abundance of food for a wide variety of predators that forage in the harbor: Ospreys, Common and Least Terns, cormorants, herons, egrets, Oystercatchers, and man.

I had set off earlier from the cove at Landing Lane, my favorite launch site on the harbor. On the east side of this cove is a huge marsh, called Great Meadows, that extends a half-mile to East Harbor. With the exception of a small island of oaks, called Bishop's Hummock, this entire area is within the intertidal zone and periodically inundated with salt water.

In stark contrast, the marsh on the west of the cove is a mere sliver. The topography here, although hardly dramatic, has enough slope to compress the intertidal zone into a narrow band and allow the upland forest of Eastern Red Cedar and Post Oak to grow close to the water's edge. This provides an excellent opportunity to examine the various plant zones of the salt marsh from the comfort of your boat.

Find a spot to pull up near the shore for a closer look at the marsh. Among the grasses, you should be able to find an odd-looking, succulent plant called Glasswort, which is edible, and, in late summer and fall, a plant with tiny clusters of very pretty purple flowers, called Sea Lavender. At the lower edge of the marsh grasses, look for shells protruding from the marsh peat. These are Ribbed Mussels, one of the most abundant animals in the salt marsh. Notice that the vertical edge of the peat (most easily seen at low tide) is riddled with holes, the work of another important and prolific marsh creature, the Fiddler Crab.

Cross the long and narrow southwestern reach of Accabonac Harbor that terminates at the Springs General Store and Pussy's Pond (a worthwhile detour for picnic supplies and a coffee) and head for another large expanse of salt marsh called Schellenger's Meadow. Along its eastern edge, a low tide reveals a series of horizontal wooden poles jutting from the marsh peat, remnants of a primitive road constructed to haul Salt Hay off the marsh.

Salt hay was an important resource for East End farmers. As far back as 1652, the Town Trustees approved 34 allotments at Great Meadows for its harvest. Salt hay had many uses, including winter fodder for livestock, and in some places livestock were turned loose to graze in the salt meadows. Longtime Springs resident Jarvis Woods, who helped harvest Salt Hay from Accabonac in the Depression era, claims that it was also used as bedding for livestock. It remained an important, harvestable resource until the mid-1900s.

Schellinger's Meadow, along with several wooded hummocks, is now protected as part of the Merrill Lake Preserve, donated in 1968 by Federic Lake, one of the founders of the Nature Conservancy's South Fork Chapter. Continue north along the preserve's shoreline, passing one of 10 Osprey nest structures found in the harbor. Accabonac has had as many as nine active nests in recent years, possibly the highest concentration of Osprey nests in the region outside of Gardiners Island. Please give the nests wide berth between April and mid-July when the nests are occupied.

Swing east and paddle over to Sage Island next, a small, low lying area that may be completely submerged during a spring tide. Pull up at the sandy spit on its west side, where Horseshoe Crabs congregate at this time of year to lay their eggs. You may notice shallow, plate-sized depressions in the sand near the high water mark—these are the nests of the Horseshoes Crabs. Several inches below the surface, mixed in with the sand grains, are greenish-gray, BB-sized eggs, up to 1,000 per nest.

The Horseshoe Crab is an interesting and harmless creature. Its long, pointed tail is used as a lever to help right itself, not to spear unsuspecting swimmers as some believe. In May and June, you may see the smaller males hitched on behind the larger females, moving about in search of suitable nesting areas. Not wanting to put all their eggs in one basket, females will deposit their 10,000 eggs in up to 10 different nests. Even so, many are lost to predation by shorebirds. At least six species of Arctic breeding shorebirds rely on the eggs to fuel their long northward migration each year.

Continue north along the shoreline of the Kaplan Preserve, another large expanse of salt meadow owned by the Nature Conservancy. Donated by the Kaplan family in 1966, it became the first preserve in the harbor and a catalyst for other private land-owners to work with public officials and private land trusts to protect the area's natural resources. To date, over 200 acres of the harbor's wetlands, beaches and woodlands have been preserved.

After passing through the Narrows, head east toward the Gerard Drive causeway. At low tide, this section of the harbor is difficult to negotiate even in a shallow draft canoe or kayak; deeper water can be found by hugging the eastern shoreline. The causeway is one of two places where Cape Gardiner is barely wider than the road itself. In 1910 a storm broke through this narrow stretch of the barrier beach, depositing huge amounts of sand on the harbor side and creating the excellent clamming flats and difficult paddling that exist today. Called the "old gutway," this breach was filled in by the Town in 1932 to create a new road to Gerard Point.

I used to portage over Gerard Drive and into the bay here, but as this is being written, the Town is installing a box culvert at the old gutway to increase tidal exchange between harbor and bay. The hope is that this will improve water quality in the harbor's north end. The culvert will be large enough to paddle through, although how much depth there will be is presently unknown. Check this out from shore before proceeding through.

Whether slipping through the new culvert or portaging, enjoy the views across Gardiners Bay of Gardiners Island, Montauk (marked by a water tower), and Napeague (marked by a radio tower) before resuming paddling. Much of the land visible from here is undeveloped. The 3,000-acre privately-owned Gardiners Island has been held by the same family since the 1600s; the "Nominicks", or high land flanking the west side of Montauk marks the forest of Hither Hills State Park; and much of Napeague, a fascinating mix of duneland, marsh, pitch pine forest, and cranberry bogs, is State parkland.

In contrast is the tightly packed development of Gerard Drive. These lots were created in 1935, prior to the implementation of zoning and planning regulations, and they have haunted town planning and zoning boards ever since. While putting a house up on stilts may protect it from storm tides, the buried cesspools do not function as they are supposed to in these situations.

Recognizing the difficult legal issues that arise when Town agencies deny building permits on severely constrained lots, Town residents have long supported open space bonds to acquire and preserve land, including a special small lot acquisition fund for lots such as these. Halfway to the inlet, at Deep Hole, is a Town park that was once the site of a Menhaden processing factory (1975–1895). Deep Hole is so-named because of the deep water so close to shore there, a feature that allowed fishing vessels to easily load and unload their catch. As with most other Menhaden processing plants on the East End, another important siting consideration was the distance to the nearest neighbor and their location relative to prevailing winds, reflecting a by-product of the processing operation, the phenomenal odors.

Further south, depending on the time of year, you may come upon a fish trap, a fish-catching structure and technique modified from one used by this area's Native Americans. The device is comprised of a fence of netting perpendicular to the shore which directs schools of fish toward deeper water and a series of funnels leading to a circular cage. Not unlike a huge lobster trap, the fish can't find the its exit and mill about until the fisherman hauls up the trap's bottom. It is an ecologically sound fishing technique that allows any unwanted catch to be released unharmed.

Near the inlet is a section of beach usually inhabited by nesting Least Terns and Piping Plovers, both federally endangered species. The aggressive and very aerial Least Terns are easy to spot, but the well camouflaged Plovers, even when calling, are difficult to pick out. Obviously, do not beach your boat near the nesting area during the critical nesting and rearing season, April through July.

A fairly strong tidal current flows through the inlet. If facing a foul current, paddling close to shore avoids the worst of it. A small commercial fishing fleet operates out of the harbor, as well as a number of recreational sailboats. These vessels have very little leeway in the narrow boat channel, so be aware of the channel's location and give them plenty of room. Gerard Point is a good place to go ashore for a picnic, to swim, or to just stretch your legs.

Prior to 1959, the harbor's inlet was located further south where the Louse Point boat ramp is today. The realignment of the inlet was quite a controversy, with some claiming relocation had more to do with politics and personal power than sound harbor management. Maintaining the inlet channel is an ongoing battle against natural coastal processes that fill in some portions with sand and shift others to less desirable locations. Just south of the ramp are moorings for the fish trap tenders and lobstermen who work the waters of Gardiners Bay.

For the final leg of the paddle, head for the narrow stretch of water between Wood Tick and Plato's Islands, continuing around the south end of Wood Tick Island through Hellgate. This final narrow passageway has deep water and is not as intimidating as it sounds. A U.S. Coastal Survey map dated 1838 shows Wood Tick Island as a peninsula off Great Meadow. If accurate, Hellgate was probably dug by hand sometime between then and 1884.

Accabonac's salt marshes, like nearly all salt marshes along the east coast, have a series of grid-like ditches that are obviously man-made. Some of the ditches were originally dug as boundary markers delineating Salt Hay leases and date back to the 1600s. Most were hand-dug under the Works Projects Administration (WPA) in the 1930s, under the pretense of dewatering and drying out the surface of the marsh at low tide, thereby eliminating potential mosquito breeding habitat.

Essentially a make work project, these mosquito ditches were dug indiscriminately, regardless of the presence or absence of mosquito breeding areas. Over the years, biologists have documented a long and growing list of problems associated with the ditches. Today, these ditches are periodically cleaned out and maintained by Suffolk County Vector Control who, currently faced with a lawsuit, are in the process of re-evaluating their mosquito control program.

One answer to the question of what to do with these ditches can be seen in the northwest corner of Great Meadows en route back to Landing Lane. Look for low dams at the harbor end of the ditches, part of an Open Marsh Water Management strategy. Constructed by Town Natural Resources staff, the simple dam is low enough to allow the incoming tide to overtop it but high enough to prevent the upland side from drying out on an outgoing tide. This enables small fish, including several that prey on mosquito larvae, to live in the upper marsh throughout the tidal cycle.

In principle at least. In practice, it has been very difficult to prevent the dams (there are now 16 in Accabonac) from leaking. As is often the case, it is much easier to destroy and disrupt natural processes than to repair and restore them. ⅄

## Mosquito Ditches

Nearly all the salt marshes on the East End are crisscrossed in a grid-like, obviously man-made, pattern of ditches. Most of these were hand-dug under the Works Projects Administration (WPA) in the 1930s, under the pretense of dewatering the high marsh surface, thereby eliminating potential mosquito breeding habitat.

The Salt Marsh Mosquito lays its eggs on the wet soils of the upper marsh, not in water. Rain or a spring tide forms small pools in which the eggs hatch and go through their larval development before emerging as winged adults. The whole process from egg to adult only takes a week, and the pool of water need only be a cupful.

The ditching was a make-work project for the unemployed during the Depression, with little oversight by biologists. Ditches were dug regardless of the presence of mosquitos, and their overall effectiveness was masked for many years by the use of DDT, a highly toxic pesticide that was sprayed over the same marshes. In many cases, the ditches themselves later became prime mosquito breeding areas if they weren't periodically cleaned and maintained.

To add insult to injury, the ditches were found to have several adverse ecological impacts on important marshland habitat, as well as the adjacent bay. In 1985, Connecticut abandoned mosquito ditching in favor of a management strategy called Open Marsh Water Management (OMWM).

New York still relies on this outdated technique. Today, 7,500 linear miles of ditches are maintained by Suffolk County Vector Control. In 2004, the Peconic Baykeeper sued over this practice, prompting the County to undertake an environmental assessment of their mosquito control program.

OMWM is an alternative method of controlling mosquitoes that relies on damming a ditch on its bay end at a height that allows tidal water over at high tide but prevents the ditch from completely draining at low tide. This transforms the ditches into linear reservoirs that allow predators of mosquito larva, such as Mummichogs and Striped Killifish, to reside in the upper marsh through the low tide cycle. There, they are well-positioned to fan out at high tide and easily access the upper marsh mosquito breeding areas.

Ditches were found to act as conduits for pollutants (e.g. road runoff, fertilizers, septic effluent) from adjacent developed upland areas to the surface waters of the harbor. In such cases the dams had the added benefit of slowing down the flow of contaminants and allowing natural biological processes to cleanse the runoff before it reached the harbor.

# 23 | NAPEAGUE HARBOR

*Amagansett, Town of East Hampton*

DISTANCE: The harbor and Hicks Island offer 6 miles of shoreline to explore.

ACCESS: 1A, 1B, and 1C) Lazy Point Road: East Hampton Town permit needed. (NOTE: NYS Parks is working on establishing an access and parking area here. In the meantime, those lacking an East Hampton Town parking permit can drop boats at one of several convenient access points and park on the road shoulder west of the sign at 3.7 miles.)

From Rte. 27 in Amagansett traveling east, continue 0.8 mile past the Amagansett Post Office and turn left onto Cranberry Hole Rd. Go 3.3 miles from Rte. 27 to Crassen Boulevard intersection on right, continue straight following "Boat Ramp" sign at next intersection, and note sign at 3.7 miles delineating point of road shoulder parking by East Hampton Town permit only. Windsurfing area and porta-johns at 3.8 miles (1A); turn left and next right to East Hampton Town boat ramp at 4.0 miles (1B).

2) Crassen Boulevard: East Hampton Town permit needed. (see Lazy Point above for directions).

3) Napeague Harbor Road: No permit needed. Traveling east on Rte. 27, go through Amagansett to the far end of the Napeague stretch and turn left across from the Sea Crest Condos onto Napeague Harbor Road. Continue to the end of the road and park near the entrance to the Walking Dunes nature trail. This narrow dead end road can be difficult to turn around on; NYS parks is considering a small trailhead parking area that would be available to paddlers as well as hikers.

NOTES: The access at Lazy Point (1A) is a popular, and crowded, windsurfing and kite boarding area. Be aware that novice kite boarders may not have the skills to avoid even slow moving kayaks and canoes. It's best to avoid this area of the harbor altogether. If launching from this spot, hug the shoreline until well clear of the boarders.

*September*

Napeague Harbor is a 1,000-acre coastal embayment surrounded largely by State parkland. With the exception of the dredged channels separating Hicks Island from Goff Point to the east and Lazy Point to the west, and a deep channel running along the harbor's northeast side, most of the water here is shallow enough to stand in. The shallow depths limit boat traffic in the harbor, a plus for paddlers, but at low tide even canoes and kayaks have to give wide berth to several large areas of shoals off the eastern tip of Hicks Island, Lazy Point, and Crassen Boulevard.

The harbor has much to offer paddlers, including a beautiful setting, great birding, and an interesting history. In addition, at this time of year it offers a sense of isolation and solitude. Surrounded by low-lying dunelands and salt marshes, and within close proximity to both ocean and bay, this waterbody also offers little protection from the wind, a consideration for paddlers and the reason for its immense popularity among windsurfers.

Launching from the beach near the windsurfers' gathering spot, I head north following the shoreline towards Lazy Point. There I meet Calvin Lester, a local bayman with a reputation, even among fellow baymen, of having an amazing ability to find and catch fish. He's after Atlantic Silversides today, working the shallows with a large seine and not doing well. Calvin's soft-spoken, chipped speech is hard to follow under the best of circumstances, and with a cigarette butt dangling from his lips he is nearly impossible to understand. Although Silversides are a popular baitfish, he seems to be saying that these will go to market in New York City and sold for consumption.

Around the north side of Lazy Point is a boat mooring area, a launch ramp, and a fairly strong tidal current. There is also a small monument to another bayman, another Lester as it happens and, come to think of it, another unforgettable character, named Tom Lester. An intimidating hulk of a man with the scariest voice this side of Hollywood, he was actually a gentle giant. Tom fished and trapped most anything that lived in the waters here: Eels, turtles, and all sorts of shellfish as well as a wide variety of fin fish. While aboard his sharpie checking his fish traps in Northwest Harbor, I learned that he once caught a River Otter in one of his fykes.

In the 1980s, Tom and his wife Cathy both got involved in efforts to preserve large tracts of vacant land around one of their favorite fishing grounds, Northwest Harbor. Cathy, a passionate and hard-working advocate of open space protection, later ran for public office and had a long career which culminated in being Supervisor of East Hampton's Town Board. The Town has been fortunate to have other baymen, such as Brad Loewen and Tom Knobel, serve in important elected and appointed positions over the years and provide their unique perspectives to challenging local issues.

The stretch of water between Lazy Point and Hicks Island is a good place to look for migrating and overwintering waterfowl and sea ducks, such as Red-Breasted Merganser, Bufflehead, and Common Goldeneye. The channel on the south side of Hicks Island was dredged in 2003–2004, with the spoils deposited on the island. This large unvegetated area will hopefully attract nesting terns (Common, Least, and Roseate), Piping Plovers, and Black Skimmers. These species nest on the island and at Goff Point most years. Keep that in mind if paddling here during the nesting season (April through July) and stay off the island and point.

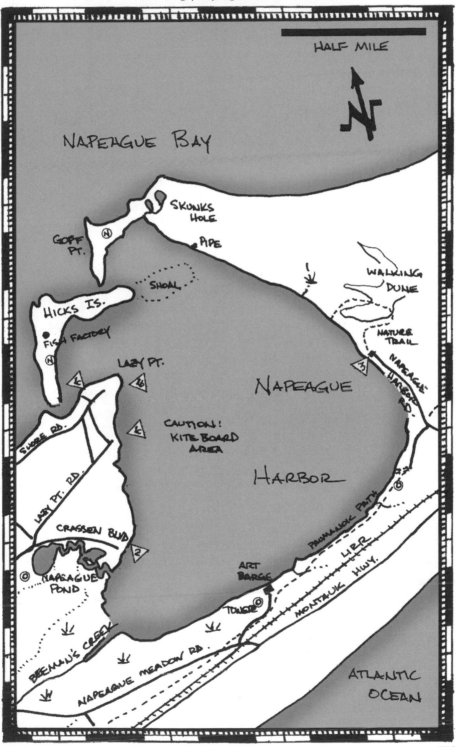

HALF MILE

NAPEAGUE BAY

SKUNKS HOLE

GOFF PT.

PIPE

SHOAL

HICKS IS.

FISH FACTORY

LAZY PT.

WALKING DUNE

NATURE TRAIL

NAPEAGUE HARBOR RD.

NAPEAGUE

CAUTION! KITE BOARD AREA

HARBOR

SHORE RD.

LAZY PT. RD.

CRASSEN BLVD

NAPEAGUE POND

PAUMANOK PATH

L.I.R.R.

ART BARGE

MONTAUK HWY.

TOWER

BREMAN'S CREEK

NAPEAGUE MEADOW RD.

ATLANTIC OCEAN

The eastern inlet is slated to be dredged next. There has been talk of abandoning the serpentine east inlet and dredging through a narrow, low section of the island to provide a much more direct route into the harbor's mooring area. As of this writing, no decision has been made.

Before heading out the inlet, be sure to check sea conditions, as Napeague Bay has a large fetch to the north and east. If facing a foul tide, most of the strong current in the inlet can be avoided by paddling as close as possible to Hicks Island's shore, where a large eddy and an opposing current forms. Keep a sharp eye out for—and stay clear of—other boats that may be more restricted in navigating through the inlet. This inlet was completely filled in after the 1938 hurricane. For the next 30 years, until the County redug the channel in 1968, Hicks Island was a peninsula-like appendage connected to the flat section of beach jutting out just west of Lazy Point.

Look for the remnants of a fish processing plant, an assortment of metal and brickwork, on the bay side of the island. This once rendered Bunker, a type of herring that seems to have more common names than any other animal I know of, into oil and fish meal. The first processing plant was built at Goff Point in 1858; ten were operating in the Napeague area, including one on Hicks Island, in the 1870s. In 1898, American Fisheries Company (despite the name, a British company) consolidated all the operations at Promised Land. In 1933 their holdings, consisting of the remaining factory and 1,300 adjacent acres stretching from bay to ocean, were bought out by the Smith Meal Company. Although the fish oil is still in demand, the factory closed in 1968 after the local Bunker fishery collapsed. In 1976 the Nature Conservancy negotiated the purchase of the property on behalf of New York State Parks, and a year later Napeague State Park was created.

Heading back inside the harbor through the north inlet, you may encounter a series of rafts moored in the deep water cove formed by the recurved spit of Goff Point. This is a shellfish grow-out station operated by the Town Hatchery in an effort to reseed its bays and harbor with Quahogs, Oysters, and Bay Scallops. Hug the shoreline as you approach Skunk's Hole, a small tidal pond probably named for the fact that it was northeast, and downwind, of the foul smell emanating from the Hick's Island Bunker factory. Just south of the tiny creek that leads into the salt pond, protruding from the beach near the low tide line, is the remnant of the two-mile-long pipeline that carried freshwater from Fresh Pond in Hither Woods to the Hick's Island factory.

Following the shoreline further south, you will encounter the northwestern flank of the famous Walking Dunes of Napeague. This fascinating area of parabolic dunes attracts Long Island's best naturalists and photographers. A Hollywood film director considered this expansive sweep of towering sand ridges a good replica of an Arabian desert. In 1922 he set up his equipment here and filmed *The Sheik*, starring Rudolph Valentino. Consider stopping at the Napeague Harbor Road access to visit the mile-long Walking Dune Interpretive Trail.

Whenever I am with a group of hikers or paddlers on the beach here someone asks, "Why is the sand so orange-colored?" The striking discoloration is exactly what it appears to be: rust. Groundwater on the South Fork, and particularly under Hither Woods, contains high levels of iron in the form of ferrous iron, a water soluble compound when immersed in the low oxygen and high acidic conditions found in the aquifer. This iron-laden groundwater moves laterally from under Hither Woods and eventually seeps into the surrounding bays and ocean, where it mixes with salt water.

Groundwater that seeps out of the sandy beach at low tide comes in contact with air, resulting in the oxidation of ferrous iron into ferric iron, a compound that is not as water soluble. This precipitates out as a solid, forming the rusty coating on the sand and rocks that is so striking. Although the same reaction takes place on the bay

### Bunker (*Brevoortia tyrannus*)

Atlantic Menhaden, known locally as Bunker, is a member of the herring family, a group of schooling fishes that includes the Shad and Alewife. They feed on plankton, filtering it from the water with their long and closely set gill rakers. Traveling in huge schools, Bunker were easily harvested by early settlers fishing from wooden dories with nets. They used the abundant, bony, and oily fish to fertilize their fields. The fish oil was later found to have a variety of important commercial uses as a base for paints, lubricants, and cosmetics, and by the late 1800s a large fishing industry developed around this species.

Steam-run trawlers soon replaced the small dories. To get the valuable oil, the fish were boiled or steamed and pressed, and the remaining fish scraps were sold as fertilizer and fish meal (food for fish farms, pets, and a supplement in cattle feed). The factories were generally located along a stretch of shoreline where deep water allowed the large fishing steamers to pull up and unload. Due to the incredible stench that emanated from these plants, they were also located as far as possible from and downwind of human habitation. In his book *The South Fork*, Everett Rattray writes that the factory smell was "strong enough to tarnish silver coins in the pockets of their employees."

Factories were located on Napeague, Cape Gardiner (Springs), Northwest Harbor near Cedar Point, and Long Beach, Orient. Between 1858 and 1898, ten fish processing plants operated in the Napeague area alone. Passersby, commenting that the area stunk to high heaven, nicknamed it the "Promised Land," a placename that remains to this day.

By the early 1900s, fishermen had to go farther afield to find Bunker. Possibly due to overfishing, the Bunker fishery eventually collapsed and the remaining plant in Napeague shut down in 1968. Paddlers can see the remnants of fish processing plants at Hicks Island, Promised Land (Napeague State Park), and Orient Beach State Park (Gardiners Bay side).

and ocean beaches north and south of Hither Woods, strong littoral currents quickly dissipate the ferric iron deposits so that they are not as discernible.

Between the southeast corner of the harbor, near an Osprey pole, and the large white structure called the Art Barge, a trail called the Paumanok Path follows the Napeague Harbor shoreline. Two simple log bridges span small, unnavigable tidal creeks that cut into the water-logged salt meadows to the south. The Paumanok Path is a regional trail that, when completed, will extend from Montauk Point to Rocky Point in Brookhaven, a distance of approximately 130 miles. As of 2004, the 45-mile-long East Hampton Town section is completed, as well as the 50-mile-long section through the pine barrens west of the Shinnecock Canal. Of the remaining 35 miles sandwiched between the canal and Sagg Road south of Sag Harbor Village, at least three quarters of the route is in place but somewhat fragmented. Local trail groups are working hard to ensure that enough land is protected to close the gaps.

The huge building practically sitting in the water on the south end of the harbor is the Art Barge. It was floated into its current location, where it hosts classes in art and photography in a very inspiring setting. The imposing steel MacKay radio tower was also relocated here, moved from Pearl Harbor following the infamous 1941 bombing. It was one of two that stood in Napeague Meadows to communicate with ships at sea. All that remains of the other is its concrete foundation, while the existing tower is the summer home of a pair of Ospreys. Their formidable nest appears as a speck approximately one-third of the way up and in the middle of the tower.

The next tidal creek that links with the harbor (large enough to warrant its own name, Beeman's Creek) is worth paddling up at or near high tide. This creek flows from the largest expanse of salt marsh in the entire harbor, and possibly the entire Peconic estuary watershed. Scan the meadows for a Red-Tailed Hawk, Kestrel, Osprey, and the rare Northern Harrier, all birds of prey which can be seen here.

Another navigable tidal creek, the unnamed outlet of Pond of Pines, intercepts the harbor just south of Crassen Boulevard. My USGS topographical map shows the original creek and outlet further west. Sometime in the last 30 years, a portion of privately-owned salt pond and marsh was dredged, creating a new creek connecting Pond of Pines with the harbor via the smaller salt pond. This apparently allowed the owner to fence off a portion of the creek on his property, effectively blocking paddlers from the waterway. I believe the fence was erected to keep clammers out of the small salt pond, where the owner once had a commercial shellfish operation.

For six years in the late 1990s, I tried my hand at raising Oysters in the shallows off Crassen Blvd. It was hard, tedious work, and I made a lot of mistakes in the first years that made it more difficult for myself. But working on the water in such an incredible setting, even in the dead of winter, was a great experience which I miss. My stab at small-scale aquaculture was done on a trial basis with the permission of the Town Trustees, and ended when they withdrew my permit. ✕

# 24 | FORT POND

DISTANCE:  The pond is 1 mile in length. A circumnavigation of the pond's shore-line is 3 miles.

ACCESS:  1) South Erie Street NYSDEC boat ramp: No permit needed. From Rte. 27 in Montauk Village, turn north at the Village green onto Edgemere Street. Make the first left onto South Erie Street. Just beyond the soccer field turn right onto an unpaved road that leads to the State-owned boat launch. Parking is on the left.

*July*

Nestled between two morainal hills, Montauk Mountain to the east and Fort Hill to the west, Fort Pond stretches nearly from bay to ocean across the narrowest section of the Montauk peninsula. It is the second largest freshwater body on Long Island, fed by groundwater seeping in from the morainal hills on each side. It occupies one of two relic glacial meltwater channels found east of Napeague, the second now occupied by Lake Montauk and Ditch Plains. These north–south trending valleys were carved by rivers flowing off the slowly receding glacier. The rivers carried tremendous quantities of sand and gravel southward onto Montauk's outwash plain which is now submerged and part of the continental shelf.

Rising sea levels, eroding bluffs, tidal currents, and littoral drift have all combined over the past 10,000 years to form sand bars across both ends of these meltwater channels. The southern end of the Fort Pond channel became separated from the Atlantic by a sand spit comprised largely of material eroded from the ocean bluffs to the east, while its northern end is separated from Fort Pond Bay by a low bar of material eroded from the Culloden Point bluffs to the east and the Rocky Point bluffs to the west.

Although Montauk is best known for its surfcasting and charter boat fishing, Fort Pond offers some excellent recreational freshwater fishing. State fisheries biologists stocked the pond with Walleye in 1997 and, in a 2001 gillnet survey, 40 were caught with an average length of 14.7 inches. The pond is also home to hybrid Striped Bass, Pickerel, Yellow and White Perch, Bullhead, and Carp, and boasts some big Smallmouth and Largemouth Bass. The deepest hole in the pond, located roughly in the middle of its northern half, measures 27 feet in depth.

Fort Pond, Fort Hill, and Fort Pond Bay are place names that refer to a Montaukett fortification whose exact location is not known. The Montauketts are a Native American tribe who inhabited an area that corresponds roughly to the boundaries of East Hampton Township. Some descendants of the Montauketts still reside here. Many place names reflect this area's long inhabitation by the Montauketts, as do several protected archeological sites, such as the Montaukett burial site at the Fort Hill cemetery and the remains of a Montaukett village at Theodore Roosevelt County Park.

From the launch ramp head southwest. Paddle close to shore to better enjoy the diverse wetland flora growing along the pond's edge, including Arrowwood, Bayberry, and Shadbush shrubs, and clusters of Tussock Sedge and various ferns. The Tussock Sedges' dense, hair-like root systems form tiny islands of cylindrical columns rising as much as a foot above the surrounding water. Interwoven among all these plants, in the form of both a woody shrub and vine, is the ubiquitous Poison Ivy.

Growing furthest out from shore, in several inches of standing water, is a tall, stout sedge whose three-sided stems (triangular in cross section) give rise to the general botanical saying "sedges have edges." Throughout most of the summer, reddish-brown, sharp-tipped spikelets that contain seeds emerge from one point along the stem, several inches below the tip. This is *Scirpus americanus*. Despite being a sedge, it goes by the common names Chair-maker's Rush, Sword-grass, and American Three-square, adding to the confusion of distinguishing among rushes, sedges, and grasses.

Rounding a Phragmites-choked point, paddle into the southernmost cove of the pond bound for Kirk Park and the Second House Museum. The park recently underwent a major replanting effort that replaced aggressive non-native species such as Oriental Bittersweet and Russian Olive with representatives of Montauk's indigenous maritime grassland community.

Second House was once, literally, the second of three houses one came upon when headed east from Amagansett. All three were initially built to house the shepherds and their families who tended the cattle and sheep that grazed on Montauk's common lands. They also provided shelter for travelers and by the mid-1880s had become popular guesthouses.

The use of Montauk as a commons for pasturing dates back to a 1655 agreement with the Montaukett Indians and continued into the early 1900s. Every spring, cattle and sheep were herded from various points in western East Hampton Town to Montauk, a two day journey. Grazing took place for the six months between May 1 and November 1, commencing in a roundup and the return livestock drive.

The shepherds lived in crude huts until 1744, when First House was constructed near what is now the entrance to Hither Hills campground. It burned down in 1909 and all that remains is its brick foundation. Second House was built in 1746 and rebuilt in 1797, while Third House (located in Theodore Roosevelt County Park) was constructed in 1806.

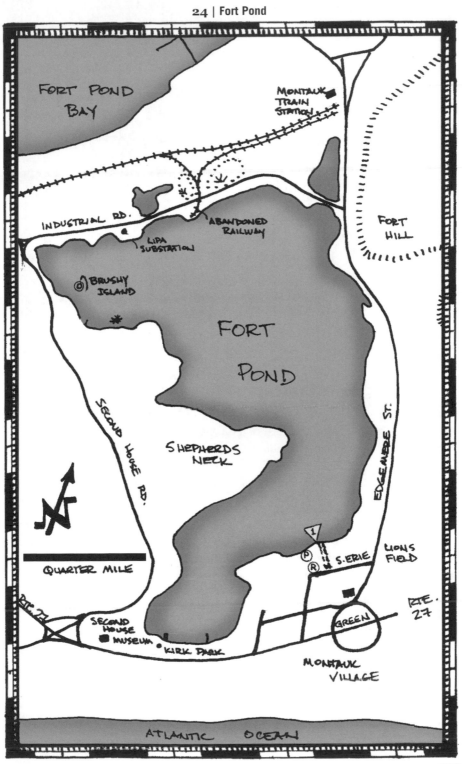

The attractive and controversial grass Phragmites.

Although the ocean is only 300 yards away, it is blocked from view by a line of dunes 15 to 30 feet tall. Excluding the primary dune, the topography between this point on the pond and the ocean rises no more than 10 feet above mean sea level, a precarious situation that was breached in the 1938 hurricane.

Turn north and paddle the west shoreline toward the point of land called Shepherd's Neck. Look for two distinct forms of common aquatic plants en route: Swamp Loosestrife or Water Willow (*Decodon verticillatus*); and Sweet-scented Water Lily (*Nymphaea odorata*). The former is a woody shrub rooted in shallow areas of the pond so that its stem can reach through the water column to the surface where its leaves collected unfiltered sunlight above the water. This type of aquatic plant is called an emergent for obvious reasons. Less obvious is the design of the arching stems. These are able to root at the tip, helping the plant spread quickly and form dense thickets over shallow areas of the pond.

The white-flowered Water Lily uses a different strategy to place its leaves in full sunlight. It uses the natural surface tension of water to support its wide, flat solar collectors. Floating-leaved plants save energy and mass normally put into a rigid stem and can colonize deeper sections of the pond than emergent plants.

Growing along the boulder-strewn shoreline of Shepherd's Neck is Smooth Alder, a small tree well-suited to the water-logged soils found adjacent to streams and lakes. Its multi-trunked growth form resembles Shadbush, also found along the shoreline of Fort Pond, but the two are easily distinguished by their fruit. Alders have a woody cone,

## Phragmites (*Phragmites australis*)

An easily recognizable plant with hollow, bamboo-like stems that can reach over 10 feet in height and are crowned with an attractive plume-like inflorescence, Phragmites is one of the most widespread grasses in the world. It is found on every continent except Antarctica. It is also widespread on the East End; it grows on every waterbody I've paddled. This was not always the case. Well-respected East End naturalist Roy Latham first reported Phragmites growing in Orient in 1900, and on the South Fork in 1920.

Recent research shows that Phragmites grew in the Northeast as many as 3,000 years ago, yet it was not as ubiquitous as it is today. Botanical inventories from the 1800s and early 1900s do not mention Phragmites at sites on Long Island that today have extensive stands of the grass. The appearance and dominance of Phragmites at many East End marshes seems to be a recent phenomenon. What happened?

Botanists have confirmed that this relatively recent surge in growth is attributed to a non-native race and genotype of Phragmites introduced to the metropolitan New York area from outside the U.S. Besides the physical characteristics that distinguish it from our native race, this exotic race is more aggressive in growth and tolerant of a wider range of soil types. Its growth via horizontal stems (rhizomes) is measured in meters, not inches, per year.

Writing about the issue in 1957, Roy Latham's words still ring true today:

> The Phragmites is a beautiful grass greatly admired by people who enjoy the landscape. Most naturalists have a dislike for it. Some detest it as an intruder. The botanist finds little worth searching for within its limits. The collecting entomologist finds it unproductive, difficult to get through to work in. The birdman fares somewhat better, for the thick stands of this reed form shelters for winter sparrows, wrens, and rails.

While Phragmites is a valuable plant in terms of stabilizing shorelines and preventing sediment and pollutants from entering the adjacent waterbodies, natural resource managers are concerned that its spread results in an overall decrease in plant diversity, as well as diversity of fauna dependant on those plants for food and shelter. Much research has focused on methods to eradicate Phragmites, or at least slow its growth, and some techniques (controlling water levels, excavating the plants and their deep root systems, applying herbicides) have been implemented here on the East End. More Phragmites control projects are sure to be implemented in the future, but this hardy plant will continue to be a dominant part of our East End landscape for many years to come.

about the size of an acorn, evident at any time of the year since the cone itself remains long after the tiny seeds have been released.

The northern side of Shepherd's Neck is quite steep and thickly vegetated with shrubs, including a number of Shadbushes. The bold shoreline gradually tapers into a small, shallow cove of emergent grasses, sedges, and rushes. On a sunny day, look for Painted Turtles basking here.

Around the next point, occupied by a day camp, is a beautiful sandy beach. Just beyond the roped-off swim area is a huge piece of granite, a glacial erratic most likely plucked off a New England mountaintop over 10,000 years ago and transported here by the slow-moving glacial ice sheet.

Just west of the rock is the pond's only island. A tangle of roots barely rising above the surface of the pond, Brushy Island is home to a couple of stunted Tupelo trees and other plants tolerant of periodic inundation. A pole topped with an Osprey nesting platform was erected by Jim Cavanagh and myself in 1990. Although it seemed like an excellent location, it has failed to attract any Ospreys. Today the pole and platform support nothing more than a thick growth of Poison Ivy, which is thriving on the island.

Not far north of the pond and Industrial Road is Fort Pond Bay. The original Village of Montauk was located on the low lying beach there until the 1938 hurricane swept most of it away. Much of the beach separating the bay from the pond is less than five feet above mean sea level and riddled with freshwater wetlands, including a large bog that was once the Montaukett's best source of cranberries. The extension of the railroad from Amagansett to Montauk in 1895, and construction of the Montauk Station and railyard, destroyed most of the bog. Many of these wetlands owned by the MTA/LIRR were recently deeded over to the Town of East Hampton for management purposes that may include future restoration work.

With Fort Pond so close to the bay, it seems that there should be an easy portage route to extend the trip into Fort Pond Bay. One possibility is a section of abandoned railway that extends to the edge of the pond. Look for the section of shoreline shored up with large, angular rocks whose sharp-edged features mark them as recent material transported here by man. Our typical rocks arrived here by way of the glacier, a slow travel process that resulted in the rocks' edges getting worn down and rounded en route.

The railway spur arcs north and west to join the main Montauk rail line in the vicinity of the Town's shellfish hatchery. This is worth investigating for a future portage route to the bay. ⋀

# 25 | LAKE MONTAUK

*Montauk, Town of East Hampton*

DISTANCE: 5 miles R/T from South Lake Drive to the inlet.

ACCESS:   1) South Lake Drive: East Hampton Town permit needed. South Lake Drive is off of Rte. 27 1.1 miles east of West Lake Drive.

2) East Lake Drive/unmarked dirt road: East Hampton Town permit needed. Located 0.9 mile from Rte. 27.

3) East Lake Drive/Little Reed Pond Outlet: East Hampton Town permit needed (non-residents can drop boats and park at the Big Reed Pond Nature Trail parking lot 0.1 mile to south). Located 2.0 miles from Rte. 27.

4) Gin Beach: East Hampton Town permit needed. At north end of East Lake Drive. Access harbor at south end of jetty or launch into Block Island Sound and paddle through inlet.

5) West Lake Launch Ramp: East Hampton Town permit needed. Located 2.0 miles from Rte. 27.

6) Star Island Road: Not posted (although owned by East Hampton Town). Located 1.8 miles from Rte. 27.

*November*

Paddling west from South Lake Drive, I come upon the mouth of Crane Creek in a small Phragmites-choked cove adjacent to the Crow's Nest Restaurant. For at least a decade there has been talk of doing a stormwater abatement project here to improve the surface water quality of Lake Montauk. South of Montauk Highway, Crane Creek is a narrow ditch that drains most of the densely developed Ditch Plains area, including road runoff and nutrients from residential septic systems. The ditch can be traced southwestward into Rhinestein Park.

Continuing counterclockwise on the lake I encounter a long finger of land separating Squaw Cove from the rest of the lake. My map lists this as Osborne Island, and a closer inspection reveals that the narrow peninsula is linked to shore by a wedge of salt marsh that is periodically flooded by a spring high tide, at which time the small cluster of shrubs is indeed an island.

Squaw Cove provides a sheltered anchorage for a small fleet of fishing dories. On the south side of Old West Lake Drive is Stepping Stones Pond, a pretty freshwater pond connected to the lake by a culvert. I've heard that before the road was built this pond flowed more freely into the lake and the actual stepping stones that allowed passage across the area are now buried under Old West Lake Drive's pavement.

This corner of Lake Montauk is the most interesting in terms of scenery and natural shoreline. Most of the lake is rimmed by small residential lots, with the northern end chock full of marinas, piers, docks, and restaurants. It seems ironic that the Montauk peninsula has so much preserved open space, but very little on the lake bearing its name.

North of Burying Place Point is a much smaller cove where Peter's Run, another freshwater creek, enters the lake. Its intermittent flow drains the swampland bordering the Montauk Downs Golf Course, whose pyramid-shaped clubhouse is visible on the western horizon.

I have no information regarding the historical significance of Burying Place Point, but several Native American burial sites were accidentally uncovered along Peter's Run in an area since named Gravesend Avenue, a half-mile to the west. There are several other Native American burial grounds in the area. One is located on the west side of the Shagwanac Hills at the end of Pocahontas Lane; the other is at the Fort Hill Cemetery near the Montauk Manor.

The Native Americans who lived in this area were called the Montaukett. I was surprised that I could not find the lake's aboriginal name in any of my references. Most maps drawn up in the 1800s label the lake Great Pond, the exception being an 1879 map of the property of Arthur W. Benson that names it Lake Wyandannee, perhaps in honor of Wyandanch, sachem (leader) of the Montauk in the mid-1600s. If true, it is also quite ironic. Benson was a millionaire sportsman from Brooklyn who purchased the entire Montauk peninsula east of Napeague Harbor for the sum of $151,000 in 1879. He also purchased the rights and claims of the Montauketts to their ancestral lands at Indian Field (now Theodore Roosevelt County Park). Some claim his dealings with the Montaukett were deceitful and unfair.

The acquisitions were key to furthering his plans to develop the peninsula, but Benson's plans for Montauk never materialized. He did succeed in removing the Montaukett from the area, and to ensure they wouldn't try to return, he had their simple wooden homes burned to the ground.

At that time, Lake Montauk had no permanent outlet to the sea. In his book *The South Fork*, Everett Rattray writes that the lake was, "until opened to Block Island Sound by dredging, another lagoon formed by a bar along the Sound-front beach. It was brackish and only occasionally open to salt water, sometimes deliberately. My grandfather and his fellow fishermen would dig a shallow trench along the beach and rig nets across the rapidly widening outflow to catch wagonloads of fish, including, they remembered, eels as thick as your arm." In this sense, Lake Montauk resembled the salt ponds along the South Fork's ocean beaches: Georgica and Sagaponack Ponds and Mecox Bay.

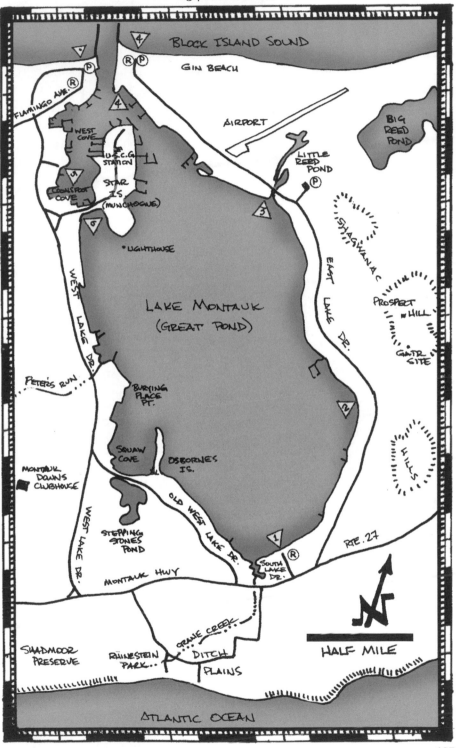

That changed dramatically in 1926 when Benson's holdings were sold to another developer, Carl Fisher, who had played a major role in the development of Miami Beach as a recreational resort and was the founder of the Indianapolis Raceway. Fisher's plan was to create the "Miami Beach of the North" at Montauk.

Many aspects of Fisher's plan were realized over the three years spanning 1926–1929, including the construction of a permanent channel between the lake and sound and a large harbor with access to deep sea fishing. For some odd reason, the dredging prompted Fisher to change the name of Great Pond to Lake Montauk; Montauk Harbor would have been more appropriate.

Ahead is Star Island, once called Munchogue for the type of reeds that grew there and now connected via a narrow causeway to the lake's west shore. Leaving it to

## The American Eel (*Anguilla rostrata*)

The American Eel has a complex and fascinating life history, parts of which are still shrouded in mystery and the subject of ongoing research. It is a catadromous species, meaning that it spends most of its life in inland brackish and fresh water, and migrates to the ocean to spawn.

On the East End, it is a long-term resident of most of the upper brackish and freshwater reaches of our tidal creeks, salt ponds, and freshwater ponds. Moving like snakes, they are capable of overland travel and have been seen making short journeys between freshwater ponds in the Long Pond Greenbelt. Eels are nocturnal, feeding at night on just about any meat, living or dead. By day they rest in bottom sediments. Their small scales are embedded into their skin, giving them a smooth surface that, along with their body shape, makes them well-adapted for burrowing and extremely difficult to grasp. In the autumn of the year they reach sexual maturity, the males (up to two feet in length) and the females (measuring up to five feet long) begin to change their topside colors from green to a silvery gray and develop larger eyes and pectoral fins, all physiological changes for their migration to sea. Over the several months that they swim to their spawning area in the Sargasso Sea, 1,000 miles away, they do not feed.

The spawn takes place in January. Little is known about their spawning behavior, but it is presumed that the adults die soon afterwards. Hatching from eggs laid amidst the floating Sargasso weed, the larvae drift north with the Gulf Stream for a year, metamorphosing into transparent glass Eels at 2.4 inches in length, and later developing pigment to become elvers. At the latter stage, they begin their journey into coastal estuaries where they overwinter. In spring they make their way up tidal creeks in search of suitable brackish and freshwater habitats. There they will reside for 5 to 20 years, growing several feet in length, before making the amazing return trip to the Sargasso Sea to spawn and die.

port, I pass by a replica lighthouse on its south end, then the Montauk Yacht Club (built by Fisher) and the Town docks and the U.S. Coast Guard Station at its northern end.

Fisher also built the Montauk Manor and the tall brick building just north of the Montauk's Village green. The stock market crash of 1929 brought an end to Fisher's Montauk Beach Development Corporation, and the end to his dream of creating the Miami Beach of the North. But his work had long-lasting consequences.

The permanent inlet surely changed some of the ecological characteristics of the lake, but I haven't located any detailed descriptions of the waterbody that predate 1926. Today the lake is known for its abundant shellfish and finfish, and remains one of the best scalloping waters on Long Island. A survey undertaken through the Peconic Estuary Program found healthy underwater meadows of Eelgrass here. It's unlikely that this marine plant thrived here prior to the 1920s.

Today, Montauk also boasts one of the largest and most successful commercial fishing fleets on the eastern seaboard. Coonsfoot Cove and West Cove bristle with boats, piers, docks, and marinas, including some large commercial vessels that you might enjoy viewing from the water. This area can be quite busy with boat traffic. Keep an eye on what's ahead as well as what's coming up astern and stay out of harm's way.

Much of the inlet's dredged material was used as fill for East Lake Drive and resulted in Little Reed Pond becoming even littler. The positioning of the culvert under East Lake Drive was of concern to the baymen not long ago. They feared that Alewives might not be able to negotiate the route up into Little Reed on their annual spring spawning runs.

Paddlers will certainly notice the network of tall wooden poles atop Prospect Hill. These are remnants of an Air Force communication facility (Ground to Air Transmission Radar or GATR site) dating back to the 1950s. As pointed out in the 1992 *Comprehensive Plan for Montauk County Park*, the GATR site is an eyesore on one of the East End's most outstanding scenic overlooks, and situated on County parkland. The publicly-owned area, with a 360° panorama of Montauk, remains gated and off-limits to the public. I recently learned that the hill is being considered for a cellular phone tower. ✕

# 26 | Montauk Peninsula Loop

*Montauk, Town of East Hampton*

DISTANCE:  10-mile loop.

ACCESS:  1) Ditch Plains Road. East Hampton Town permit needed. Located 0.3 mile from the West Lake Road–Rte. 27 intersection. There are three ocean access points here: the Town beach parking area (with restrooms), the East Deck Motel (the west side of the narrow lot), and an unpaved parking area sandwiched between the motel and a trailer park (0.9 mile from Rte. 27).

See the Lake Montauk chapter for access points to the harbor and Block Island Sound. Kayaks can be launched from the beach at Turtle Cove. Surf and current conditions there can be dangerous. Park at the Montauk Point State Park lot and carry to beach via footpath. Launching is currently prohibited from the north side of the State park.

*October*

Tracing the ocean shoreline east from Ditch Plains to Montauk Point, then west along Block Island Sound to the inlet at Lake Montauk, and south through the inlet to the Town park at South Lake Drive, describes a ten-mile-long paddle that is just one mile short of looping back on itself. The paddling route includes six miles of parkland, the tallest ocean bluffs on Long Island, and the historic Montauk lighthouse on the easternmost point of New York State.

The route also includes stretches of challenging open water subject to ocean swells, wind, and strong currents, so a little planning is a good idea. Tidal currents at the Point and along Block Island Sound are the strongest. A flood tide can flush a paddler and boat around the Point and all the way to and through the Lake Montauk inlet. Conversely, an ebb tide, although not providing as strong a push, can propel one through the inlet and east to the Point.

Other trip-planning considerations are winds and surf conditions. Strong wind against tide generates sizeable standing waves at Shagwong Point and North Bar, and big ocean surf can make launching or landing challenging. Depending on your ability, you may find these situations fun or intimidating.

On a late October day, John Todaro and I set out to do the route in nearly ideal conditions. The water is still fairly warm, the surf small, and the air clear, sunny, and still. We launch from the beach at Ditch Plains into knee-high surf and, once clear of

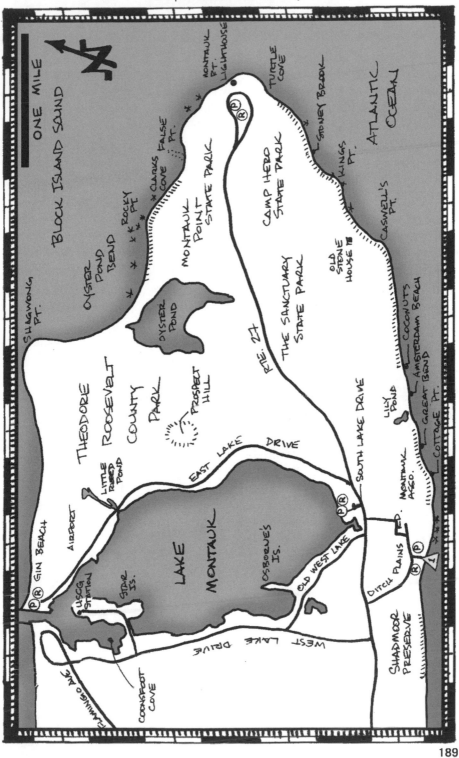

the breaking waves, turn east to follow the shoreline around the Point in a counter-clockwise direction. Our plan is to paddle around to South Lake Drive and jog the mile to Ditch to pick up the car.

Clearing the Ditch Plains jetty that marks one of the most popular surfing spots in Montauk, we pass a construction crew busy working on the very low section of bluff that separates a trailer park from the ocean. With an average annual erosion rate of one foot per year, the trailers are perched precariously close to the surf. Coastal experts have determined that bluff erosion at Montauk stems from a combination of factors that include sea level rise, wave action, and groundwater trapped in clay layers that seeps through the bluff face. Apparently the latter can be somewhat controlled by lining the bluff face with filter cloth, which is what appears to have been installed at the trailer park.

Rounding Cottage Point, the oceanfront bluffs increase in size, tapering in height again east of Great Bend until they disappear altogether at Amsterdam Beach. Landward of Cottage Point, a cluster of distinctive shingled homes are visible over the shrubby Montauk moorland vegetation. This is the historic Montauk Association property acquired by Arthur Benson, and designed and laid out by Frederick Law Olmstead and Sanford White in the 1880s.

Local surfers refer to Great Bend as Cavett's Cove, a reference to the well known entertainer who resides in the Association. There are no surfers here today, but we pass close by two snorkelers spearfishing among the rocks in the clear, calm water.

The modest, white-washed cottages at Amsterdam Beach were once part of another celebrity's estate—the artist Andy Warhol. This setting is unlike anywhere on Long Island's south shore. Much of his wetland-riddled property is now owned by the Nature Conservancy and being managed for rare plants including the federally endangered Sandplain Gerardia (*Agalinis acuta*). The cottages are privately-owned, as are over 100 acres of vacant land to the west and north. The latter is one of the largest vacant parcels in East Hampton. A proposed subdivision of the property is getting careful scrutiny by the Town Planning Board, and several environmental groups are lobbying for its acquisition.

Amsterdam Beach is named for the steamer that went aground and wrecked here in October 1867. Another ship, the schooner Elsie Fay, wrecked on the rocks east of Amsterdam in February 1893, spilling its cargo of coconuts onto the beach and giving rise to the beach's name: The Coconuts. In those days, most everything from shipwrecks was salvaged and put to use, including the coconuts which were collected and eaten.

In striking contrast to the Warhol cottages and Association houses is an industrial-looking residence that looms over the moorland landscape just west of Caswell's Point. Designed by a nationally-renowned architect, the multi-towered structure certainly stands out. I wish it didn't.

The author at Turtle Cove south of the Montauk Point Lighthouse.

Just east of Caswell's Point is the remains of the Stone House, now perched precariously close to the edge of the bluff, and another bluff stabilization project. This one is a combination of filter fabric, wooden terracing, plantings, and a rock revetment at the foot of the bluff where it meets the ocean. This attempt to counteract the natural forces of bluff erosion has been in place for over a decade and may have bought some time for the homeowner. However, one difficult design challenge with these erosion control projects is their beginning and ending points. Where natural bluff meets altered bluff, the altered bluff has shown signs of failure.

Another problem, an aesthetic one, is the loss of the naturally fluted bluff face. This much-photographed bluff feature, called a hoodoo, is the result of different erosion rates for the material which the bluff is made of. Sand wears away faster than pockets of clay. I've heard that a coating of salt spray also plays a role in the irregular sculpting of the bluff.

The bend or cove that the Stone House overlooks is called Lightboat Bend, and its midpoint marks the western boundary of Camp Hero State Park. Straddling the park boundary is the highest point of the ocean bluffs (85 feet). From there, with good visibility, the bluffs of Block Island can be seen 13 miles to the east.

Looming over the parkland is a huge radar tower. Camp Hero was established in 1942 as part of our Coastal Defense System to protect the approaches to New York City and Long Island Sound. The Camp was used for a variety of military purposes, including anti-aircraft artillery training and air traffic surveillance. The latter was aided by the construction of the large radar tower in late 1960, but made obsolete

## Atlantic Silverside (*Menidia menidia*)

Beginning in May, great schools of adult Silversides congregate in the upper reaches of our bays and harbors to spawn. The tiny, spherical eggs adhere to one another, forming lumpy masses, and hatch in as few as eight days depending upon the temperature of the water. At first, the young feed primarily on crustacean zooplankton; over time their diet becomes more omnivorous and includes detritus and algae along with small fish and insects. As adults, they will follow an incoming tide into the salt marsh grasses to feed on the abundant marsh snails found there.

On the other side of the predator–prey balance sheet, Silversides are consumed by terns, herons, cormorants, Skimmers, flounders, and Bluefish, to name a few. But the importance of Silversides in the estuary ecosystem is more than that of a link in the food chain: it is an important link between the highly productive intertidal salt marsh and the deeper, offshore areas of the estuary, including the ocean itself.

Silversides are one of the most abundant of our estuarine fish. Over the course of the summer, the tremendous numbers of developing juveniles convert the energy and productivity of the salt marsh into a huge, mobile biomass. During the fall, these schools move offshore into deeper bay and ocean waters to overwinter. This movement drives the fall run of Bluefish, attracting the attention of winged and two-legged piscivores as well. As such, Silversides play an important ecological role as a net exporter of the salt marsh's summer productivity.

with advances in satellite technology and closed in 1982. The tower and several other structures with historical significance have been incorporated into the park's interpretive trail system.

On the west side of the rocky reef that marks King's Point I stop to dig out my camera and take a few photos. While fiddling with the camera, I realize that there is a significant current pulling me east into the rocks and breaking waves. This surprises me. Longshore or littoral currents along the ocean beach are not tide-driven but wind- and wave-generated, and neither is very evident today.

Once a littoral current is set in motion, it develops its own momentum and can continue for a time after the wind and waves have dissipated. That may be what I am experiencing here, although I wonder if I am close enough to the point to be feeling the pull of the incoming tide this far west. Longtime Montauk surfer Russell Drumm claims that an incoming tide can pull, quite strongly, northeasterly from the excellent surf break on the west side of Turtle Cove.

King's Point is one of a half-dozen rocky promontories on the Montauk coastline east of Ditch that jut out seaward. One might assume that these natural boulder

The Atlantic Silverside is a key link among salt marsh, estuary, and pelagic ecosystems.

fields would protect the bluff areas immediately landward, and result in the rocky points eroding slower than the adjacent shallow coves. But according to the coastal geologists who wrote *Living with Long Island's South Shore*, this is not so. Although the boulder fields break up wave energy, this is offset by the fact that waves focus more of their energy on the shallower bottom contours of promontories than on the deeper water of adjacent coves.

This phenomenon is exploited by surfers. They will launch from shore at the deep part of a cove, where the paddle out through the breakers is easiest, then paddle right or left towards the rocky promontory where the waves peak, and line up for a high energy ride. The bottom line is that the promontories and coves erode and retreat at the same rate, thus maintaining an irregular shoreline, and excellent surf breaks. It also contradicts one of the basic rules of coastal processes: shorelines tend to straighten over time.

An hour after launching at Ditch Plains we turn into Turtle Cove, where a number of fishermen wave hello. Lines are being cast from shore and boats, a surprising number threading through fly rods, in hopes of hooking one of several large fish species that are on the move. This annual ritual defines autumn for many East Enders. The fishermen seek Striped Bass and Bluefish. The predatory gamefish seek schools of Atlantic Silversides and Herring that are now migrating out of the bays and along the ocean shoreline.

An incoming tide pulls us around the point where we cross an imaginary boundary between the Atlantic Ocean and Block Island Sound. On a flood tide the northwesterly current just east of the lighthouse can reach 3.3 knots, close to the speed we had averaged over the 3.5 miles from where we launched. We were very happy to be riding a fair tide here.

On the north side of the lighthouse, we keep a sharp eye out for the large glacial erratics that lie just below the surface a surprising distance from shore. On a day with ocean swells of any size, watch for breaking waves here and at North Bar off False Point. Even a southerly swell will make it around the point and send breaking waves along the Block Island Sound shoreline, although they will lose quite a bit of height as they wrap around the Point.

The shallow bight that marks Clark's Cove was the anchorage and unloading area for lighthouse supplies during the 1800s when shipments were made by coastal schooners. The lighthouse was built in the 1790s, and for the first 50 years the shipments included whale oil to fuel the light. Although far from an ideal harbor, both North Bar and False Point offer some protection from ocean swells, and the bottom contour marking a fathom of water is quite close to the beach, facilitating landing and unloading.

A section of steep bluffs begins on the west side of Clark's Cove and extends into Oyster Pond Bend. Rocky Point is the midpoint of the low bluffs and is marked by a cluster of large pieces of granite, called the Stepping Stones, just offshore from the beach. Quite a few are shaped and positioned in a way that allows seals to haul out on them and bask in the winter sun. In ideal conditions (windless, sunny, low tide) I've counted as many as 35 Harbor Seals adorning these rocks. Most of the seals arrive in this area from the north by December, and we are not surprised to encounter none this trip.

At the sandy beach on Oyster Bend we pull ashore for a break. Protected from a west wind that is starting to blow fairly hard, and offering a beautiful view over Oyster Pond, the narrow beach that separates the pond from the bay makes a great lunch stop. Also taking advantage of the lee here are small flocks of Common Eiders and White-Winged Scoters, newly arrived migrants from nesting areas up north. Another northerner, this one swimming and diving off by itself, lets loose with a series of odd, haunting calls. The intriguing sound conjures up images of canoe tripping in New England and Canada. It is, of course, the Common Loon. Called Mookwa by the Cree, the name translates as "spirit of the northern waters." How fitting!

Oyster Pond fills via small freshwater creeks draining parkland to its east, south, and west: Montauk Point State Park, Camp Hero State Park, the Sanctuary Preserve, and Theodore Roosevelt County Park. Every so often, naturally and without a helping hand from man, storm waves and/or high pond water levels cut a channel through the beach, draining a portion of its brackish and fresh waters at low tide and getting a shot of salty seawater on an incoming tide. The low salinity of this coastal pond is perfect for Oysters, and they grow prolifically here. You might consider portaging into the pond and exploring this remote gem before continuing west.

Back in the boats, we hug the low coastal bluffs of Theodore Roosevelt County Park for some protection from the westerly wind that has now formed white caps on the bay. Not far ahead is Shagwong Point and a tide rip that can generate sizeable breaking waves. Wind is working against tide when we arrive, and John swings wide around the point to avoid the worst of the steep-sided waves. He'll also get a stronger push from the flood tide further from shore.

I cut the corner closer to shore and begin paddling westward into the teeth of a more than 15-knot wind, holding a direct line on the Lake Montauk inlet. Despite the wind and white-caps, we cover the two-mile length of Gin Beach in good time. Soon we are paddling through the busy inlet, staying close to the rock jetty and out of the way of the many fishing boats entering and exiting the harbor.

Lake Montauk is an important fishing port, and most of the action is at its north end. As we proceed south we pass docks and large commercial boats on either side, as well as a number of waterfront restaurants that would make a nice dinner stop. Also here, on the north end of Star Island, is the U.S. Coast Guard station.

Further south, just past Star Island, we have the lake pretty much to ourselves. En route to our take-out at South Lake Drive we pull alongside a bayman's dory. He is working from the boat with a bull clam rake, and is clearly frustrated with changes in the lake over the last two decades that have hurt his livelihood. He gives us an abbreviated and intense discourse on the loss of scallops, changes in fishing regulations, the loss of underwater land for clamming, waterfront development, mosquito spraying, and even changes in attitudes towards baymen by newcomers.

While there are a lot of unanswered questions, it is easy to see why the man feels under siege from all quarters. The bayman has been part of the local waterfront scene here for many years, and will hopefully survive in some shape or form in the future. ✕

# IV | THE ISLANDS

# 27 | COECLES HARBOR'S MARINE WATER TRAIL

*Shelter Island*

DISTANCE: 5 miles R/T.

ACCESS: 1) Burns Road: No permit needed. From the South Ferry, take Rte. 114 north to the first intersection (a rotary). Go straight through the rotary onto Cartwright Road, continue for 0.8 mile and turn right onto Burns Road. Park at end. Pick up a map at the water trail kiosk there and launch from the wooden ramp.

*September*

Situated on the northeast corner of Shelter Island, Coecles Harbor is a large embayment measuring two miles in length and over a half-mile in width. Connected to the harbor are several small tidal creeks and picturesque coves worth exploring. Separating the harbor from Gardiners Bay are Ram and Little Ram Islands, interesting landforms that form the bulk of its northern shoreline. No longer true islands, Ram and Little Ram are mounds of glacial deposits now connected to each other as well as to the mainland of Shelter Island by sand formations called tombolos.

I had explored the Ram and Little Ram Island side of the harbor years ago, so on this visit I decide to paddle along the harbor's southern edge. This would enable me to check out the interpretive water trail there. Jay Damuk of Shelter Island Kayak Tours, who helped organize the water trail, informed me that the trail began at the Burns Road launch ramp, so that's where I head.

Off to one side where the road meets the ramp is a small, attractive kiosk providing information about the water trail and maps for paddlers to take along with them. Armed with map and binoculars, I set off in a southwesterly direction for Foxen Point. Along the way are two interpretive stations, each marked by numbered white and green buoys corresponding to various aspects of the history and ecology of the route as described in the water trail brochure.

I've been told that the interpretive water trail was the brainchild of Nature Conservancy Board Member Jim Jordan. The Nature Conservancy, Town of Shelter Island, and Shelter Island Kayak Tours worked together to make this interesting idea a reality. Not unlike terrestrial nature trails, the goals of the water trail are to educate, foster an appreciation for the natural world, and encourage good stewardship. I believe this is the first interpretive water trail on the East End.

Most of Foxen Point and the north arm of Congdon Creek was acquired and protected by the New York State Department of Environmental Conservation in the 1970s. The water trail guide instructs you to paddle from Foxen Point directly over to Foxen Creek. I suggest you make a detour first. Turn west and paddle Foxen Point's southern shoreline deep into the north arm of Congdon Creek. It's as pretty a stretch of shoreline as you'll find anywhere on the harbor.

Just west of an Osprey nesting tower near the point is a huge piece of pink granite, a glacial erratic, split in two. At high tide you can paddle right through the narrow crack separating the two pieces of rock, one of which has a small Marsh Elder shrub growing precariously atop it. A bit further west is an old Eastern Red Cedar whose branches are quite bare. It appears that the edge of the low bluff it sits on has eroded away, exposing and damaging its root system. Only a few tufts of evergreen needles remain, revealing a smooth, silver-gray, beautiful trunk.

A small hummock of cedars and oaks owned by the Nature Conservancy protects the Creek's largest expanse of salt marsh on the hummock's landward side. The tall Cordgrass (*Spartina alterniflora*) is decked out with yellowish seeds, each slightly smaller than a rice grain. These will drift with the tidal currents and perhaps establish a new patch of salt marsh elsewhere in the estuary.

Circling back towards Fox (not Foxen) Point, I pass by another Osprey nest, this one constructed in an Eastern Red Cedar snag. A closer look reveals that the snag is not completely natural. Someone has added several branches in order to make a more secure and enticing nesting platform. Apparently it worked. However, I've been told that this year's clutch was predated on by Raccoons.

Skirting around the tip of Fox Point, I head into the southern arm of Congdon Creek for a look at the commercial fishing fleet. At the west end of the Creek is the Town Dock. A number of large fishing and sailing vessels are berthed here, and paddlers should be aware that these boats may not be able to maneuver outside the boat channel. Stay alert and out of the way.

At the Town Dock, I about-face and head east to rejoin the water trail. Nearly all of Coecles Harbor's southern shoreline, over two miles in length from Town Dock to Sungic Point, is owned and managed by the Nature Conservancy. This is part of the Mashomack Preserve, a 2,000-acre mosaic of fresh and marine wetlands, fields, and forests that comprises one quarter of the total land mass of Shelter Island. It makes for great touring by canoe or kayak.

At water trail buoy #4, which marks the entrance to Foxen Creek, I turn in for another worthwhile side excursion. At its extreme south end where the creek's waters are well protected from the wind, huge schools of small baitfish (under three inches in length) put on a spectacular synchronized swimming exhibition. Easily observed in the clear water of late September, they move slowly in tight formation beneath my boat. Suddenly they scatter in all directions, some choosing to dart straight up to the surface and into the air to avoid hungry predators. Every so often

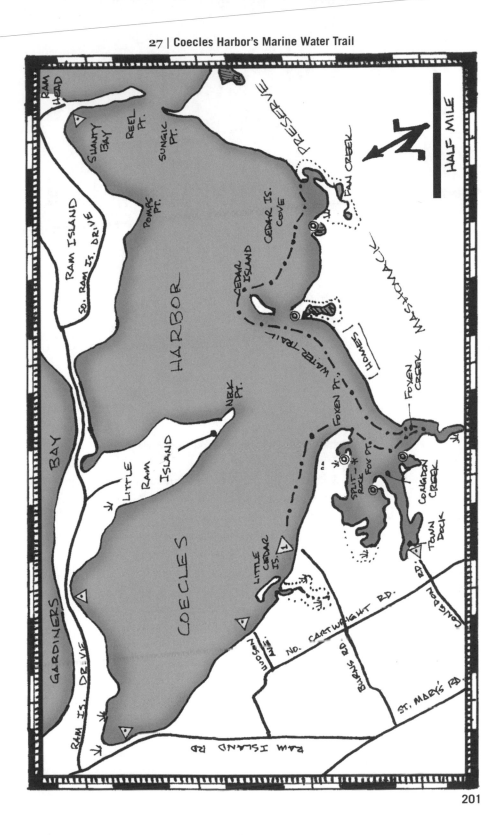

The tombolo at Jessup Neck, Morton National Wildlife Refuge.

the predator, most likely a small Bluefish, also bursts out of the water in hot pursuit of its airborne prey.

Back in the main part of the harbor, the water trail continues east past some docks and clusters of houses that were constructed before Mashomack Preserve was established by the Nature Conservancy. At the next point, opposite Cedar Island, there is a pretty salt pond that I am able to poke into on the incoming tide. The narrow inlet is very shallow and barely navigable. Stalking the shallows for food here are a Great Blue Heron and two Snowy Egrets, while several Greater Yellowlegs work the landward edge of the marsh and the exposed mudflats. Speaking of mudflats, be careful to avoid getting stranded in this shallow pond on a dropping tide. The walk to the harbor, although short, would be a messy affair.

Cedar Island, deeded to the Town of Shelter Island by its last owner, Gregory Taylor, is a nice place to go ashore to stretch your legs or have a picnic. Be aware that on a spring low tide this island is temporarily connected to the nearby point by a tombolo. If headed further east, you may have to paddle around the island's north side.

The furthest and finest section of the water trail is Fan Creek. From a distance, the creek's entrance is not easy to pick out but it can't be missed if you approach by paddling close along the shoreline of Cedar Island Cove. Once inside, the narrow creek and its thin ribbon of salt marsh wind their way into the inland forest of Mashomack

## Tombolos

"Tombolo," stemming from the Latin for burial mound, is a lovely Italian word used by geologists to refer to a sand beach or bar connecting an island with the mainland or other islands. There are many examples of tombolos on the East End: the sandy isthmus connecting Jessup Neck to Noyac, the Ram Island causeway on Shelter Island, Long Beach, connecting North Haven and Noyac, and the beach linking Little Hog Neck with the rest of the North Fork are just a few. One of the largest tombolos on the South Fork is Napeague, the five-mile-long sandy stretch connecting Montauk and Amagansett.

Tombolos are composed of material eroded from both the island and mainland it now links. Once washed into the sea, the material is transported by wind and tide-generated shoreline currents to form sandy spits at either end. Once the spit grows long enough to span the distance between two islands, or an island and the mainland, it is referred to as a tombolo.

The movement of sand doesn't stop with the formation of the tombolo. Erosion, transport (called littoral drift), and deposition is fairly constant. The only variable here is the rate of change: rapid and dramatic with a nor'easter, slow and subtle with our prevailing southwesterlies.

In many cases, one side of the tombolo is more protected from wind-driven waves than the other, resulting in quite different plant communities on each side. Exposure to frequent storm waves inhibits growth of intertidal vegetation, and a barren but beautiful beach backed by dunes will form. The more protected side can support the growth of Cordgrass, and a salt marsh will develop. In this way, tombolos are miniature versions of our oceanfront barrier beaches.

Earth science writer Andrew Alden notes:

> Tombolos are temporary things, mostly because the islands don't last long. The sea makes quick work of them, geologically speaking, wearing them down to the waterline in a few thousand years. Then the tombolo loses its protection and disappears.

Preserve. Here I encounter thousands of Salt-marsh Snails (*Melampus bidentatus*) seeking refuge from the incoming tide by climbing tall stalks of Cordgrass. Although quite conspicuous clinging to the narrow blades of grass during or near high tide, they appear to be absent in many of the salt marshes out here. This is the first place I've seen these small, air-breathing gastropods on the water trail today.

Tucked far up the creek at water trail station #13, surrounded by a picturesque salt marsh, I turn to the trail brochure and read: "#13 End of the Line, Beginning of the Food Web." Time to return home. ✕

# 28 | WEST NECK CREEK

*Town of Shelter Island*

DISTANCE: 4 miles R/T. The trip can be extended another 4 miles by including West Neck Harbor, Dickerson Creek and Menantic Creek.

ACCESS: There are seven access points on West Neck Creek, and another five on West Neck Harbor and Menantic Creek. Two are described here.

1) Wades Beach: Town of Shelter Island permit needed. This is a pretty spot with rest rooms, picnic tables, barbecue grills, lots of parking and a beautiful sandy beach for launching. To reach it from the South Ferry, follow Rte. 114 (Ferry Road) for 0.75 mile and turn left onto Midway Road. Follow the signs to Wades Beach.

2) Daniel Lord Road: No permit needed. From South Ferry, follow Rte. 114 for 1.9 miles and turn left onto Smith Street. Go to end and turn right onto Menantic Road. Daniel Lord Road is on the left.

---

*October*

Although pleasant summer-like weather continued into the middle of this October, and winter seemed very far away, we received a brief reality check over Columbus Day weekend. A cold front pushed the mild, warm air out to sea and replaced it with a more seasonally appropriate air mass of Canadian origin. Cool and dry, it was as crisp and tart as a freshly picked apple. Well, I thought at the time, there it goes. Summer is really over. As if to emphasize the point, the wind blew hard out of the northwest, adding a significant wind chill factor into the mix.

The wind is our main concern as Deb Reed and I set out for a late afternoon paddle on Shelter Island. We decide to take a double kayak instead of the more comfortable canoe, as the former sits much lower in the water and is less affected by the wind. Our destination is West Neck Creek, a narrow waterway tucked in the southwest corner of Shelter Island with good protection from a northwesterly blow over most of its length.

Driving up to the South Ferry terminal, a quick glance at the wind driven waves erases any idea of paddling over from North Haven. Although the crossing to Shelter Island is a short, 10-minute paddle, and the entrance to West Neck Harbor only another 20 or so, today it would be a wet and wild one. We opt to take the ferry and launch into a more sheltered stretch of water.

Taking an indirect route to the access point at the end of Daniel Lord Road, we enjoy some beautiful late-afternoon views over Dickerson and Menantic Creeks, and

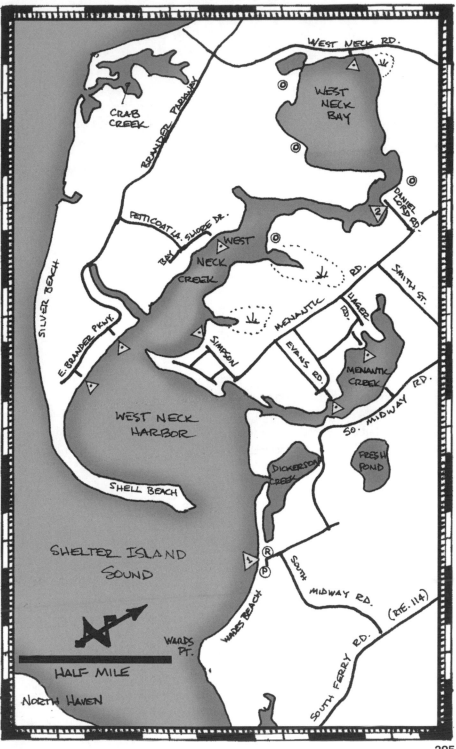

WEST NECK RD.

CRAB CREEK

BRANDER PARKWAY

WEST NECK BAY

PETTICOAT LA. SHORE DR.

DANIEL LORD RD.

2

BAY

WEST NECK CREEK

SILVER BEACH

MENANTIC RD.

SMITH ST.

WAGER RD.

E. BRANDER PKWY.

SIMPSON

EVANS RD.

MENANTIC CREEK

WEST NECK HARBOR

SO. MIDWAY RD.

FRESH POND

SHELL BEACH

DICKERSON CREEK

SHELTER ISLAND SOUND

1

R

P

South

MIDWAY RD.

WARDS BEACH

(RTE. 114)

HALF MILE

WARDS PT.

SOUTH FERRY RD.

NORTH HAVEN

over a picturesque horse pasture on Smith Street. Shelter Island still has that special, undefinable feel that belies its location a stone's throw from the Hamptons. Yet we note that the lack of a bridge has not kept the residential building boom at bay.

Finally on the water, we set off to explore West Neck Bay first. The bay, a circular pond less than a half-mile in diameter, is the headwaters of West Neck Creek. Both creek and bay have depths in excess of 10 feet spanning their entire length, allowing fairly large boats to navigate their waters. This aspect of the waterway was exploited early on in Shelter Island's history, as described in Everett Rattray's *The South Fork*:

> Shelter Island's Quakers traded too; vessels carried timber and dried cod to the West Indies, returning with rum and salt, and some good-sized hulls were built in some unlikely places on their island, as on the banks of narrow West Neck Creek, a tidal stream winding in from Peconic Bay a mile and more northward into a deep circular pond, making a perfect anchorage then and now.

Today, West Neck Creek's "unlikely place" reputation refers to its being a hot spot for brown tide algal blooms. Despite the number of years and talented scientists devoted to this mysterious and devastating phenomenon, aspects of this event remain frustratingly unclear.

While the bay's size and limited fetch keep waves to a minimum, there is little in the way of protection from the wind until we reach the lee near West Neck Road. Cormorants, Black-backed Gulls, and Herring Gulls are resting on pilings here, keeping a nervous eye on us as we paddle by.

Turning into a narrow opening in the salt marsh, we paddle into a small cove with a sandy beach and picnic area. This, we learn, is privately owned and restricted to residents of the Harborview Acres neighborhood. The sun, now quite low in the sky, illuminates a patch of Saltwort, or Salicornia, and a small clump of Salt Marsh Asters. Both add a splash of color to the various shades of green in the marsh. The former shines in its brilliant autumn color, a deep crimson-red, while the aster's splash of color, a pale-purple, is the product of its late-blooming flowers.

Back out in the main part of the bay, we paddle back towards the creek, making good time with the brisk tailwind, noting a few Osprey nesting structures en route. Passing my truck and our starting point, we hug the creek's east shoreline and poke around the two small coves (unnamed as far as I know) that reach east towards Menantic Road. Both are quite pretty with a large expanse of salt marsh set against a backdrop of forest. Great Blue Herons take flight as soon as we clear the narrows at the entrance to each cove. The snags in these quiet nooks probably serve as overnight roosting areas for the herons, whose wingspans dwarf those of the gulls.

We set off to explore one more cove that nearly touches Brander Parkway and appears to have been dredged and bulkheaded. Crossing to the west side of the creek to enter this narrow cove, the wind manages to pick the water droplets off the raised blade of the paddle and place them in my lap with amazing precision. Funny how that works!

By the time we are back out on West Neck Creek, twilight has given way to night and darkness is upon us. We set out for Daniel Lord Road, a mile away and, as I have often found whether paddling, cross country skiing, or sailing at night, it is difficult to judge one's distance and speed. That, and the fact that I am in good company enjoying a beautiful star-lit night, results in our paddling right by the take-out before realizing where we are. ✕

## Great Blue Heron (*Ardea herodias*)

Readers who have managed to plod through all the trip descriptions in this book may have noticed the frequency with which I've reported seeing Great Blue Herons. There are several reasons for this, one of which, obviously, is that this bird is quite common on the waters of the East End. Another is that it is such a large, striking, and hard to overlook animal. And a third reason is that I never tire of seeing this awesome creature on the water.

Standing four feet tall, with a wingspan of six feet, the Great Blue Heron is quite a sight to behold as it takes flight from the edge of the salt marsh. If you are lucky, you will be treated to one or more of its hoarse calls before it disappears. I first heard its "FRAAAAHNK!" croak one evening while setting anchor in a cove on the coast of Maine, and thought I was in the company of some sort of prehistoric creature.

Like the other herons and egrets found on the East End, the Great Blue stalks shallow waters for anything it can grab with a lightening quick flick of its long neck and spear-like bill. Fish, frogs, crabs, and even rodents have been known to disappear down its gullet.

Great Blue Herons form colonies, called rookeries, in which they build stick nests in the tops of trees. The rookeries I have visited up north were in beaver ponds, with the nests constructed in snags near the middle of the pond. The last rookery documented on Long Island was at Gardiners Island in 1900. They nest north of here in Connecticut and Rhode Island, and west of here in Westchester County and New Jersey. Why they do not nest anywhere on the East End, where there appears to be suitable habitat, is a mystery to me.

Another mystery is how this bird survives the winter here. It can be found on the East End throughout the year, but its numbers are highest here during the winter months. Ironically, this is when the bulk of its prey (small fish and crustaceans) is buried in the marsh muds or overwintering in the deep water of the bays and ocean, well out of reach. On several mid-winter paddles, I have followed its tracks along the bottom of a shallow tidal creek that shows no signs of marine life. It must not be easy, as evidenced by the number of Great Blue Heron carcasses that are reported by winter's end.

# 29 | SHELTER ISLAND CIRCUMNAVIGATION

*Town of Shelter Island*

DISTANCE: 17 miles.

ACCESS: The following access points are keyed to the accompanying map:

A) Shelter Island:

1) Thompson Road
2) Seagull Lane
3) North Silver Beach
4) Bootleggers Alley
5) Rocky Point Road
6) Crescent Beach
7) Carousel Lane
8) Orient Lane
9) Dawn Lane
10) Ram Island Drive

B) South Fork:

11) Rte. 114/North Haven: Limited parking area on left (west) side of road. No permit needed. Launch from sandy beach west of the ferry slips, and stay well clear of the ferries.

C) North Fork:

12) Greenport Train Station: No permit needed. From Greenport's central business district, head west on Rte. 25/Front Street. Turn left on 4th Street. Cross railroad tracks and make next left into parking area and drive to far end. Although bulkheaded, there is a sandy beach that is suitable for launching.

NOTES: This long paddle can become a really long paddle if you don't factor in tidal currents when planning this trip. According to Eldridge's *Tide and Pilot Book*, ebb and flood currents off Jennings and Paradise Points run 1.5 knots, while those between North Haven and Shelter Island (in the vicinity of the South Ferry) can reach 2.5 knots. Considering that most canoes and kayaks average 2–3 knots, these currents are formidable. Although you can avoid bucking the worst of a foul current by hugging the shoreline, its best to plan your trip to take maximum advantage of a fair tide, or at least to minimize paddling against a foul tide.

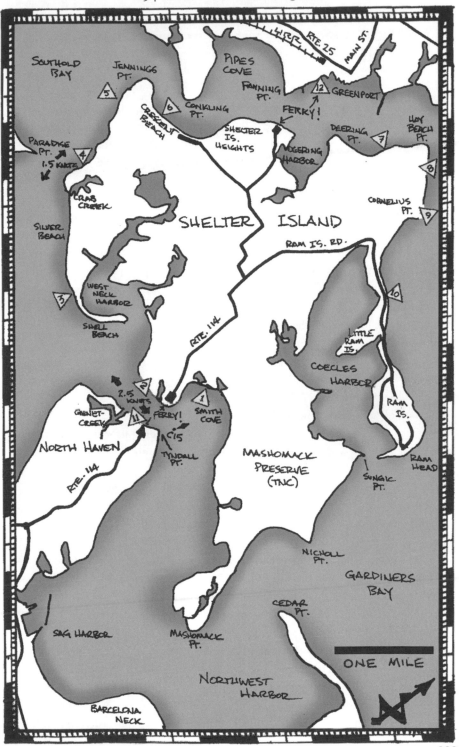

*November*

Paddling with Russ Tillman is always an adventure but, so far, this early November outing around Shelter Island is going quite smoothly. Riding an incoming tide, we have covered the first seven miles of the journey quicker than we thought possible, and pull our boats up on the beach near Crab Creek for a rest, a bite to eat, and to wait for the ebb tide.

Our trip planner, Russ had checked the tide table and calculated that our best bet would be to launch from the Little Ram Island causeway and head northwest, making a counter-clockwise circumnavigation. "If we depart at 11:00 A.M.," he explained with the chart laid out before us, "we can ride a favorable flood tide to the narrows between Paradise Point and Crab Creek, reaching it just when the tide changes, and then ride a favorable ebb tide through Shelter Island Sound and around Mashomack Point. With a one-to-two-knot boost from the current, we'll have no problem covering the distance in five or six hours, wind permitting." Sounded like a good plan.

It is a perfect day, with an insignificant breath of wind out of the north. Finding a nice stretch of sandy beach to load and launch our boats, we shove off: Rob Battenfeld in a newly purchased fiberglass Current Design Solstice sea kayak, Ron D'Allessandro and Russ in a We-No-Nah racing canoe, and Judy Cooper and myself in an Old Town Discovery canoe. Paddling a short distance out into Gardiners Bay, we turn left and head northwesterly along the tombolo connecting Little Ram Island to the bulk of Shelter Island.

Rounding Cornelius Point, there is a perceptible pull on our boats as the flood tide squeezes through the narrows created by it and Long Beach Point (marked by the lighthouse known as Bug Light, visible a mile to the northeast across this western edge of Gardiners Bay). Turning southwestward at Hay Beach Point, the light northerly wind combined with the accelerating tidal current shoots us effortlessly past the Greenport waterfront, quiet this late in the year, and the nearly vacant Deering Harbor. We pause momentarily to give one of the North Ferry boats wide berth before continuing on through its wake and abeam of Pipes Cove, off to starboard.

Closer by, to port, are the steep bluffs of Shelter Island Heights. Towering 180 feet above our small craft, the elevation of these kames seem to be magnified by several steep, unvegetated sections bordering the water. At the south end of the Heights, the bold shoreline transforms into a long, flat, and very attractive sandy beach called Crescent Beach, spanning three quarters of a mile in length to Jennings Point.

Perched at the far end of the strand is the Pridwin Inn, a popular destination for paddling friends during the summer months. We would meet after work at the launch area on Rte. 114 in North Haven (at the South Ferry terminal), and paddle to the Pridwin's all-you-can-eat barbecue dinner. With the long summer days, the five-mile paddle was easy to complete in daylight. After gorging ourselves with food and drink and enjoying the sunset over the North Fork, we would make the return trip by moonlight, starlight or under the cover of darkness. A fun outing!

Too early to stop, we paddle close to the outer bend that gives Crescent Beach its name and where the tidal current would be strongest. This area of the waterway, right up to Jennings Point, has the feel of deep water, and the chart soundings back that up: 80 to 90 feet of water depth.

Approaching Jennings Point, the water takes on characteristics of a big river with huge glacial erratics scattered about near the shore, strong eddy lines, and some wild-looking boils. Canoes and kayak are swept around the point and propelled towards Southold Bay before the current diminishes somewhat. We adjust our course to a southerly heading and set our sights on the next point of land near Crab Creek.

The narrows between Crab Creek and Paradise Point marks an interesting phenomenon. This is where the flood tide travelling between the North Fork and Shelter Island meets the flood tide travelling between the South Fork and Shelter Island. We had hoped to hit this point at high tide, a point when the flood tide we rode in on peters out and the ebb, which would carry us south and west around Mashomack Point, begins to flow.

As we paddle into an opposing current, it is obvious that we are a bit early. We know that we can make fairly good time against the tide by hugging Silver Beach, which we have done many times en route to and from the Pridwin. But I calculate that we have covered seven miles in under two hours, and of the remaining ten miles of paddling we are confident that we will be riding a fair tide in the form of a two-knot current over most of the next leg—the seven and a half miles through Shelter Island Sound, around Mashomack Point, and out into Gardiners Bay.

The trip now looks like a piece of cake. Over the objections of Russ, who views every paddling trip as a physical workout and never likes to stop, I suggest we go ashore for some food and rest and wait for the ebb to set in. Russ is unanimously overruled, and the first mistake of the trip is set in place.

With lunch eaten and the ebb tide beginning to flow, we no longer have an excuse to lounge on the beach. We are also getting cold. The effort of paddling has kept the November chill at bay, and hidden the fact that the temperature has been steadily dropping. Eager to warm up, we set off at a brisk pace, westward bound along the sandy shoreline of Silver Beach.

Tides, the vertical rise and fall of the water column, can create substantial horizontal tidal currents through narrows and over shoals. Tide and current, working in concert with wind-generated waves, do remarkable things over time. One is rearranging huge amounts of sand. As someone who loves to pore over maps and charts, and spend time sailing, surfing, and paddling, I am fascinated by the complex, dynamic nature of littoral processes.

Beyond Silver Beach and past a stretch of bulkheaded shoreline and docks, we come abreast of a good example of a deposition site: Shell Beach. How do you explain the presence of this long, narrow hook of sand reaching from west to east across West Neck Harbor? This coastal barrier beach, as well as the long spit directly across the water on North Haven separating Genet's Creek from Shelter Island Sound, seem to indicate a net transport of sand from west to east.

Perhaps wind is the overriding factor here. Our prevailing southwesterly wind may be driving the net littoral drift on the north side of the Sound, sculpting a gentle arc of beach which is expanding northeasterly. Over on North Haven, in the lee of the prevailing southwest wind, the development of the Genet Creek barrier beach may be driven by northwesterlies: our strongest (albeit less frequent) winds. But even these theories lead to more questions than answers. For example, why hasn't a spit developed on the west side of Smith Cove, which seems to have a similar exposure to tide, current, and wind as West Neck Harbor?

The interrelationships between wind and tide are complex ones, made even more so by the capricious nature of storms. Gradual but steady shoreline changes over the years may be completely reversed by a major storm, wiping out a decade's worth of sand accretion overnight, or reestablishing a beach at the foot of what had always been considered an eroding bluff. This can confound even astute professionals of coastal geology. More than once, I've heard their conclusions debunked by baymen who, relying on decades of daily observations in lieu of aerial photographs and sediment samples, have raised some valid counter points.

Everett Rattray's book *The South Fork* offers some hard-to-believe historical insights on this topic. As we are being swept along the passage between Shelter Island and North Haven, in 40 feet of water, I think of Rattray's claim that this channel could have been waded by horses 300 years ago. He also mentions Manhansack Island, located somewhere between Sag Harbor and Mashomack Point. Today, no such island can be found on the chart.

Within sight of the South Ferry crossing, we're making close to four knots over the ground, the result of the synergy of paddle and tidal forces. The ferries deal with the strong currents here by steering a course well upcurrent when leaving the slip, then using the current to angle gradually down toward the landing. The resulting course is a huge arc; to a first time passenger, it must appear as if the Captain has left the wheel.

Paddling close by C15 off Tyndall Point, we cut across open water for a direct line to Mashomack Point. The point, and the land mass east of Smith Cove, are all part of the 2,000-acre Mashomack Preserve. Comprising one quarter of the entire island of Shelter Island, the preserve was acquired by the Nature Conservancy in 1980. In addition to tidal creeks and marshes, swamps and ponds, meadows and woodlands, this beautiful preserve has 10 miles of coastline. Our "as the crow flies" course from the South Ferry has not taken full advantage of this wild stretch of waterfront, so we steer closer to land as we approach Mashomack Point, and hug the preserve's eastern shoreline all the way to Nicholl Point.

Mashomack, once home of the Manhasett Indians, translates as "where they go by boat," so this is certainly an appropriate way to view the preserve. Although it is now late afternoon, none of our party is in a hurry to finish. It seems as if our cars are just around the bend, and we slow the pace markedly to enjoy our incredible surroundings. Both the wind and the water are calm and quiet as we pause to listen to the mournful wail of a nearby Common Loon and take some photos. At the water's edge, a young Raccoon is sorting through the flotsam and jetsam left by the receding tide, completely unperturbed by our approach. In contrast, a White-tailed doe dressed in her drab gray-brown winter coat disappears quickly and quietly into the adjacent forest. Making our way slowly northward along Gibson Beach in this tranquil setting, each of us is lost in our own thoughts. Mine includes, "Why rush?"

Turning the corner at Nicholl Point, a very brisk northwest wind breaks the spell. We are going to have to really work for these last three and a half miles of the trip. Not only is the wind against us, but the fair ebb tide that has propelled us around Nicholl Point is now an foul ebb tide pushing us away from the entrance to Coecles Harbor. Hugging the shore, we manage to get some protection from the wind and tide and make Sungic Point without too much trouble. But what we see ahead is not a pretty scene.

The wind is whipping up white caps inside the harbor. Imagining the conditions outside Ram Head, Judy and I opt for the inside passage. Russ is dead set on completing the trip as planned. I can just see him thinking, "Well, it's not really a circumnavigation if we cut off Ram Island!" Momentarily tempted to argue this technical point, I give in to a sense of urgency to get moving. We'll debate this matter later over a beer. It seems the wind has increased in just the few minutes we huddle at Sungic Point. Russ convinces his canoe and business partner, Ron, to paddle the outside route. Meanwhile, Rob has donned his spray skirt and seems keen to test the seaworthiness of his new sea kayak in the wind and waves. Off they go.

I'll take a foul tide over head winds in a canoe any day. Paddling into Coecles, we have both. After clearing the narrow entrance, Judy and I head for the south side of Ram Island, hoping it will provide a slight break from the full force of the wind. Not only is there absolutely no relief from the wind, but the slot between Little Ram Island and Ram Island seems to create a wind tunnel. The only hints of a lee are the finger piers and docks. We dodge behind these to rest before poking out from the

## Common and Red-Throated Loon (*Gavia immer*) and (*Gavia stellata*)

I was pleasantly surprised to see, and hear, Common Loons on my first paddles in Gardiners Bay many years ago. Among the repertoire of its wild vocalizations is an eerie wail that is probably the origin of the Loon's Cree Indian name, "Mookwa," which translates as "Spirit of the Northern Waters." For myself, this handsome bird evokes memories of canoe tripping in northern Maine and Canada, and its company on the waterways of the East End was very welcome.

Both Red-throated and Common Loons are found here in fairly large numbers during the winter months, with several East End bird counts registering them in the hundreds. Much smaller numbers of Common Loons stay through the summer months, mostly in the outer bays such as Gardiners and Block Island Sound. These are one and two-year-olds that are not ready to breed and nest.

Loons are perhaps the strongest underwater swimmers of any bird found in this area. Known as the Great Diver in Britain, it can reach depths of 600 feet and remain underwater for 40 seconds. Unlike most birds' bones that are hollow as a weight-saving design for flight, Loon bones are solid, the extra weight being an advantage for diving. One of its features that maximizes swimming efficiency—its large, webbed feet positioned as far aft as possible—is a liability on land: it cannot stand and walk. Like a fish out of water, the Loon must resort to pushing itself around on its chest and belly.

seaward end and paddling furiously for the next one. Leap-frogging from dock to dock, we are finally within sight of the causeway, soaked and completely exhausted.

Unbeknownst to us, our painfully slow progress is being watched by a couple from their living room window. Seeing us literally inching our way along, they run outside to meet us when we tuck into the lee of their dock. "Where are you two headed?" they shout over the roaring wind. Judy points ahead and I yell, "Our car is parked on the causeway!" "Well, come ashore, we'll drive you over there."

We had stubbornly plodded on thinking we had no option but to continue; now that one is being offered, we are ashore in a flash. Five minutes later, huddled in front of a wood fire with a cup of hot tea in hand, the wet and wild Coecles Harbor paddle already seems like a distant memory.

The rest of our party, Ron, Rob, and Russ, also becomes a distant memory. For a while anyway. Enjoying some island hospitality from our hosts, the Demerests, and drying the last patches of wet clothing before the fire, we eventually wonder how the rest of the crew is faring. As we learn later, although Judy and I had a very difficult finish ON the water, the others had a very difficult finish IN the water!

Hundreds of Common and Red-throated Loons overwinter on the East End.
This beached loon may be suffering from lead poisoning, a common affliction
from ingesting lead fishing sinkers.

That's right. Not wanting to scratch their brand new, beloved boats in the surf-strewn rock garden just off the causeway, all hands had jumped overboard into the cool November water. I'll bet that was Russell's idea. Shielding their precious boats from the glacial erratics with their bodies, they had scrambled through the surf and slippery boulders. Cold and drenched from head to toe, they had made it to dry land still holding onto their gleaming, scratch-free craft. Serves them right, I thought, for buying such expensive boats. So ended the paddle around Shelter Island, "the island sheltered by islands." I guess that phrase doesn't really apply to Ram Island. ✗

# 30 | ROBINS ISLAND

DISTANCE:  From the South Fork access point, the trip around Robins Island is 7 miles R/T. It is a 5.5-mile R/T paddle from the North Fork.

ACCESS:  1) North Sea Road: No permit needed. From Rte. 27 near Southampton Village turn north onto North Sea Road and follow it for 4.2 miles (avoid the right turn onto Noyac Road) to a dead end on Little Peconic Bay.

2) New Suffolk Beach: Southold Town permit required. From Rte. 25 in Cutchogue turn south on New Suffolk Road (10.3 miles east of Rte. 105). Travel 1.6 miles from Rte. 25, turn left onto Jackson St. and continue to end. Park is on the right.

NOTES:  The entire island, including the intertidal zone, is privately owned. Do not plan on being able to land and get out of your boats.

Strong tidal currents, up to 2.4 knots, develop in the North and South Race. When combined with an opposing wind, rough seas can form.

---

*Circumnavigating the "Jewel of the Peconics"*

Forming a natural boundary between Great Peconic Bay and Little Peconic Bay, Robins Island makes an excellent destination for experienced paddlers. Since it is privately owned and off-limits to visitors, the 435-acre island referred by many as the "Jewel of the Peconics" is best explored by slowly cruising along its shoreline in a shallow draft boat. A canoe or kayak is ideally suited for the trip.

A circumnavigation of the island can be done from either the South Fork or the North Fork, with the latter offering a shorter and more protected crossing. The South Fork route involves a nearly mile-long open water crossing each way to and from Cow Neck.

The position of Robins Island between the two forks causes it to act as a poorly-fitting plug that restricts tidal flow between Little and Great Peconic Bays. This, in turn, results in swift currents off the island's north and south points, labeled the North Race and South Race on charts. While neither Race gets the type of wild sea conditions sometimes found in The Race between Long Island Sound and Block Island Sound, a tide against wind situation there can be challenging for inexperienced paddlers and canoeists.

Wind, tide, equipment, and abilities should be carefully considered in planning this trip. If conditions look questionable at the start, there are plenty of protected

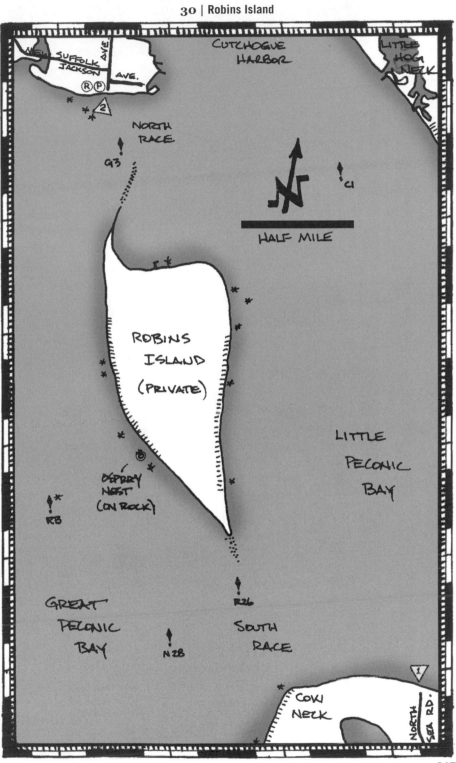

waterways to paddle nearby. The Scallop Pond–Sebonac Creek estuary and North Sea Harbor on the South Fork and the tidal creeks emptying into Cutchogue Harbor on the North Fork are great alternative areas to explore.

*The Eldridge Tide and Pilot Book* lists a maximum current in the South Race of 2.4 knots. You wouldn't want to paddle against that, and you shouldn't have to do so. The worst of the current is a fairly restricted area directly in line with the southern point of Robins Island and the point at Cow Neck. At a short distance to either side of that line, the current greatly diminishes.

From North Sea Road on a flood tide, paddle on a course directly for the south end of Robins Island to take advantage of the current. On an ebb tide, you have two choices. Paddling west close up against the Cow Neck shoreline before starting the crossing puts you directly in the South Race perpendicular to the current and requires an adjustment for getting set to the east. The other option is to paddle a northerly course out into Little Peconic Bay well east of the South Race, and turn west once you're clear of the current and can take advantage of the big eddy off the southeast side of the island.

Once across, be aware that even the island's intertidal zone is privately owned and there is no public access or landing permitted. The long sandy spits at either end of the island may be inhabited by nesting shorebirds. The material that forms these beaches started out in the sandy bluffs on the island's east and west sides. Over time, waves have pulled portions of the bluff into the sea and tidal and wind-driven currents have redeposited the sand on the island's tips. This process continues today and results in a gradual reconfiguration of the island's outline.

Look for the small holes near the top of the 50-foot-high bluffs that mark the nesting cavities of bank swallows and note the interesting patterns of sedimentation in the bluff face. Robins Island is a recessional moraine deposit, meaning it is comprised of material left behind by a glacier that was melting and retreating northward. The island, as well as Shelter Island, Gardiners Island, Little Hog Neck, and Great Hog Neck, were all formed at the same time in this manner.

The glacier also left behind some large rocks, called glacial erratics, and a huge one supports an Osprey nest just off the island's west side. Near the island's north point, the sand spit encloses a small pond. There are several small ponds and wetlands on the island, and some are host to rare species and unusual specimens. A species listed as "endangered" in New York State, the Eastern Mud Turtle, was discovered here in 1994. Subsequent field work by biologist Norm Soule determined that the island hosted the largest population of Mud Turtles in the state.

A Poison Sumac measuring nearly three feet in circumference and an unusually large American Elder are also found in the wetlands. The former has been designated a New York Champion tree, the largest of its kind in the State. The island's Native American name, Anchannock, translates as "land well wooded" or "place full of timber," which implies that it may have been home to many other large trees long ago. As with most of the East End, the island was completely cleared many years ago and today is covered with second growth.

The island's future, and even its ownership, was hotly disputed in the 1980s. Several development plans were put forth and discussed, while groups unsuccessfully lobbied for public acquisition and preservation. In 1994 the island was acquired by Louise Moore Bacon and, working with the Nature Conservancy, a management plan was drawn up. The plan includes a conservation easement over several environmentally significant areas, limits construction to already disturbed areas, and prohibits future subdivision.

Mr. Bacon has also worked with professionals to develop an ecological restoration plan for the island, and much of that work has been completed. It appears that the partnership between the Nature conservancy and landowner has been a successful one, and it may ensure that the island remains the "Jewel of the Peconics" well into the future. ✕

## What Is East End Sand Made Of?

Our East End shoreline is comprised of two very different materials: partially decayed plant matter in the form of peat, and sand. The former is limited to areas protected from wave action where salt marsh grasses can develop. The latter makes up the bulk of our coastline, including our spectacular ocean beaches.

Sand grains are minerals that have been broken down from rock over many years and several different physical and chemical processes. Our beach sands are very light-colored, reflecting the predominance of the light-colored, glass-like mineral quartz, which accounts for 90% of our sand. Quartz, a very hard and nearly indestructible material, is the principal mineral of the earth's crust, and the main component of granite. Granite is the most common rock in the New England mountains, an area that the last glaciers scoured and scraped, transporting rock and sand south to form the terminal moraine later called Long Island.

A close look at the sand on our beaches reveals a number of other colors. The light tan mineral is feldspar, purple is garnet, mica sparkles like tiny pieces of a mirror, and the greenish-black grains are hornblende. A small magnet is useful to separate out the tiny black grains of magnetite that resemble the filings in the game "etch-a-sketch."

Each of these minerals has its own density. A strong steady wind can remove the lighter minerals, such as quartz, leaving behind some interesting and pretty purple-and-black patterns on the beach made by the heavier minerals magnetite and garnet.

# 31 | CARTWRIGHT ISLAND

DISTANCE: 3.5 miles R/T including circumnavigating the island.

ACCESS: 1) Barnes Hole Road: East Hampton Town Permit needed. From Rte. 27 east of Amagansett Village, turn north onto Abrahams Landing Road, cross the LIRR tracks and turn left onto Old Stone Highway. Barnes Hole Road is 1.5 miles on the right. Continue to end.

2) Louse Point: East Hampton Town Permit needed. From Rte. 27 east of Amagansett Village, turn north onto Abrahams Landing Rd., cross the LIRR tracks and turn left onto Old Stone Highway to Louse Point Rd. (2.4 miles). Turn right. Boat ramp and parking are at 3.1 miles.

*July*

Cartwright Island, named for B.C. Cartwright who established the first Menhaden fish processing factory at the Promised Land in 1872, is the southernmost of a chain of tiny unnamed islands that form a seven-mile-long archipelago off the southern tip of Gardiners Island. At high tide, much of the archipelago disappears entirely. With the ebb, shoals formerly awash and barely navigable by kayak are transformed into a broken chain of sand and pebble beaches.

The see-saw action of tides pushing water back and forth between Napeague and Gardiners Bays creates strong currents, standing waves, and eddies. Small channels bisecting the shoals, and the tiny islands themselves, are constantly changing and shifting with time. Big storms may overtop an island, removing its sparse plant cover, or temporarily wipe out the island itself. It is a wonderful a place to explore in a canoe or kayak.

Barnes Hole and Louse Point are the closest launching sites for a paddle over to Cartwright Island. Although the one-and-a-half-mile passage can be made in a half-hour by kayak, don't let that fact lull you into going off unprepared. Since it is an open water crossing, a few things should be considered. Be sure to get an up-to-date weather forecast. The one-and-a-half-mile stretch of water between Cartwright Island and your point of return is a significant amount of fetch that is capable of building a formidable sea.

Even with a good forecast, be prepared for a sea breeze on the return trip. This is a local weather phenomenon that builds in the afternoons and may not be in the weather forecast. It is a southwesterly wind that is often much stronger than a breeze. Finally, keep in mind that the tidal currents move roughly north and south, perpen-

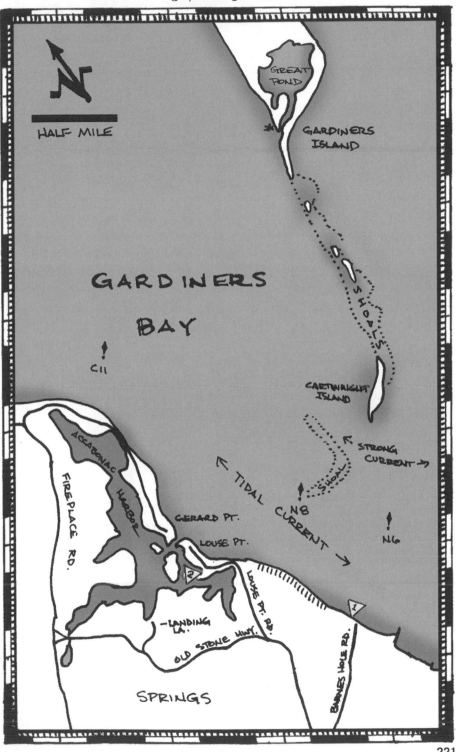

dicular to your direction of travel, so adjust your course accordingly. Eldridge lists the maximum current at 0.4 knots in this general area, but the slot of deep water just off the southern tip of Cartwright moves a lot faster than that.

Cartwright Island can be difficult to locate on the horizon from the low vantage point of a kayak. Try locating it from a high point of land on the beach before launching, and use one of the string of six navigational buoys marking the deepest channel between Gardiners Bay and Napeague Bay as an aid. N6 lines up well on a course from Barnes Hole Road, and N8 is useful in navigating from Louse Point. The latter buoy also marks the western edge of a large crescent-shaped shoal. (Once, returning from Cartwright by the light of a full moon, I paddled into an area of small breaking waves in the middle of Gardiners Bay. Momentarily disoriented, I realized that I had paddled over the shoals near N8 at the low end of a spring tide cycle.)

On this paddle over from Barnes Hole Road, the set of an incoming tide becomes more pronounced as we approach the island's south point, sweeping us past a small flock of Double-crested Cormorants stretching their wings towards the late afternoon sun. In the lee of the southwesterly breeze, we paddle the calm flat waters along the island's north side. There, out of the grip of the tidal current, the bay bottom drops quick and steep from shore to 14 feet of water.

Drifting along the sandy shoreline, we watch a scene reminiscent of Alfred Hitchcock's *The Birds*. The island, as well as the sky above it, is filled with hundreds of screaming terns. An endless stream of the noisy birds circles in for a landing, most with small silvery fish in their pointed beaks, as another endless stream of empty-beaked terns departs. Ashore, successful fish-catchers are mobbed by one or two aggressive young terns who, although now capable of flight, still rely on daily handouts from Mom and Dad. We are also aware of something that even Hitchcock couldn't have replicated on film: the strong aroma emanating from a colony of fish-eaters.

Due in part to its remote location—free of four-legged predators and four-wheeled vehicles—and the rich fishery resources close at hand, this sparsely vegetated island is an attractive and productive summer home for a large collection of shorebirds including Common Terns, Least Terns, Roseate Terns, Black Skimmers, and American Oystercatcher.

It wasn't always so. Author Everett Rattray offers an interesting historical perspective of the island in his book *The South Fork*. Prior to gaining its current name, the island was one of several Ram Islands found on the East End, in reference to the fact that these small islands, "at least at certain seasons and most especially with gruff rams, rampageous hogs, and bellowing bulls… made suitable lockups for the lust-maddened creatures." Those kind of neighbors would have sent the birds elsewhere.

Having spent much of my free time over the past 15 years paddling canoes, kayaks, and surfboards along the coast here, I am well aware of coastal processes and

Black Skimmers employ a very unusual fishing technique.

## Black Skimmer (*Rynchops niger*)

Skimmers have one of the most interesting bills, and hunting techniques, of any bird I'm familiar with. What appears at a distance to be a thick, sturdy bill is quite the opposite. The Skimmer's lower mandible is longer than the upper and paper-thin, providing minimal drag as it slices through the water for prey. Unlike other birds, the lower mandible is fixed to the skull, a design that makes it rigid and prevents it from being wrenched off as it skims, and the upper is movable, enabling it to snap shut and trap a fish felt by the lower. To compensate for the wear and tear of skimming, the lower mandible grows at roughly twice the rate as the upper.

Skimmers rarely see their fish prey. Since they hunt by feel and not by sight, Skimmers are not limited to fishing during daylight hours. In fact, I encounter them most often at dusk and rarely see them fishing in daylight. With this unusual fishing technique they can take advantage of the daily vertical movement of fish and greater numbers found near the surface during the night.

the dynamic nature of our littoral zone. Yet I was shocked to read that this tenuous silver of land once had a cattail marsh!

Rattray describes the island during his younger years as being dotted with three-to-four-foot-high piles of twigs and rubbish, the ground nests of the fish-hawk or Osprey. Later, for a couple years during World War II, "there were sand pyramids bulldozed up over the Osprey nests on Cartwright, targets for the machine guns, rockets, and bombs of steel-blue Grumman fighters…"

Another kind of invasion was taking place during World War II: the expansion of the Great Black-Backed Gull's nesting range southward into New York. It's southernmost breeding location in 1921 was Nova Scotia. In July of 1942, local naturalist LeRoy Wilcox banded the first young hatchlings on Long Island at a nest on Cartwright Island. Forty-three years later, in 1985, a survey limited to Long Island's south shore beaches and offshore islands found 6,948 nesting pairs.

Turning away from the island, we watch a pair of large, long-winged birds gracefully flying in tandem just inches over the water. Every so often they reach down and drag their odd, orange-and-black bills through the water's surface. One of my companions thinks it may be a young-of-the-year and its parent, the latter sharing its unorthodox fishing technique with its offspring. These unusual-looking birds are Black Skimmers, and we realize there is a large colony of them nesting in the center of the island.

Black Skimmers, along with most of the island's other nesting birds, are monitored as part of the intensive, annual *Colonial Waterbird and Piping Plover Survey* of nesting sites on Long Island. While the feisty rams and destructive bombers are gone, the island's ecological integrity is now jeopardized by those who are likely to love it to death. "Ignorance is bliss" aptly describes the boater who, several years ago, set up a campsite on the island in the middle of nesting season. I sailed by a scene I could not believe: cooler, tent, lounge chair, roaring bonfire, and excited dog running amok in the nesting area.

Kayakers and canoeists can be part of the problem or, as knowledgeable and responsible stewards, part of the solution. The choice is ours. Cartwright makes a great destination for a paddling trip, but please take only photographs and leave nothing but your wake. *This is private property.* ✕

# 32 | GARDINERS ISLAND

*Springs, Town of East Hampton*

DISTANCE:  A circumnavigation of the island from any of several Gardiners Bay launch sites in Springs is 16 miles.

ACCESS:  1) Fireplace Road: East Hampton Town permit needed. From Rte. 27 in East Hampton Village, turn north onto North Main Street (there's a windmill at this intersection), go under the train trestle, straight ahead at the traffic light and make your next right onto Springs–Fireplace Road (0.6 mile from Rte. 27). Continue to dead end on Gardiners Bay (6.6 miles from Rte. 27).

2) Louse Point Road: East Hampton Town permit needed. From Rte. 27 east of Amagansett Village, turn north onto Abrahams Landing Rd., cross the LIRR tracks and turn left onto Old Stone Highway to Louse Point Rd. (2.4 miles). Turn right. Boat ramp and parking are at 3.1 miles.

3) Barnes Hole Road: East Hampton Town permit needed. From Rte. 27 east of Amagansett Village, turn north onto Abrahams Landing Road, cross the LIRR tracks and turn left onto Old Stone Highway. Barnes Hole Road is 1.5 miles further, on the right. Continue to end.

NOTES:  Gardiners Island, including its intertidal zone, is privately owned. Landing anywhere on the island is prohibited.

*October*

Gardiners Island is simply an amazing place. I don't think it has an equal anywhere on the eastern seaboard. Ospreys nest here in greater numbers than anywhere else on Long Island. Many types of shorebirds, including some rare species, nest on the island's sandy spits. Wild turkeys forage in oak woodlands that some claim to be old growth forest. Seals congregate among the rocks off its eastern shore. And, as late as 1930, Bald Eagles nested there. If the eagle were to return to nest in the Long Island area, my bet is that it would choose a site on Gardiners Island.

The island's history matches its rich and interesting flora and fauna. Its Native American name, Manchonak, translates as "island of the dead," a reference to an incidence of distemper or yellow fever that killed those residing on the island. It was uninhabited in 1639 when Lion Gardiner purchased it from Wyandanch, the leader, or Sachem, of the Montauketts. Captain Kidd visited the island in 1699. Legend has it that he buried treasure there. The 3,000-acre island has remained in the Gardiner family to this day, in many ways unchanged over the past 350 years. It is a timeless relic on a much changed, and still quickly changing, East End of Long Island.

It is a clear autumn day in 1989 when I first set out to explore the island's shoreline. We are a crew of seven in three canoes. Our plan is to launch from Louse Point and set an easterly course for Cartwright Island, a tiny sliver of sand at the southern end of a string of shoals and sand bars connected to Gardiners Island. This would be the shortest distance across Gardiners Bay, a mile-long open water crossing. From there we would work our way north along the shoals to Gardiners Island itself.

A few in our party—Rick Whalen, Judy Cooper, and myself—have briefly set foot on the secluded island at the invitation of one of the family owners. George Velmachos is familiar with some of the island's coastline from various fishing excursions in the vicinity. I am not sure if Kurt Billing, who hails from North Sea, has ever been on or near the island, but he is always game for an adventure. The rest of the crew, Kurt's longtime friend Jay Huber and Jay's girlfriend Nancy Hand, have never heard of the place. Nor is it clear they have ever paddled a canoe before.

As we carry boats down to the water and prepare to leave, I learn that Nancy is the daughter of one of my mother's best friends—quite a coincidence. I also learn that this is Jay and Nancy's first date. That, in my experience, is a proven recipe for disaster. With that in mind, I make sure Nancy and Jay have an experienced paddler in the stern of their canoe before we set out.

The wind is light out of the northwest, perfect for the time being but forecasted to increase in strength later in the day. We'd have to keep an eye on that, especially for the return crossing. The crossing of Gardiners Bay is absolutely delightful. We paddle in a close convoy, enabling all seven of us to converse and banter. Along the way we encounter a group of Common Loons, most likely recent arrivals from their nesting grounds further north, which treat us to a delightful chorus of calls and stir up memories of paddling adventures in Maine and Quebec.

An incoming tide pushes us north so that we reach the section of shoals roughly halfway between Cartwright Island and Great Pond. Turning left, we head northeasterly and hug the west edge of the barely exposed sandy spit that, at high tide, is punctured with ever-changing navigable breaks connecting Napeague and Gardiners Bays. To the west lies a wide shelf of shallows, much of it less than 10 feet deep, over which loose flocks of diving ducks and other sea birds quietly bob and dive. Along with the loons, we note Long-tailed Ducks, Red-breasted Mergansers, Double-crested Cormorants, and Scoters in the mix.

In his book *The South Fork*, Everett T. Rattray refers to this area as The Shoals, a place that, "must have been one of the world's great feeding grounds for sea ducks....On or in the bottom grow the clams, mussels, periwinkles, moon snails, slipper shells (quarterdecks, "deckuhs" to the Bonacker) which comprise the diet of the sea ducks, divers one and all."

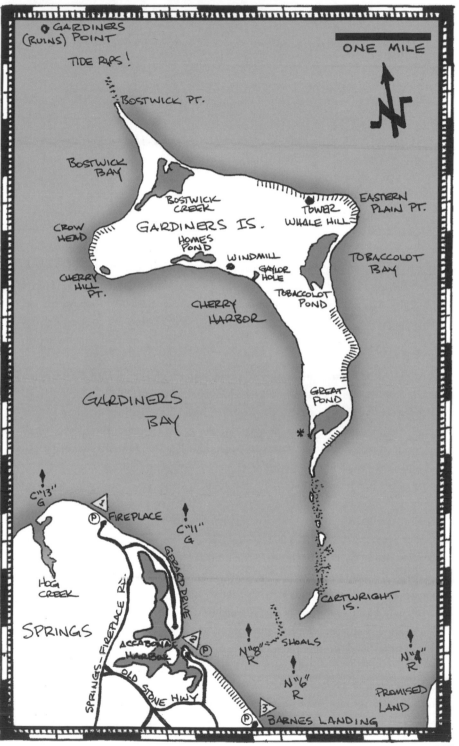

GARDINERS
(RUINS) POINT

TIDE RIPS!

ONE MILE

BOSTWICK PT.

BOSTWICK
BAY

BOSTWICK
CREEK

GARDINERS IS.

TOWER
WHALE HILL

EASTERN
PLAIN PT.

CROW
HEAD

HOMES
POND

WINDMILL

GAYLOR
HOLE

TOBACCOLOT
BAY

CHERRY
HILL
PT.

TOBACCOLOT
POND

CHERRY
HARBOR

GARDINERS
BAY

GREAT
POND

C"13"
G

FIREPLACE

C"11"
G

HOG
CREEK

SPRINGS

CARTWRIGHT
IS.

GERARD DRIVE

SPRINGS-FIREPLACE RD.

ACCABONAC
HARBOR

OLD STONE HWY

N"8"
R

SHOALS

N"6"
R

N"4"
R

PROMISED
LAND

BARNES LANDING

227

Describing a day of stringing for coots at The Shoals 60 years ago, he continues:

> This is a lonely place… greenish water, blue sky, a little yellow sand in the offing on Ram Island or Cartwright proper, and in those days, the fish-hawk nests, piles of twigs and rubbish three or four feet high but looming taller in the horizontal seascape. The hills of Gardiner's Island, brown in gunning season, are too far away to impose.

Some aspects of that scene have changed over the years. The numbers of diving birds have diminished, Cartwright Island's Osprey nests are gone, and the island has succumbed to tide and storms that have redistributed much of its sands over the sub-tidal portions of The Shoals. Yet Rattray's wonderful description of a lonely place of greenish water, blue sky, and a little yellow sand in a horizontal seascape still rings true.

At the huge glacial erratic which acts as a natural buoy marking the entrance to Great Pond, we turn into its narrow inlet and enjoy riding the swifts of an incoming tide. Great Blue Herons, Great Egrets, and the smaller, black-legged, yellow-footed Snowy Egret stand like sentries, tall and immobile, as we pass by. Reaching the far, eastern end of the pond, we are pleasantly surprised to find a new channel cut through the narrow barrier beach, and slide our canoes over the shallows into Napeague Bay.

In the lee of low sandy bluffs, we raft up for a snack and discussion. We've made good time and discuss the idea of continuing on up the eastern side of the island, toward Tobaccolot Bay. Earlier in the summer I had accompanied bayman Calvin Lester as he made his rounds checking lobster pots scattered about that small embayment. It was a beautiful stretch of water, and one that I wanted to revisit. All hands agree and we paddle on.

In the small bay just east of a simple grass landing strip and wind sock that serves as the island's airport, we weave through a rock garden of glacial erratics—some of which, in another two months, will be adorned with basking seals. The shoreline here is a steep, sandy bluff, 20 to 30 feet high. With a long fetch in the easterly quadrant, waves driven by nor'easters erode the bluffs and power a littoral conveyor belt that delivers the sand south to the shoals and spits we paddled by earlier in the day.

Abeam of Tobaccolot Pond, the bluff ends, but a low continuous dune ridge unfortunately blocks our view of the largest body of freshwater on the island. The shoreline bluffs reappear at Eastern Plain Point, this time rising dramatically to over 60 feet in height and forming the seaward flank of Whale Hill. A tower perched precariously atop the bluff here once provided an excellent lookout for ships and spouting whales; today it is home to a pair of nesting Barn Owls.

Approaching the north end of the island, the tall bluffs gradually taper until, abreast of Bostwick Creek, we feel the full strength of the northwest wind, now much stronger as forecasted. It is late afternoon, and time for another decision: turn around or continue around the island? A quick look at the chart reveals that turning around at this point is the longer of the two choices. But no one likes the look of the long, upwind paddle that lies ahead.

The chart also reveals that a paddle across Bostwick Creek would shave a full two miles off our return trip. Technically, that means a portage across private property, but the portage is a mere 100 feet across a bare, sandy beach. The carry would take no more than a few minutes, and we didn't count on being challenged in October.

We were. The moment our canoes hit the beach a truck pulls up and a no-non-sense character, apparently the Gardiners Island caretaker, informs us that we are on private property. "Please, couldn't we just carry our boats across the beach?" I plead, "We'll be gone in a minute." A largely one-way discussion ensues. I point out that we only want to paddle across Bostwick Creek and repeat the short portage on the west side into Bostwick Bay. Trespassing, true, but an ever-so-slight transgression that could surely be overlooked.

"Nope," is the firm reply to each of my points, including the weather, our route, the time of day, and the extra paddling and time required to clear the northern spit of Gardiners Island. In the end a disappointed and tired crew picks up their paddles and points their canoes towards Bostwick Point, a mile to windward.

Racing a setting sun, we paddle hard into a brisk wind off our port bow. Thankful that the low sand spit is protecting us from the stormy sea if not the wind, Rick Whalen points out something else we should be thankful for: the blizzard of 1888. That storm created a permanent breach between Gardiners Point and Bostwick Creek, establishing a new point (Bostwick), a new island (Gardiners Point) and, more importantly at that moment, saves us two miles of paddling.

Finally rounding Bostwick Point, with the wind and waves slightly abaft our beam, we make good time across Bostwick Bay towards Cherry Hill Point, and surf, paddle, and sail the final three-mile leg to our landing at Fireplace Road. Although we miss exploring the four-mile stretch of shoreline between Cherry Hill Point and Great Pond, there are no complaints among the crew for taking a shortcut back to the Springs.

Darkness has set in by the time we step ashore, and the tired and cold crew look forward to a hot shower and dinner. The parting words from Nancy and Jay are, "Well, that was interesting but I don't think I'll do it again!" Yet, something clicked on that first date. They are now happily married with four kids. ✕

To many, the Osprey is simply an awesome bird to watch. To some, it is also a harbinger of spring. Among those with a more intimate knowledge of its recent history and fate, the Osprey is a symbol of much more. Based on 14 years of studying and working with our South Fork Ospreys, I offer the following lessons learned from this interesting bird:

## Lesson #1: The Interconnectedness of Things

In the 1940s, the breeding population of Ospreys along the coast between New York and Boston was estimated at 2,000, or 1,000 active nests. In 1969, that same population had plummeted to 300 birds, or 150 active nests. Even more worrisome were the numbers of young produced from those nests. An intensive study on Gardiners Island in 1966 revealed that among its 60 active nests only 4 young were produced. What had happened?

This decline in numbers and productivity correlated with the spraying of the pesticide DDT in our salt marshes, which began in 1945. While highly effective in its purpose of killing mosquitoes, DDT accumulated in the tissues of small fish, such as Mummichogs, that fed on mosquito larvae, and in the tissues of larger fish that preyed on Mummichogs, eventually finding its way into the tissues of animals at the very top of the food chain, including the Osprey.

## Lesson #2: Biomagnification

At each higher level in the food chain, DDT became more and more concentrated in the fatty tissues to the point where, in 1948, it began to affect the reproductive success of the Osprey. Apparently, at certain concentrations in the its tissue, DDT inhibited the female's ability to produce normal egg shells; the shells were too thin to support the weight of the incubating parents.

A study of an estuary near Long Island Sound measured the dramatic change in the concentration of DDT among the different levels in the estuarine food chain. An initial dosage of DDT in the estuarine water of 0.000003 parts per million (ppm) registered 0.04 ppm in zooplankton, 0.5 ppm in Mummichogs, 2 ppm in Needle Fish, and 25 ppm in Ospreys. This process, called biomagnification, resulted in a concentration of DDT in Ospreys that was *10 million* times more than that of the estuarine waters into which the DDT was sprayed.

## Lesson #3: Science, Politics and the Chemical Industry

By the mid-1960s, scientific evidence pointed to DDT as the cause of low reproductive rates in Ospreys and other birds of prey. This information, combined with rising human health concerns, the publication of Rachel Carson's classic work *Silent Spring* (1962) and, ironically, increasing insect resistance to the pesticide, resulted in its prohibition.

DDT use was banned in New York State in 1971, and in the rest of the United States the following year. DDT continues to be used in other countries, especially third world countries where malaria is prevalent. Debates regarding its use in saving human lives versus its environmental impacts still rage today. And recently, criticism has been leveled at the validity of the original scientific research that correlated DDT use with a decline in Osprey productivity.

## Lesson #4: The Resilience of Nature

It took a decade after DDT was banned, but through the 1980s and 1990s, Ospreys showed a slow but steady recovery. Young birds from the East End were used to reintroduce Ospreys to areas formerly occupied before the DDT-induced population crash. Encouraging? Yes! But here is a sobering note: our current Osprey population figures for all of Long Island are equal to the pre-DDT (1930) population for Gardiners Island alone.

There is still much work to be done, including habitat protection through public acquisition and open space planning, restoring water quality and degraded marshes, reestablishing wetland buffer areas and Eelgrass beds, and undoing the ecological damage of the grid-like pattern of mosquito ditches.

## Lesson #5: Ignorance is Bliss

Many waterfront property owners would love an Osprey pole to call their own, and over the years I have been asked to assess many residential sites for one. In an unfortunately large number of cases, I find a huge, overbuilt house and pool with all the energy-sucking amenities, landscaping designed to least resemble our East End environment, and an emerald green lawn sloping down to the bay.

All these lifestyle choices are somehow rationalized as quality of life necessities, yet the connections to overconsumption and good stewardship are somehow ignored. Of course, these homeowners don't spread the cocktail of insecticides, fungicides, herbicides, and fertilizers over their manicured lawn; they pay someone else to do it.

# 33 | GARDINERS POINT (THE RUINS)

*Springs, Town of East Hampton*

DISTANCE: 10 miles R/T from Springs; 8 miles R/T from Orient.

ACCESS: 1) Fireplace Road: East Hampton Town permit needed. From Rte. 27 in East Hampton Village, turn north onto North Main Street (there's a windmill at this intersection), go under the train trestle, straight ahead at the traffic light and make your next right onto Springs–Fireplace Road (0.6 mile from Rte. 27). Continue to dead end on Gardiners Bay (6.6 miles from Rte. 27).

2) Orient Point: No permit needed. Follow Rte. 25 to its eastern end 8 miles east of Greenport. Bear right after the Cross Sound Ferry office and follow the road to the parking area on the left. Launch on the gravel beach to the left (and stay well clear of the ferry docking area.)

NOTES: Do not plan to land on Gardiners Point. It is an important bird nesting area. Do not disturb the colony during nesting months (April through July). Landing on the island is prohibited at all times. The route from Orient is subject to more tidal current. Try to take advantage of an ebb tide on the paddle out, and a flood on the return.

*August*

Concerns about our later-than-planned departure and the tide rips off Bostwick Point (the north end of Gardiners Island) disappear as quickly as the Springs shoreline once we fall into the rhythm of paddling. An Osprey circles nearby, dives with a great splash, comes up empty-taloned and quickly repeats the process. Soon after the second splash it is airborne again, this time with a large fish in its feet. Seems like a good omen if one believes in such things.

Conditions are perfect. A moderate southerly wind is helping us along towards our destination five and a half miles to the north. This sea breeze will likely fade as the sun drops lower in the western sky and we begin the return trip. And the late-afternoon, clear blue sky holds promise for a spectacular sunset and moon rise later in the evening. If all goes well, we will not be far from my truck at the north end of Fireplace Road when the sun dips below the horizon.

From the low vantage points of our kayaks, our destination is nowhere visible on the northern horizon, so we decide on a course for the west side of Gardiners Island, specifically the bold, sandy bluff near Cherry Hill Point known as Crow Head. Not far off to port is Crow Shoals, its western edge marked by buoy R14. I am surprised to hear that stumps are visible there at extreme low tides, evidence it was once *terra*

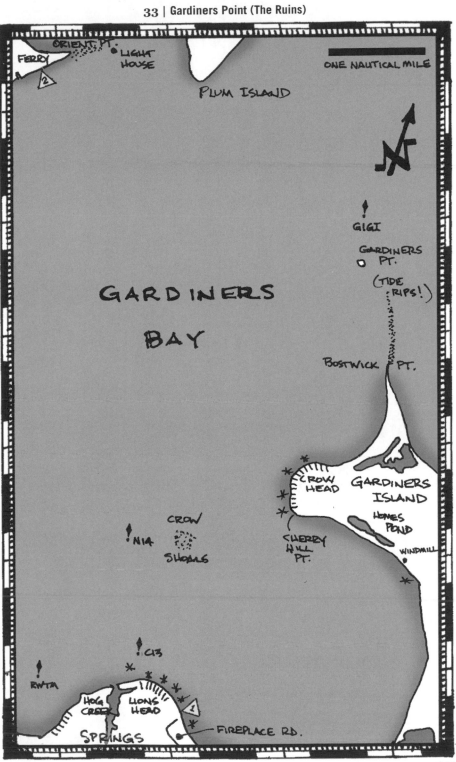

ONE NAUTICAL MILE

ORIENT PT.
FERRY
LIGHT HOUSE
2
PLUM ISLAND

N

GIGI
GARDINERS PT.
(TIDE RIPS!)
BOSTWICK PT.

GARDINERS BAY

CROW HEAD
GARDINERS ISLAND
HOMES POND
WINDMILL

CROW
N14
SHOALS
CHERRY HILL PT.

C13
RWTA
HOG CREEK
LIONS HEAD
1
FIREPLACE RD.
SPRINGS

*firma*. Aside from a rock that rises to within three feet of the surface, my chart shows at least seven feet of water on the shoal.

Soon we are paddling over a school of aquatic piscivores and beneath a flock of aerial ones. The latter I can identify as Common Terns, and the slim silvery fish protruding from many of their beaks are probably Atlantic Silversides. I call over to George Velmachos, my paddling companion and an experienced salt water fisherman, to identify the aquatic predator creating the boiling water around our boats. "Bluefish!" he yells over the noisy feeding frenzy of birds and fish.

In addition to seasonal migrations, Bluefish schools regularly move locally in and out of bays and inlets. These latter movements are triggered by changes in the tide, weather, and food supply, and are most likely what we are witnessing from our kayaks.

Nearing Cherry Hill Point, a huge glacial erratic comes into view just offshore. Judging from the uniform coat of whitewash, or guano, over its upper surface, it is a popular resting spot for seabirds, including the Double-crested Cormorants inhabiting the tree-top nests at the edge of Homes Pond, a mile to the east. George and I decide to pass inside the erratic and, as we paddle, a conversation about the relative merits and drawbacks of sea kayak travel ensues.

Both of us suffer from back ailments related to tight hamstrings and a variety of old back injuries. We can usually ignore it, but there's something about the confinement of a sea kayak, and the inability to change the position of one's legs, that exacerbates the situation. I can sit in a canoe all day, but after an hour or two in a sea kayak all I can think about is getting to shore and stretching my legs.

I am of the opinion that the discomfort is a tradeoff for the kayak's speed and low wind resistance. George isn't convinced. He is paddling a sea kayak that he had recently helped his wife Callie build. A graduate of a wooden boat-building school in Maine with a number of completed watercraft, including several sea kayaks, under his belt, he feels the problem might be solved with a different seat, thigh bracing, and foot rest adjustments.

We both agree that we would be much further from our turn-around point had we embarked in a canoe. We are passing beneath the bluffs of Crow Head on a course for Bostwick Point, more than halfway to our destination, Gardiners Point (also known as "The Ruins"), which is now visible on the horizon at 11 o'clock.

"The Ruins" refers to the remains of Fort Tyler. Built in 1898, it was part of a coastal defense system that included forts at nearby Plum Island and Great Gull Island. These were designed to protect New York City from a Spanish naval attack by way of Long Island Sound and Hell Gate. Over the years it has been used as a target for military planes to practice their shooting and bombing skills, and reduced to rubble. Hence the nickname.

The Ruins sits in a spectacular setting on a tiny sliver of sand far from the South Fork, North Fork, and even the island to which it was once connected, Gardiners. A lighthouse occupied the site during Sag Harbor's whaling era, guiding large sailing vessels around the north end of Gardiners Island on their way to and from port. This remains the preferred route to and from Sag Harbor for deep draft vessels today, as the channel between Gardiners Point and Plum Island is wide, deep, and stable. In contrast, the route around the south end of Gardiners Island, while navigable, is a maze of shifting shoals bordering a very narrow channel.

Back then the lighthouse marked the northern tip of Gardiners Island, then called Gardiners Point, until the blizzard of 1888. A gale associated with the blizzard breached the narrow spit of land, moving enough sand to submerge its northern half (one mile in length) under three feet of water. The end result was a new northern tip of Gardiners Island, called Bostwick Point, and a new island in Gardiners Bay.

Rafting up at Bostwick Point, George and I pull out some water, food, and the nautical chart before heading out on the final leg of the trip. I am a bit apprehensive of the tidal currents between here and the Ruins, now clearly visible as a long line of breaking waves and confused chop. George has a lot of experience fishing in this area, and feels confident that the best approach to the Ruins on a flood tide is from the smooth water on the west side of the rips. This, he pointed out, will position us downstream of the chop and avoid any possibility of getting drawn into it.

I prefer the eastern side, arguing that the western route will not allow us to compensate for the incoming tide and current, and we might be swept so far west that we will end up having to paddle head on into the current to make the island. George counters that the deep water on the west side of the rips will negate the current. I later learn that he was right.

In the end, the discussion of how to approach the island is decided by the current itself. We inadvertently drift well west of the shoals while struggling to resecure George's spray skirt. Paddling through deep water, we are able to take a straight line to the Ruins with negligible set, arriving within two hours of departing from Fireplace Road.

Despite the sore backs and cramped legs, it is an excellent evening adventure. We circle what's left of Fort Tyler, and learn of yet another interesting aspect of this small piece of the East End: its importance as a bird nesting colony. Although nesting season is over for the year, signs on the island proclaim it a tern nesting area. I later learn that over 100 terns make a home here each year, including a fairly significant number of the federally endangered Roseate Terns. A habitat restoration project at the Ruins, completed for the 1995 nesting season, apparently has shown some success.

We are also treated to a spectacular moonrise and sunset, both happening nearly simultaneously, on the return trip. And, back home, we are treated to that deepest of deep sleeps brought on by a long paddle and the fatigue of many obscure, little-used muscles. ✕

### Double-crested Cormorant (*Phalacrocorax auritus*)

These large, primitive-looking, dark birds are easily identified by their characteristic postures: in water they sit so low that only their necks and heads are visible, on land they stand with wings spread wide, and in air they often fly in V-shaped formations, resembling a silent flock of Canada geese.

Cormorants are unusual among the seabirds for their lack of oil glands to waterproof their outer feathers. This decreases the bird's buoyancy and accounts for its low-in-the-water posture. It is also an advantage in diving and pursuing its main source of food, fish. On the downside, it results in heavy, waterlogged feathers and awkward, laborious flight. Hence the outstretched wing stance: a method of drying out.

This poses an interesting question. Is the lack of oil glands a primitive feature, or a sign of an advanced evolutionary adaptation? No one seems sure, but there is no doubt that the Cormorant is a proficient piscivore. Other adaptations that enable it to swim underwater with great speed and dive to depths of 70 feet include the extra webbing found between the rear and front toes (all four toes are webbed, a feature shared with all members of the Pelecaniformes Order), and the location of its powerful legs far aft on the body, a feature it shares with other strong swimmers such as loons and penguins. When Double-crested Cormorants find a school of fish, they sometimes synchronize their pursuit by forming a curving line, herding the school as they dive underneath it. I've seen them do this at Water Fence, off the north side of Hither Woods.

Although found on nearly every East End waterway that has fish, the Double-crested Cormorant nests in only one location here, Homes Pond on Gardiners Island, and that nesting colony was established only recently, in 1983. The nests are flimsy collections of sticks in the tops of trees. Locating the colony is a simple matter of looking for a large stand of dead trees; the nutrient-rich guano excreted by the nesting birds burns the leaves and eventually kills the tree itself. After toppling over, the birds may continue to nest in suitable limbs. During the nesting season you may smell the colony before sighting it, as its trademark guano scent is powerful stuff.

A census of the colony in 1985 revealed 210 Cormorant nests. That number increased to 600 in 1988 and shows no signs of tapering off. Local biologists and fishermen have taken note of this increase with some concern. Paul Spitzer, a biologist who has studied the Gardiners Island Osprey population for many years, surmises that the growing number of Cormorants there are outcompeting the Osprey for a limited food resource, namely Menhaden, and are indirectly responsible for the recent dip in Osprey nesting productivity. It is an interesting theory that warrants further investigation.

# 34 | PLUM ISLAND–GREAT GULL ISLAND–LITTLE GULL ISLAND

*Orient Point, Town of Southold*

DISTANCE:  14 miles R/T.

ACCESS:  1) Orient Point: No permit needed. Follow Rte. 25 to its eastern terminus eight miles east of Greenport. Bear right after the Cross Sound Ferry office and follow the road to the parking area on the left. Launch on the gravel beach to the left (and stay well clear) of the ferry docking area.

NOTES:  The following passage is found in *A Cruising Guide to the New England Coast* by Roger Duncan and John Ware: "Plum Gut is a vicious piece of water, where seven knot currents come together forming a tide rip that can run as high as ten knots." Tide rips can also be encountered in the Sluiceway between Plum Island and Great Gull Island, and the narrow passage between Great and Little Gull Islands. These strong tidal currents create large standing waves and conditions not appropriate for novice paddlers. When combined with opposing winds, the spectacular tidal rips and standing waves are challenging even for experienced kayakers.

When planning an outing through this notorious stretch of water, note that the NOAA tables don't refer to times of slack water but instead list times for the minimum before flood and the minimum before ebb. These calculations relate to the fact that there may not be a time when there is no current at all, but rather a time when the current is minimal before it begins to flow in the opposite direction. Also keep in mind that the times of minimum and maximum currents are not synchronized at each of the passages. For example, when the tide begins to turn at The Race and the current is weakest there, a 3.4-knot current is pouring through Plum Gut.

Not far on either side of the narrow passages that regularly register 3–5 knots of current are waters that remain relatively calm with currents in the 1–2 knot range. A longer course that swings wide of the narrows may prove to be the quickest route when bucking a foul tide or confronting wild seas.

Access to Plum Island and Great Gull Island is strictly prohibited, and landing on Little Gull Island can be dangerous. Plan on being in your boat for the entire trip.

*November*

Tucked in a quiet eddy behind the Orient Point lighthouse, appropriately nicknamed the Coffee Pot, we review our game plan. Protected first by Orient Point and then by the rocky shoals comprising Oyster Pond Reef, we have experienced very little current since leaving the beach near the ferry terminal. But, just before reaching the Coffee Pot, it has become quite apparent that we are not dealing with a slack tide. Plum Gut and the brunt of an ebb current lie ahead of us.

"Let's try to hold a course in line with the Plum Island water tank," I suggest, "and adjust as needed depending on what the tidal rips are like." From the low vantage point of my sea kayak, the crossing doesn't look bad in terms of standing waves. But the current here on the edge of the Gut is powerful, and I am not at all certain how feasible it will be to hold that ferry line. My companions, Russ Tillman and John Todaro, nod okay and, with that odd mixture of anxiety and excitement I often feel when about to embark on an outdoors adventure, we set off.

The adventure we have planned is a paddle out to Little Gull Island, a 14-mile-long round trip from Orient Point by way of Plum Island and Great Gull Island. En route, we will be crossing several stretches of notoriously treacherous water. Plum Gut, the Sluiceway, the Race, and a narrow bit of water between Gull and Little Gull Islands are four passages that connect Long Island Sound with Gardiners Bay and Block Island Sound. With each tidal cycle, huge amounts of water rush through these constricted passages, creating strong currents and powerful eddies. And, depending upon the tidal stage and wind strength and direction, large standing waves can develop. We will be crossing three of the four passages.

We will also be getting a close look at three historic lighthouses and three fairly remote islands. One houses the secretive and controversial Animal Disease Center recently (June 2003) transferred to the Department of Homeland Security; another is home to the largest nesting population of Common and Roseate Terns in the western hemisphere, and a research station manned by the American Museum of Natural History.

The three islands comprise the western end of an archipelago that extends northeasterly from Orient Point to Watch Hill, Rhode Island and includes Fishers Island. These islands, along with a low ridge running along Long Island's north shore, are somewhat related—they were formed by a glacial ice sheet over 20,000 years ago. Collectively they are called a moraine.

The crossing of Plum Gut from the Orient lighthouse to the nearest point of land on Plum Island is three quarters of a mile. The first quarter-mile is quite

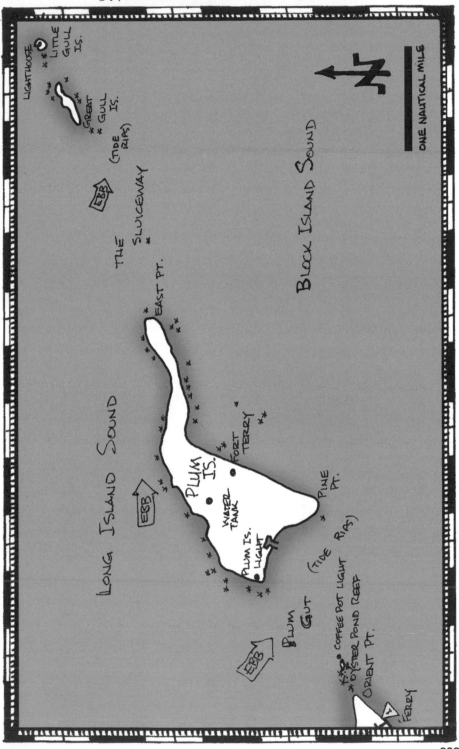

straightforward, with lots of moving water but no standing waves. Despite the current, we are holding our course for the Plum Island water tank and not getting set to the east.

Then a line of white caps appears just ahead. As we get closer, they turn into large, closely-packed, steeply-sided waves, some of them breaking and sending white foam cascading down against the current and into a deep trough. "Let's stick close together!" I yell over to the others. That is the last I see of them for awhile.

Leaning into a curling wave, I stop paddling for a moment to brace as it breaks over my shoulder and cockpit and sends me surfing sideways for a few uncomfortable seconds. This does not feel good. I steer slightly to the left, away from the waves, so that they break over my starboard quarter, and paddle and surf northeasterly across the Gut. With my focus riveted on bracing, balancing, and the next wave approaching, my vision is limited to the immediate area within 15 feet of my boat. Everything else is a blur, and I lose sight of my companions.

Fortunately, it is over in a matter of minutes. Pulling into a big eddy behind the Plum Island lighthouse, we take a breather and relax. Looking back, it appears we have paddled through the worst stretch of the standing waves. I make a note that the shortest route across this stretch of water is not necessarily the best one. Just a bit further north of our line the water, while moving fast, has barely a ripple on its surface. There, in the flat water, a large fleet of recreational fishing boats has congregated.

What draws the fishermen are large Bluefish and Striped Bass lurking beneath the surface. The carnivorous fish, in turn, are drawn here by schools of small baitfish: Herring, Bunker, and Silversides, among others. Near the bottom of this food chain, and the attraction for the baitfish, are small planktonic organisms, lots of them, a virtual soup of algae and algae-eaters. The small plankton are particularly prolific here due to the strong tidal currents that flow from deep to shallow water, causing a phenomenon called upwelling where nutrients from the bottom rise towards the surface, and sunlight, to be converted into food by phytoplankton. Take a look on your chart at the dramatic change in depths at Plum Gut: 300 feet on the Gut's northwestern side, 75 feet at its middle, and 190 feet to the southeast. And that's over a distance of only one mile.

Our next decision is whether to paddle the north or south side of Plum Island. That is an easy one. We had some local knowledge from George Velmachos, another paddling friend who has spent a lot of time fishing in this area and who advised us that an outgoing tide would push us along the north side at a good clip and almost directly towards Great Gull Island. The only problem is bucking the tide and getting around the point near the Plum Island lighthouse.

That is easier than it looks. We stay close to shore, where the foul tide is weakest and a rock garden of huge glacial erratics provides plenty of helpful eddies. This exercise reminds me of working my way upriver on a canoe trip, leap-frogging and ferrying from one eddy to another. Soon, we are home-free and riding a fair tide along the north shore of Plum Island. With Plum Gut behind us, our thoughts turn to the Sluiceway. What lies in store for us there?

As we clear the northern side of Plum Island, I wonder how clearly we will be able to discern our next mark, Great Gull Island, three miles to the east. Sea kayaks and their occupants sit very low in the water, a great advantage in rough water and strong winds. But for sighting distant landmarks on our East End's largely horizontal landscape, the view from a kayak is quite limited.

But even a swimmer would have been able to pick out our destination. The Little Gull Island lighthouse, an 80-foot-tall granite tower, looms large on the horizon directly in line with Great Gull Island.

Off to starboard is a long arm of Plum Island that ends with a point of land appropriately named East Point. We had planned to pull in close to shore there in order to look over the two-mile stretch of water between the point and Great Gull Island. Although my two companions and myself are hoping to complete a round-trip paddle including Little Gull Island, none of us are willing to commit to crossing the Sluiceway without first having a close look at the conditions there.

There is barely a ripple in the Sluiceway, and Russ Tillman makes the obvious call before we even reach East Point. "Let's stay further offshore, away from East Point, and take better advantage of the ebb tide!" The outgoing tide pushes us on a nearly perfect course towards our destination.

We paddle a course that keeps us just north of a straight line drawn between East Point and Great Gull Island, and in deep water. South of that line is a series of shoals and rocks, and potentially fast water. As we continue east, I am surprised that the ebb current isn't pulling us south into the Sluiceway, but the calm conditions lull me into not thinking about it any further.

Within a quarter-mile of Great Gull I realize what has happened. Plum Island is focusing most of the ebb current into the eastern end of the Sluiceway. Before we know it, we have been sucked well south of Great Gull and, abandoning the idea of cruising along the island's north shore, paddle hard through some tide rips to gain the huge eddy on the island's south side.

We aren't the only ones seeking refuge in the eddy. There, resting and feeding along the eddyline, are large flocks of Common Eiders and Scoters. These hardy seabirds birds have recently arrived from their nesting grounds along the coast of Maine and the Canadian Maritimes, and will spend the entire winter here in Gardiners Bay and Block Island Sound without touching land.

Now well protected from the current, we skim close by the southern shoreline of Great Gull Island to get a good look at the unusual site. As with nearby Gardiners Point and Plum Island, a fort was built here in 1898 during the Spanish–American war to protect shipping entering and exiting the eastern end of Long Island Sound.

The military outpost was also used during World Wars I and II as part of our coastal defense system, but abandoned in 1949.

The fort's ruins remain and part of the military facility is used today to house biologists studying the island's most famous inhabitants: Roseate Terns. The island's history as a tern research station is nearly as long as its military history. American Museum of Natural History ornithologist Helen Hayes has been involved in research at Great Gull Island since 1966. The island boasts the largest nesting concentrations of Roseate and Common Terns in the western hemisphere: 1,600 pairs of Roseates and 10,000 pairs of Common Terns. Roseate Terns are listed as a federally endangered species; Common Terns are faring better but still listed as a threatened species in New York State.

Over the past 37 years, biologists stationed at the island during the nesting season (May through July) have banded a quarter of a million terns. In the 1980s, vegetation encroaching on the nesting areas led biologists to reintroduce the Meadow Vole to the island. As the population of this prolific grass-eater exploded, vegetation was reduced, and tern nesting increased, marking the experiment as a success.

No terns are evident during our early November paddle, having already flown south to their overwintering areas in South America. But a dozen Harbor Seals swim alongside us, appearing as interested in watching us as we are in observing them. They escort us to the east end of Great Gull, and continue to watch from a distance as we angle toward a sharp eddy line. The line delineates a strong ebb current coursing through the narrow passage between the two Gull Islands, which we quickly ferry across.

Little Gull Island is tiny and its lighthouse takes up a good chunk of its footprint. On its northwest side are the remains of a small dock and protected beach where we make for shore. I am particularly thankful for the calm conditions that allow us to make an easy landing, as I can sense that it is usually not the case on this exposed island. And it is definitely time to exit the kayak and stretch the legs and back.

The first lighthouse was constructed here in 1804; the present structure was built in 1869. Back in those days the lighthouses were manned by a keeper and his family. In 1815, the keeper was ashore when a September hurricane carried away much of the island. His wife and four children watched the storm from the lighthouse windows… imagine that!

While we rest, eat, and explore the two-acre pile of glacial and man-made rubble that comprises Little Gull Island, I try to make some sense of the tides we are experiencing. We departed Orient Point and crossed Plum Gut at 9 A.M. which, according to the NOAA tide tables, was close to the middle (three hours after the start of) of an outgoing, or ebb, tide. As a general rule, the time of high or low tide corresponds to times of slack water, meaning the time when tidal current is nil, and the mid-point in time between high and low tide corresponds to times of maximum tidal current.

Paddlers Russ Tillman (left) and John Todaro (right) take a break on the south side of Plum Island.

Forget those general rules when planning a crossing of Plum Gut, the Race, or the shoal waters found between the two. Fortunately for us, Plum Gut's aberrant ebb tide reaches a maximum velocity in the first quarter of the roughly six-hour tidal cycle, or one and a half hours after the start of the ebb, well before we even launched from the beach near the Cross Sound ferry terminal. The flood, or incoming, tide, on the other hand, follows the mid-point rule: maximum current is three hours after the flood begins and three hours before the ebb.

Watching the current rip around the shoreline of Little Gull Island I learn something even more unusual about the tides here: the ebb current continues for two hours after low tide!

After spending an hour on the island, it is time to go. The ebb tide is still running but much diminished. With luck, it will soon turn and we will ride the flood tide back to Orient Point. We made the seven-mile passage to Little Gull in only two hours, and it seemed too easy. But we still have to get back, and that means recrossing the Sluiceway and Plum Gut.

Russ Tillman is ready to go first and easily paddles through the small rips just west of Little Gull. John Todaro and I watch him set a southwesterly course that puts him quite far off to the south of Great Gull Island to take best advantage of the impending flood current for the return trip. John and I linger for a few more photographs, then paddle directly towards Great Gull Island, making the third-of-a-mile crossing in a matter of minutes.

We want another close look at this island that we have both heard so much about. In addition to being the site of a well-known, long-term study of Roseate terns, it has recently become one of the largest winter seal haulout sites on the east coast of the U.S. The bulk of our seal visitors are Harbor Seals, but Grey, Harp, Ringed, and Hooded species are also in the mix. The dozen whiskered faces that watch us paddle by Great Gull Island are all Harbor Seals, a small number compared to the mid-winter population here. In recent years, researchers have estimated Great Gull Island's winter seal numbers at 1,000 individuals, or one-fifth of the entire Long Island population.

Halfway across the Sluiceway Russ rejoins us. I paddle over to a navigational buoy to get a close look at what the tide is doing and am surprised to find it still ebbing, although quite weak. This buoy is not on my chart; it appears to be in the vicinity of Middle Shoal Rock, probably to steer boats into the Sluiceway's deepest water and well east of Bedford Reef and Old Silas Rock.

Soon we are on the south side of Plum Island's East Point. A spectacular rock garden of huge glacial erratics entices us closer to shore, and the calm conditions allow us to weave through and around the massive chunks of granite. I have an ulterior motive for paddling among the rocks: I am looking for a suitable slab on which to land and stretch my sore back.

Given the current state of affairs on Plum Island, even landing on the beach for a few minutes is out of the question. But, given the state of my lower back, it takes quite a bit of persuasion from John to prevent me from paddling to shore. John swears a vehicle is tracking our progress from the island, and he wonders aloud if the helicopter overhead is doing the same.

Since 1954, the 840-acre island has been used by the U.S. Department of Agriculture as a research and quarantine center to study foreign animal diseases with the goal of protecting our farm industry. In June 2003, the island and its highly classified facilities were transferred to the Department of Homeland Security.

What actually goes on there has been the subject of much wild speculation and accusations among the general public. Adding fuel to those long-burning fires are recent allegations of mismanagement by the federal government itself, as found in a report recently filed by the General Accounting Office.

Bill Smith, head of the environmental organization Fish Unlimited, relayed some disturbing information regarding the island. Their sewage treatment plant, which discharges into Plum Gut, has been cited many times for not meeting the conditions of its discharge permit. The island's three incinerators, which destroy infected animals, periodically belches black smoke into the air. Bob DeLuca of the Group for the South Fork agrees that the federal facility is facing some serious environmental issues. The Group has joined a growing list of organizations called Concerned Citizens for Safety and Security on Plum Island to pressure government officials to address them.

East of the rock gardens, the shoreline transforms into a pretty sandy beach that arcs southwesterly towards Pine Point. At this sandy bend a number of brick buildings constructed in 1899 are visible. This is another fortification, called Fort Terry, built during the Spanish–American war that also served as a military post during World War I and World War II.

According to the writings of naturalist Roy Latham, the construction of the fortifications at the turn of the century spelled doom for the largest colony of Ospreys on the east coast. He cites pre-1900 sources in a claim that Plum Island's colony was larger than Gardiners Island's. Latham writes, "The laborers working on that project developed a liking for Osprey eggs. The nests, situated on the ground and in low trees, as well as in the island's big white cedar swamp, were very accessible."

As we approach Pine Point we can see that the flood tide has begun. Strong tide rips have set up just south of the point, and we paddle off into them without hesitation. Not far off in the distance is our destination.

Plum Island soon falls astern. I have learned much about this mysterious island's interesting history, and have seen its beautiful shoreline up close. I am glad to know there are folks lobbying for better stewardship of its natural and historic resources, and I hope they are successful. Someday I'd love to paddle over and explore its Atlantic White Cedar swamp, perhaps when it is designated Plum Island National Wildlife Refuge. To borrow a line from *Suffolk Life* newspaper editor David J. Willmott, Sr., "And why not?" ✕

## Seals

If you venture out onto the bays between early December and late April, you are likely to encounter these inquisitive marine mammals. The latest census data I've seen (1999) had the Long Island population at 6,000, with 2,000 overwintering in the vicinity of Great Gull Island off the North Fork. Although the largest numbers are seen in winter, seals have been reported throughout the year and some researchers speculate that a few have given birth to pups on Long Island.

The East End's seal population increased dramatically over the past decade, most likely the result of decreased hunting up north. A bounty on seals in Massachusetts was in place as recently as 1962, and one in the Canadian maritimes was not lifted until 1976. The federal Marine Mammal Protection Act of 1972 further protected seals in the U.S. We may be witnessing an expansion of seals into their historic range as their core populations up north increase.

Five different species of seals have been recorded on the East End. I'm told that the most common seals are the Harbor Seal (*Phoca vitulina*) and the Gray Seal (*Halichoerus grypus*), but the different species are difficult to distinguish in the water, including (as I've learned from leading seal programs at Montauk Point) the young Gray Seals from the adult Harbor Seals. The southernmost breeding area for Gray Seals is not far away: Nantucket Island. Pups are born there in late December and January and weaned by February. Soon after, young Grays begin to show up here. The closest regular pupping area for Harbor Seals is further up the coast in New Hampshire and Maine. Their pupping season is late April to mid-June.

Seals are well-adapted to the cold, marine environment. A thick layer of blubber, comprising roughly one-third of their body mass, insulates them from the cold water. Their torpedo shape not only conserves heat by minimizing surface-to-volume ratio but makes them fast and efficient swimmers. Heat is also conserved in the design of their blood vessels, which form a type of heat exchanger that allows the skin and flippers to have a much lower temperature than the animal's core and its vital internal organs (not unlike that found in birds, enabling a gull to stand on ice with its uninsulated feet).

Their hemoglobin-rich blood combined with their myoglobin-rich muscles enable seals to store large amounts of oxygen for long, deep dives. Dives up to thirty minutes and 1,400 feet deep have been recorded for Harbor Seals. Diving and swimming are crucial to feeding. Seals prey on many types of fish, crabs and squid.

As graceful as they are in the water, they are extremely awkward on land. Watching one maneuver onto one of their haulout rocks favored for basking can be comical. So why bother? According to biologists, basking behavior is primarily associated with thermoregulatory balance, a term for energy conservation. Water is much more efficient at conducting heat away from an organism, even a thickly blubbered seal, than air. Seals can conserve calories (and maintain that torpedo figure) by hauling themselves out of our 35°F sea water and basking in the 20°F air!

Basking may be associated with other functions, such as reducing skin parasites. And even the hardy seals have a bottom line: when the wind chill hits -15°F, or rough seas make snoozing on the rocks impossible, they won't bother coming out.

Paddlers need to know that the Marine Mammal Protection Act of 1972 prohibits any harassment of these animals, including any act that alters their natural behavior. Keep a safe distance from haulout sites so that basking seals are not disturbed.

To report a stranded or injured marine mammal or sea turtle, call the Riverhead Foundation Hotline: 631-369-9829.

# Appendix: Paddling Resources

## I | MAPS AND CHARTS

Whichever map or chart you prefer to use, make a copy of the specific area you wish to explore (reduce or enlarge as needed, and be sure to include the scale and north arrow) and leave the expensive originals at home.

### Charts

I have found that nautical charts, due to their scale, have limited use for exploring the East End's waterways. The exceptions to this rule are routes that involve crossing the larger bays or paddling to offshore islands (Gardiners, Cartwright, Little Gull). In those cases, having a chart with the location and description of navigational aids is important.

A waterproof chart at a 1:100,000 scale (*#67: Peconic and Gardiners Bays*) that covers the entire area of this book except western Shinnecock Bay and the upper Peconic River can be ordered for $21.95 plus shipping from **Waterproof Charts** (1-800-423-9026 or *waterproofcharts.com*). I find this chart difficult to read even on land, but I'll pack an enlarged xerox of the specific area I'm paddling (e.g. Robins Island) in my waterproof and see-through map case.

Two NOAA paper charts (*#12358: Shelter Island Sound and Peconic Bays*, and *#13209: Block Island Sound and Gardiners Bay*) cover the East End at a 1:40,000 scale. Their large sizes (36" x 45" each) make them a bit unwieldy on the water, but they are beautiful works of art and make excellent wall hangings!

### Five Town Topographic Maps

These excellent, detailed maps were created by the Suffolk County Department of Health Services for the five East End towns (Riverhead, Southold, Shelter Island, Southampton, and East Hampton). They depict contours at five foot intervals and were mapped at a one inch to two hundred feet scale that is ideal for small tidal creeks such as Alewife Brook and Goose Creek, or small ponds such as Mill Pond and Long Pond. These can be ordered by phoning the County at 631-852-4114 and requesting an index (free) or the entire set of maps on a CD ($50) to be sent by mail. From the index, you can order maps ($5 each) through the same number.

*USGS Topographic Maps*

These are the most useful maps for most of the inland waterbodies and harbors described in this book (e.g. Sagg Pond, Accabonac Harbor, Sebonac Creek). These 1:24,000 scale maps can be ordered online at *store.usgs.gov* or by phone at 518-486-1092 (call before noon).

Each map costs $6 plus shipping. Many local libraries have these maps in their reference sections, and copies can be made from them. Eighteen maps cover the area described in this book, and are titled as follows: Wading River, Riverhead, Eastport, Quogue, Mattituck, Mattituck Hills, Southold, Orient, Plum Island, Greenport, Shinnecock Inlet, Southampton, Sag Harbor, East Hampton, Gardiners Island West, Gardiners Island East, Napeague Beach, Montauk Point.

*Road Maps*

A good road map of the East End is essential. The best map for the South Fork is made by **Streetwise** and is usually available at local bookstores. Their maps of Southampton and East Hampton Towns can be ordered at *streetwisemaps.com* or 800-497-1314. Unfortunately, they do not make a map of the North Fork and you will have to settle for the **Hagstrom** map, also available at most local bookstores.

For Shelter Island, get yourself a copy of the excellent free map produced by the Shelter Island Chamber of Commerce. It includes all of the many boat access sites on the island, as well as other useful information. Contact them by mail at Box 598, Shelter Island NY 11964, by phone at 631-749-0399, or online at *shelter-island.net*.

## II | ACCESS AND PARKING PERMITS

*Town of Shelter Island*
(631-749-0291, *www.shelterislandtown.us*)
The majority of the many access points on the island (approximately three dozen), called landings (roads that dead-end on the water), do not require a permit to use or park. **Parking Permits** are needed at Town bathing beaches (Wades Beach, Shell Beach, and Crescent Beach), and are available at Town Hall.

*Town of East Hampton*
(631-324-4142, *www.town.east-hampton.ny.us*)
Nonresidents can obtain a **Launch Ramp Permit** for $50 which allows them to launch and park at any of the many town-owned launch ramps. Residents need to obtain a free **Beach Parking Permit**.

*Town of Southampton*
(631-728-8585, *www.town.southampton.ny.us*)
Parking permits are available through the Town's Parks and Recreation Department, or can be purchased at any of the town's staffed beaches. **Resident Parking Permits** are $20/year (discounts provided for EMS volunteers and seniors). **Nonresident Parking Permits** are $150/year or $15/day.

*Town of Southold*
(631-765-1800, *southoldtown.northfork.net*)
Permits are available through the Town Clerk's office, Norman E. Klipp Park, Town Beach, and New Suffolk Beach, or at a number of local shops. **Resident Parking Permits** are $6/year. **Nonresident Parking Permits** are $100/year or $12/day. (At the town's website, go to "Local Places of Interest" and select "Parking Permits.")

Note: Southold's beach parking situation is complicated by the fact that certain beaches belong to the Park Districts and do not come under Southold Town jurisdiction. At the town's website, go to "Local Places of Interest" and select "Parks and Beaches" for more information on both the Town Beaches and Park District Beaches.

*Suffolk County Parks*
(631-584-4949, *www.co.suffolk.ny.us*)
Any County park that has facilities and is staffed requires a **Green Key** for access (e.g. Shinnecock Inlet East in Southampton Village, Indian Island in Riverhead, and Cedar Point in East Hampton). There may be an additional parking fee as well. The Green Key must be purchased in person. This can be done at the park with proof of residency (for the county resident rate). $20 for residents, $35 for nonresidents. There are discount rates for Seniors and emergency services volunteers. (At the town's website, go to "Departments" and select "Parks.")

## III | EMERGENCY CONTACTS

(For life-threatening emergencies, dial 911.)
Southold Town Police . . . . . . . . . . . . . . . . . . . . . . . . . . . . . . . . . . . . . . . 631-765-2600
East Hampton Town Police . . . . . . . . . . . . . . . . . . . . . . . . . . . . . . . . 631-537-7575
Shelter Island Police . . . . . . . . . . . . . . . . . . . . . . . . . . . . . . . . . . . . . 631-749-0600
Riverhead Town Police . . . . . . . . . . . . . . . . . . . . . . . . . . . . . . . . . . . 631-727-4500
Southampton Town Police . . . . . . . . . . . . . . . . . . . . . . . . . . . . . . . . 631-728-3400
U.S. Coast Guard—Shinnecock Bay . . . . . . . . . . . . . . . . . . . . . . . . 631-728-0078
U.S. Coast Guard—Montauk . . . . . . . . . . . . . . . . . . . . . . . . . . . . . . 631-668-2773

## IV | WILDLIFE AND NATURAL RESOURCE CONTACTS

*Public Agencies*

U.S. Fish and Wildlife Service . . . . . . . . . . . . . . . . . . . . . . . . . . . . . . .631-581-2941

N.Y.S. Department of Environmental Conservation . . . . . . . . . . . . . .631-444-0310

Suffolk County Parks . . . . . . . . . . . . . . . . . . . . . . . . . . . . . . . . . . . . . .631-854-4949

East Hampton Town Natural Resources Department . . . . . . . . . . . . .631-324-0496

Southampton Town Department of Land Management . . . . . . . . . . .631-287-5710

Southampton Town Bay Constable . . . . . . . . . . . . . . . . . . . . . . . . . .631-287-5717

Riverhead Bay Constable . . . . . . . . . . . . . . . . . . . . . . . . . . .631-727-4500 ext. 317

Southold Bay Constable . . . . . . . . . . . . . . . . . . . . . . . . . . . . . . . . . . .631-765-2600

*Private Organizations*

Peconic Baykeeper . . . . . . . . . . . . . . . . . . . . . . . . . . . . . . . . . . . . . . .631-727-7346

Group for the South Fork . . . . . . . . . . . . . . . . . . . . . . . . . . . . . . . . . .631-537-1400

The Nature Conservancy . . . . . . . . . 631-329-7689 (Shelter Island 631-749-1001)

Peconic Land Trust . . . . . . . . . . . . . . . . . . . . . . . . . . . . . . . . . . . . . . .631-283-3195

## V | TIDES AND CURRENTS

Until I learned how to navigate the internet, I bought a copy of the *Eldridge Tide and Pilot Book* each year to look up times of high and low water, and to plan my full moon paddles. This useful reference book can be found in many marinas, marine supply stores, or by calling 617-742-3045. Now I use the web site *tbone.biol.sc.edu/tide* for tidal and moon phase information.

Mean tidal range on the East End is listed as 2.5 feet. Listed tidal heights and times of low and high tide can be thrown off significantly by strong winds. A hard wind out of the east will push water up into the bays, creating higher than normal tides and delaying the ebb tide. Conversely, a hard and prolonged west wind creates lower than normal low tides and can delay the onset of the flood tide.

Strong tidal currents are found at most inlets, as well as at narrows in the bay. The most notorious currents are found along the archipelago of islands just east of Orient Point on the North Fork. There, in the narrows linking Long Island Sound and Gardiners Bay, expect to find 3–5 knot currents and large, steep, standing waves. The races on either end of Robins Island, and the stretch of Shelter Island Sound between the island and North Haven, register 2.5 knots of tidal current.

When paddling against the current at an inlet, stay close to shore where there is often a helpful countercurrent, or eddy. If not, the current is usually weakest in the shallower water close to shore. Where there is a bend in the inlet, the current will be strongest on the outside of the bend and weaker on the inside track. And there's always the option of carrying, or portaging, if the current proves too much.

## VI I CAMPING

There are two Suffolk County campgrounds situated on East End bays: Indian Island County Park (631-852-3232) is at the confluence of the Peconic River and Flanders Bay in Riverhead, and Cedar Point County Park (631-852-7620) is on Northwest Harbor in East Hampton.

Hither Hills State Park campground (631-668-2554) in located on the ocean in Montauk, a short distance from Napeague Harbor and excellent paddling in Gardiners Bay and Block Island Sound.

## VII I INNS, MOTELS, SIGHTSEEING

There are many waterfront inns, bed and breakfast establishments, and motels which could be used as a base to explore the East End's waterways. This area also boasts many interesting attractions worth visiting: museums (maritime, natural history, and art), lighthouses and other historical structures with interpretive displays, and an aquarium. Many of these can be accessed by canoe or kayak. The local chambers of commerce are a wealth of information on places to stay and visit.

North Fork Chamber of Commerce . . . . . . . . . . . . . . . . . . . . . . . . 631-298-5757
Riverhead Chamber of Commerce . . . . . . . . . . . . . . . . . . . . . . . . 631-727-7600
Hampton Bays Chamber of Commerce . . . . . . . . . . . . . . . . . . . . . 631-728-2211
Southampton Chamber of Commerce . . . . . . . . . . . . . . . . . . . . . . 631-283-0402
East Hampton Chamber of Commerce. . . . . . . . . . . . . . . . . . . . . . 631-324-0362
Montauk Chamber of Commerce. . . . . . . . . . . . . . . . . . . . . . . . . . 631-668-2428

The websites of all the above, and much more, can be accessed online at *www.eastendcommunity.com*.

Also check *Peconic.org* for a list of local environmental organizations, updates, and new information.

# REFERENCES

*http://www.chesapeakebay.net/info/american_eel.cfm*

Berrill, N. J. and Jacquelyn. *1001 Questions Answered About the Seashore*. New York: Dover, 1957.

Brown, Lauren. *Grasses: An Identification Guide*. Boston: Houghton Mifflin Co., 1979.

Bull, John. *Birds of the New York Area*. New York: Dover, 1964.

Caduto, Michael J. *Pond and Brook: A Guide to Nature in Freshwater Environments*. Hanover, NH and London: University Press of New England, 1990.

Cronin, William. *Changes in the Land: Indians, Colonists, and the Ecology of New England*. New York: Hill and Wang, 1983.

Cryan, John F., and John L. Turner. "The Peconic: Pine Barrens River." *The Heath Hen* 2.1 (1995): 1–22.

Ehrlich, Paul R., D. S. Dobkin, and D. Wheye. *The Birder's Handbook*. New York: Simon and Schuster, 1988.

Emery, K. O. *A Coastal Pond: Studied by Oceanographic Methods*. Woods Hole, MA: Oyster Pond Environmental Trust Inc., 1997.

Gosner, Kenneth L. *A Field Guide to the Atlantic Seashore*. Boston: Houghton Mifflin Co., 1978.

Halsey, William. *Sketches From Local History*. Southampton: Yankee Peddler, 1966.

Harlowe, William M. *Trees of the Eastern and Central United States and Canada*. New York: Dover, 1957.

Hendrickson, Richard G. *Winds of the Fish's Tail*. Mattituck, NY: Amereon Ltd., 1996.

Johnson, Ann F. *A Guide to the Plant Communities of Napeague Dunes*. Mattituck, NY: Mad Printers of Mattituck, 1985.

Jorgensen, Neil. *A Sierra Club Naturalist's Guide to Southern New England*. San Francisco: Sierra Club Books, 1978.

Kopper, Philip. *The Wild Edge: Life and Lore of the Great Atlantic Beaches.* New York: Times Books, 1979.

Kozlowski, Gregory. *The Sweet Water Angler: The Official Newsletter of the DEC Long Island and NYC Freshwater Fisheries Management Units* 8.2 (2001).

Lamont, Eric. "Early Collections of Phragmites from Long Island, New York." *Long Island Botanical Society Newsletter* 7 (1997): 9–10.

Latham, Roy. "Phragmites." *Long Island Naturalist* 6 (1957): 26–27.

Lawlor, Elizabeth P. *Discover Nature at the Seashore.* Harrisburg, PA: Stackpole, 1992.

Leatherman, Stephen P. *Barrier Island Handbook.* University of Maryland Coastal Publication Series, 1988.

Long, Robert P., William and Barbara Wilhelm. *Canoeing the Peconic River.* Cutchogue, NY: Peconic Publishers, 1983.

Maryland Department of Natural Resources. *Mute Swans in Maryland: A Statewide Management Plan.* 2003.

McCormick, Larry R., O. H. Pilkey, Jr., W. J. Neal, O. H. Pilkey, Sr. *Living With Long Island's South Shore.* Durham, NC: Duke University Press, 1984.

Moyle, Peter B. *Fish: An Enthusiast's Guide.* Berkeley, CA: University of California Press, 1993.

Mulvihill, William. *South Fork Placenames.* Sag Harbor: Brickiln Press, 1995.

Newcomb, Lawrence. *Newcomb's Wildflower Guide.* Boston: Little, Brown and Co., 1977.

Oysterponds Historical Society. *Historic Orient Village.* Orient: Oysterponds Historical Society, 1976.

Pasquier, Roger F. *Watching Birds.* Boston: Houghton Mifflin Co., 1977.

Perry, Bill. *A Sierra Club Naturalist's Guide to the Middle Atlantic Coast.* San Francisco: Sierra Club Books, 1985.

Petry, Loren C. and Marcia G. Norman. *A Beachcomber's Botany.* Chatham, MA: The Chatham Conservation Foundation, 1968.

Poole, Allan. *Ospreys: A Natural and Unnatural History.* New York: Cambridge University Press, 1989.

Rattray, Everett. *The South Fork: The Land and the People of Eastern Long Island.* New York: Random House, 1979.

Robbins, Ken and Bill Strachan (Eds.) *Springs: A Celebration.* East Hampton: The Springs Improvement Society, 1984.

Robins, C. Richard, and G. Carleton Ray. *Atlantic Coast Fishes.* New York: Houghton Mifflin Co., 1986.

Sibley, David Allen. *The Sibley Guide to Birds.* New York: Knopf, 2000.

Sirkin, Les. *Eastern Long Island Geology: History, Processes and Field Trips.* Watch Hill, RI: Book and Tackle Shop, 1995.

Sterling, Dorothy. "Our Cape Cod Salt Marshes." *The Association for the Preservation of Cape Cod Informational Bullletin* 6 (1976).

Stokes, Donald and Lillian. *A Guide to Bird Behavior: Vol. 1-3.* Boston: Little, Brown and Co., 1983.

Strahler, Arthur. *A Geologist's View of Cape Cod.* Orleans, MA: Parnassus Imprints, 1988.

Symonds, George W. D. *The Shrub Identification Book.* New York: William Morrow, 1963.

Teal, John and Mildred. *Life and Death of the Salt Marsh.* New York: Random House, 1971.

Tyning, Thomas. *A Guide to Reptiles and Amphibians.* Boston: Little, Brown and Co., 1990.

Villani, Robert. *Long Island: A Natural History.* New York: Abrams, 1997.

Zarillo, Gary. *Dynamics of Mecox Inlet and Resulting Effects on Adjacent Beaches.* 1985.

Zinn, Donald. *The Handbook for Beach Strollers From Maine to Hatteras.* Chester, CT: Globe Pequot Press, 1985.